Immigration, Social Integration and Crime

The problem of social control has constituted the acid test for the entire issue of immigration and integration. But whilst recent studies show that in Western Europe the crime rate for non-nationals is three, four or more times higher than that of the country's 'own' citizens, academic interest in these statistics has been inhibited by the political difficulties they raise. *Immigration, Social Integration and Crime* addresses this issue directly. Providing a thorough analysis of immigration and crime rates in all of the main European countries, as well as examining the situation in the US, Luigi Solivetti concludes that the widespread notion that a large non-national population produces high crime rates must be rejected. Noting the undeniably substantial, but significantly variable contribution of non-nationals to crime statistics in Western Europe, he nevertheless goes on to analyse and explain the factors that influence the relationship between immigration and crime. It is the characteristics of the 'host' countries that is shown to be significantly associated with non-nationals' integration and, ultimately, their involvement in crime. In particular, Solivetti concludes, it is 'social capital' in the host societies – made up of features such as education, transparency, and openness – that plays a key role in non-nationals' integration chances, and so in their likelihood to commit crime. Supported by extensive empirical data and statistical analysis, *Immigration, Social Integration and Crime* provides an invaluable contribution to one of the most pressing social and political debates – in Europe, and elsewhere.

Luigi M. Solivetti is Professor of Sociology at the Faculty of Statistics of the Sapienza University of Rome. He has carried out research work in the fields of Social Control and Social Change, extensively publishing at the international level.

Contemporary issues in public policy
Series editors: David Downes and Paul Rock
London School of Economics

This series of books is intended to offer accessible, informed and well-evidenced analyses of topical policy issues – from the national health through women's work to central issues of crime and criminal justice – as a counterweight to the manner in which they tend to be presented in political and public debates. The mass media can be sensationalizing and overly-simple. Many observers and commentators are too engaged politically or professionally to take a dispassionate stand. By contrast, what is offered here is considered expert commentary laid out in a literate and helpful manner. Moreover, in the wake of globalization, the revolution in information technology and new forms of regulation and audit, an immense proliferation of data has occurred which can swamp all but the most experienced and duly sceptical analyst. Providing an excellent core for teaching in social policy, criminology, politics and the sociology of contemporary Britain, the series is also intended for politicians, policy-makers, journalists and other concerned people who wish to know more about the world they live in today.

Available:

Key Issues in Women's Work
Catherine Hakim

The Police and Social Conflict
Nigel Fielding

UK Election Law
Bob Watt

Child Sexual Abuse: Media Representation and Government Reactions
Julia Davidson

Forthcoming titles:

Health and the National Health Service
John Carrier and Ian Kendall

Mental Health and Crime
Jill Peay

Immigration, Social Integration and Crime

A cross-national approach

Luigi M. Solivetti

Routledge
Taylor & Francis Group
a GlassHouse book

First published 2010
by Routledge
2 Park Square, Milton Park, Abingdon, Oxfordshire OX14 4RN

Simultaneously published in the USA and Canada
by Routledge
711 Third Avenue, New York, NY 10017

A GlassHouse book

Routledge is an imprint of the Taylor & Francis Group, an informa business

First issued in paperback 2011

Typeset in Sabon by
Glyph International

British Library Cataloging in Publication Data
A catalogue record for this book is available
from the British Library

Library of Congress Cataloging in Publication Data
Solivetti, Luigi M.
    Immigration, social integration, and crime : a cross-national approach / Luigi M. Solivetti.
        p. cm.
    "A GlassHouse book."
    Includes bibliographical references and index.
    ISBN 978-0-415-49072-6
    1. Europe—Emigration and immigration. 2. Social integration—Europe.
    3. Crime—Europe. I. Title.
    JV7590.S66 2010
    304.8'4–dc22
                                                2009045002

ISBN13: 978-0-415-49072-6 (hbk)
ISBN13: 978-0-415-69774-3 (pbk)
ISBN13: 978-0-203-88078-4 (ebk)

Contents

Illustrations

Figures

Charts

Tables

Foreword

David Downes and Paul Rock

The centuries-old issue of immigration has, for the past few decades, been revived as a growing and disturbing element in relation to questions of integration, crime and punishment. However, much as it may have figured in public discourses, usually as a symptom of increasing destabilization, but at times as, in itself, a direct cause of crime, rational and informed debate has been handicapped by the sheer difficulties of assembling, let alone analysing, adequate data on the interplay between immigration, crime and punishment. A particularly complex set of problems, both technically and conceptually, are involved in distinguishing between different groups of immigrants: non-nationals as distinct from those granted citizenship; those from within the European Union and those from without; and how to define and measure with some rigour trends across national boundaries even within Europe itself. In this path-breaking book, Luigi Solivetti tackles these problems not only systematically but in key respects for the first time. First published in Italy in 2004 by il Mulino, this edition has been updated and much expanded as well as lucidly translated.

In the context of globalization, a term which often obscures as much as it reveals, the twenty-first century had long been in prospect as an era of the mass movement of people, escaping as refugees from despotic regimes or from relative or – less often than is supposed – dire poverty for better civil protections and economic prospects in the developed world. Yet the presumption that immigration portends a rise in crime and growing social disruption is at best a distraction from constructing humane policies of asylum and resettlement; at worst a recipe for what Stan Cohen termed both moral panic (1972) and states of denial (2001). As Solivetti makes clear, the gains to the host society from immigration, and the crimes committed against the migrants in their society of origin, as well as in the process of migration, are viewed as far less compelling.

Despite the odds against it, this study provides grounds for cautious optimism. Solivetti analyses the fullest data set so far assembled on cross-national trends in Europe and the USA to demonstrate that the more welfare-oriented and socially protected the society, the more levels of crime and punishment among non-national immigrants are modified. This conclusion complements the recent work of Nicola Lacey (2008) on political economy and punishment, and that of Wilkinson and Pickett (2009) on the links between egalitarian social and economic policies and relatively lower rates of virtually all social problems and punitive 'solutions'. This is not wishful thinking or partisan cherry-picking of the data, but close-grained social science. There is a clear narrative here which we ignore at our peril.

Luigi Solivetti is a social scientist whose work has spanned social anthropology – one of his major studies, *Equilibrio e Controllo in una Societa Tradizionale [Balance and Control in a Traditional Society]* Rome, Istituto Italo-Africano & L'Harmattan, 1996) was an ethnography of social control and community relations in northern Nigeria – sociology, criminology and social statistics. He thus brings to bear on the vexed topics of immigration, integration, crime and punishment an unusual sensitivity to and expertise in the human realities beneath the surface of demographic trends.

References

Cohen, S. 1972. *Folk Devils and Moral Panics.* London: Macgibbon and Kee.

Cohen, S. 2001. *States of Denial: Knowing about Atrocities and Suffering.* Cambridge: Polity.

Lacey, N. 2008. *The Prisoners' Dilemma: Political Economy and Punishment in Contemporary Democracies.* Cambridge: Cambridge University Press.

Wilkinson, R. and Pickett, K. 2009. *The Spirit Level: Why More Equal Societies Almost Always Do Better.* London: Allen Lane.

Acknowledgements

The author wishes to thank Enrica Aureli, Françoise Bliek, Susanna Garroni, Eugenio Sonnino, Peter Spring and Enrico Zaghini for all their help and advice during the writing of this book.

Introduction

Here you are free and you have pride ...
Long as you stay on your own side!
Free to be anything you choose ...
Free to wait tables and shine shoes!
(R. Wise and J. Robbins,
West Side Story, 1961)

Literature, working on personal experience, sometimes rapidly grasps what the social sciences laboriously study. In his novel *The Road to Los Angeles*, the writer John Fante, familiar as he was with emigration from personal experience, regarded it from a viewpoint far removed from sentimentality or mawkishness. When Fante touches on the social problems revolving round emigration, his descriptions are as distasteful as they are illuminating. The novel's protagonist, Bandini, has known, like the author, the immigrant's sufferings, and cannot easily forget how at school his classmates called him *wop* and told him he should have stayed back home. And when he finds himself working in a revolting fish cannery, together with Asian immigrants only recently arrived, the first thing he does is to call the person working next to him *nigger*; and to explain just what he had in mind, he says to him: 'You are a damn foreigner ... I was born right here in good old California' (Fante 1985).

It would be just as well to begin by asking ourselves what chance there is for us to end up like the protagonist of Fante's novel. There's no lack of reasons for concern. In *good old Europe*, as Bandini would put it, there has been a significant influx of immigrants in recent years. Countries with a long tradition of emigration have found themselves insensibly turned, almost without them realizing it, into countries of immigration. Countries with a population conditioned, homogenized even, by centuries of living together, with common cultural and religious characteristics, or at least with differences polished by habit, have suddenly found themselves living cheek by jowl not with *one* foreigner, a figure that excites curiosity and in general benevolence (like Pocahontas), but with foreigners *en masse*. Many have had the unnerving sensation, a quite novel one for them, of finding themselves the sole native occupants on board a bus or other means of transport whose passengers are all immigrants. Or they find themselves on a street frequented only by immigrants. The sense of disorientation, or even unease, that they usually derive from such an experience is not due merely to the mass character of the phenomenon, but also the consciousness that these people are not tourists: in other words, they are not in transit, but are here to stay.

This first impression, however, is likely to be accompanied with other considerations. We may begin by noting that this is a phenomenon that cannot be understood or defined within national frontiers. The dimension in which this phenomenon needs to be placed is transnational; and, for our purposes, it is that of Western Europe. Now, many in Europe itself consider the European Union merely a series of accords for the free circulation of goods and, subordinately, for alleviating the hassle that people had to go through whenever they crossed the frontiers. A fundamental policy of the European Union, however, consists also of the free movement of EU citizens: it consists in giving citizens of the individual countries the chance to seek better opportunities of work and life elsewhere within the wider frontiers of the European Union. The current presence in all EU countries of non-nationals, who are nonetheless citizens of the European Union, represents a phenomenon that presumably will not be reduced but on the contrary become increasingly significant, to the point of producing, in an admittedly distant future, situations in which the majority of some countries will consist of non-natives. Luxembourg, for example, seems already far advanced in this direction.

It should be noted, at the same time, that this policy of the free circulation of EU citizens has paradoxically coincided with the growth of immigration to the EU of those coming not from the EU itself but from countries very distant in terms of geography, culture, economic development, religion and so on. Indeed, immigration from non-EU and non-European countries has far outstripped – with one or two exceptions – immigration within the EU. If we look at the EU as a whole, EU non-nationals form only a third of all non-nationals; and of the remaining two-thirds roughly half consist of non-European non-nationals.

The combination of immigration from EU countries and that from non-EU and non-European countries has had the cumulative effect of Western Europe assuming a role in international migration of which few Europeans themselves are conscious. Western Europe has received, at least since the early 1990s, an annual influx of immigrants far outstripping that of the USA (see Chapter 3.3), i.e. that of the country that represents *par excellence*, in the public consciousness, the *land of immigration*.

Immigration to Western Europe, moreover, represents a far from transitory phenomenon: there are good reasons for assuming that it will be of long duration. For some of its underlying causes are becoming ever more pronounced, and ever more pressing.

In the first place, while the overall gap between the advanced economies as a whole and the backward economies as a whole has not grown any wider in recent years – indeed the rapid development of countries such as China, Malaysia and Brazil has reduced it – the gap between the two extremes represented by the richest countries and the poorest countries of the world has at the same time dramatically widened. Now, the countries of the EU represent the most affluent bloc in the world with an annual average income (GNP) of over $30,000 per capita. And this bloc is geographically closest to the poorest bloc, situated in sub-Saharan Africa, with an annual average income of approximately $500 per capita. The bloc of EU countries is also close to other poor and turbulent regions, such as the Middle East and North Africa, where, if we exclude the oil-producing countries and Israel, the GNP is in general of the order of $1,500–3,000 per capita; and such as the former Communist countries of Eastern Europe. The latter present three negative conditions that have repercussions on the phenomenon of emigration: a level of average income that is low, at least in comparison with that of Western European countries; often a deterioration in living standards (lower income, greater economic inequalities, lower life expectancy) since the disintegration of the Soviet Union; and a breakdown of the internal equilibria that had also enforced rigid controls on internal and international emigration. We can therefore identify a situation characterized by an ever more pronounced *economic and social differentiation* between Western Europe on the one hand and the Third and former Second World, on the other. It should be noted that this differential is dissimilar from the one that led to the mass emigration of Western Europeans 50 or 100 years ago. Those emigrants went to America or to other European countries to earn more money, let's say twice what they could have obtained if they had stayed at home. But the emigrants from the so-called developing countries who seek their fortunes in Western Europe today are inspired by the not unrealistic hope of earning ten times what they could possibly obtain in their homelands. So we can safely predict that this *differential* will give rise to a growth in pressure on the phenomenon of migration to the countries of the EU. An improvement of the economic conditions now taking place in many developing countries will also contribute to this growth in pressure. For, paradoxical as it might seem, and contrary to what might be thought, extreme poverty is more an obstacle than an incentive to emigration. True, it is especially the inhabitants of the poor countries that tend to emigrate; but among these the poorest and the most ignorant are impeded by their very condition of indigence. Migrations, like revolutions, start when conditions begin to get better. A growth – albeit a relative growth – of the income and education for the masses in the developing countries will make emigration a more viable option; and the decrease in the cost of air travel will have the same effect.

In the second place, the demographic factor is presented as a factor at least as critical. Western Europe is overall a demographic area characterized by an insignificant variation of its indigenous population. The natural variation of the population (i.e. the difference between live births and deaths) fell from 0.7 per cent to 0.1 per cent from 1950 to the start of the twenty-first century; and some countries (Germany, Italy, Sweden) have for years been in a phase of negative variation (with the number of deaths outstripping that of births). In contrast, the annual average growth of population in the poorest countries is around 2.5 per cent. Many of these countries have a variation of 3 per cent or more; in other words, a rate equivalent to a doubling of their population within a time span of 23 years or less. At the same time, we have an ageing European population, characterized by age groups comprising a population share that tends to be similar from one group to another, combined with a decreasing percentage of the young population and that of working age. By contrast, the structure of the age groups in the poorest countries is drastically skewed in the other direction, and the percentage of the working population is growing. Over 50 per cent of the population in these countries are below the age of 20; and over 25 per cent are aged between 14 and 29. So the population in the poorest countries predominantly consists of children, adolescents and young adults, i.e. those who represent the part of the population most exposed to the problems of social, economic and professional integration, and more prone to look around for alternatives. From 1985 to 2005, the population of working age between the ages of 20 and 39 in EU countries has decreased by 5 per cent (and is expected to further decrease in the years ahead); it has increased by more than 50 per cent in the developing countries.

All this can be summed up with the concept of the existence of a *demographic differential* between Western Europe and the Third World. The consequences of this *differential* for the current and future trend of the phenomenon of migration are easy enough to grasp; on the one hand, the reduction of European demographic growth and the lack of natural replacement of Europe's young age groups are translated into lack of manpower, and this in turn into a demand for an immigrant workforce; on the other hand, the masses of youths in the developing countries represent an enormous reservoir of potential emigrants.

Those who wish to derive from this situation the image of a Western Europe as a fortress besieged by ever larger armies of foreigners would, in our view, be distorting the economic and social reality. To remain at the metaphorical level, we could speak, more plausibly, of an island of prosperity and opportunity (in terms not only of economic opportunities but also of political rights and civil liberties) towards which many coming from less privileged areas are attracted. The image of the fortress under siege would tend, in particular, to conceal the contribution that many of these immigrants have already been making for years to this prosperity and to the efficient functioning of the socio-economic organization of Western Europe. Already in the decade 1950–60, the first boom of European economic development drew advantage (not in all European countries, admittedly, but undoubtedly in some of them) from the contribution of the huge numbers of non-national workers employed, especially in the industrial sector. Today, the situation is more homogeneous: in all the countries of Western Europe, and at the same time in almost all sectors, the contribution of non-nationals to the economy is significant. Some sectors, in particular such as harvesting/fruit picking, home helps, hotels and restaurant staff, carers for the elderly and street traders, use the immigrant workforce in a particularly significant way; work that is sometimes regular, sometimes irregular, but in any case a significant contribution to the labour market. The history of migration, besides, shows that immigrants enrich, rather than impoverish, the host country, as is shown by the development and prosperity achieved by countries preponderantly of immigration such as the USA, Canada and Australia; that immigrants normally constitute a better motivated and more enterprising group than natives in the workplace; and that they aspire to material prosperity and therefore consume, thus expanding the professional and economic opportunities of the indigenous population.

Having said that, we cannot fail to point out that the control of immigration and the integration of immigrants pose serious and growing problems for the countries of the EU. Those who think the problems at issue here are relatively trivial, merely 'banal' aspects of the budget allocated to welfare, or social security, would be mistaken. It is enough to bear in mind that immigration has forced, and continues to force, a reflection on the principles of contemporary liberal theory: and in particular a re-definition of the extension of those human rights (political rights, civil liberties, economic rights) that ought to form the normative core of relations between State, individuals, and groups. The problems of immigration, for example, have highlighted the obstacles encountered in trying to put into practice the affirmation that the individual possesses an inherent *inviolability* (namely, a series of inalienable rights) based on ideals of justice, over which not even the reasons of insufficiency of welfare should prevail (Rawls 1971). This difficult (and in some respects painful) re-definition of human rights when they have regarded non-nationals emerged with particular force subsequent to the crisis induced by the economic recession of the 1970s, and has assumed various forms: restrictions on international mobility; curbs on the residence permits granted to non-nationals already present in Western Europe; resistance by governments and various political groups to the requests of non-nationals for naturalization, participation in political life, and equality with citizens in terms of right to state benefits; and so on (Petilli 1993).

The position of the various European countries in terms of these restrictions is however, highly differentiated, because they present some basic parameters of the phenomenon of migration that are far from homogeneous.

A first aspect of differentiation consists of the scale itself of immigration in the various European countries. There are countries such as Belgium, Germany, France, Austria, Sweden and Switzerland (not to mention Luxembourg, which forms a case of its own in view of its small demographic size), in which the percentage of non-nationals is decidedly high, from 5 per cent to almost 20 per cent of the total resident population. By contrast, other countries, such as Italy, Spain and Portugal, presented down to the 1990s a non-national population equivalent to only 1–2 per cent of the resident population.

These marked differences in the percentage of foreigners in relation to the local population are a matter of considerable interest. It is presumed they are correlated with other differences between the various European countries: differences in terms of the policies adopted towards non-EU immigrants, legacies of the colonial past, and also economic and social conditions.

One difference that undoubtedly merits attention is that of the historical development of immigration. Some European countries present a long tradition of accepting waves of immigrants. France already had, by the early 1920s, a huge population of non-nationals, equivalent to roughly 4 per cent of the total population. This percentage had risen to 6.5 per cent by 1931; after the Second World War and to the present day the figure has not significantly changed, even though the origin of the non-national population has dramatically changed. Germany has had, since the second half of the 1960s, a sizeable population of non-nationals; by the early 1970s it had risen to *c.* 4 per cent of the population and continued to grow substantially in the following years. Even higher percentages were registered during the same years in Belgium. Switzerland had hosted a sizeable non-national population (higher than 10 per cent of the total) already in the period before the First World War; and by the early 1960s had once again returned to similar figures, before embarking on a further expansion. More modest but nonetheless significant percentages were registered in Great Britain already by the early 1960s. By contrast, other countries, such as Italy or Spain, down to the 1980s registered a percentage of non-national population substantially lower than those of the countries we have just cited, and lower than 0.5 per cent.

In turn, the evolution of the phenomenon of immigration is also very dissimilar in terms of the immigrant share of the resident population. Thus, countries with a still low percentage of non-nationals may be characterized by a rapid growth of their influx of immigrants. This is important for the central aspect of our analysis: namely, for integration and social control. A rapid growth of immigration is an aspect that allows us to predict, *ceteris paribus*, greater difficulties for the integration of new immigrants within the host country.

Other significant differences consist of the country of origin of immigrants. The origin of immigrants in the various countries, whether they are non-Europeans, or non EU-citizens, represents a strikingly heterogeneous phenomenon. There are countries such as Germany, Luxembourg and Ireland in which non-European immigrants form a small minority of the total number of immigrants, whereas in other countries, such as Italy and Portugal, they form the majority. There is no correlation, however, between the immigrant share of the resident population and the distance from Europe of the countries whence they come. Countries with a low percentage of immigrant population may have to come to terms with immigrants in large part coming from remote areas, not only from a geographical but also from a social, cultural and economic point of view. The problem of the integration of these immigrants will present presumably greater difficulties than those posed by immigration from less distant areas.

Apart from these differences between the various countries – differences that nonetheless remain significant – the criminality of non-nationals represents not only a more striking, or more immediate, aspect of the problem of integration, but also the critical point of all the social balances that affect immigration. The criminality of non-nationals represents a tipping point, in two senses: the point at which the problems of integration of non-nationals themselves risk shifting the conduct of immigrants towards antisocial adaptation; and, simultaneously, the point at which the hospitality – often cautious – of the indigenous population is transformed into hostility towards the *alien*. A reflection of this is the fact that in the countries of Western Europe the issue of the control of immigration and the criminality connected with it has progressively assumed a central role in the electoral policy of governments and oppositions in recent decades, often contributing in a decisive manner to their success or their fall.

Ever since the late nineteenth century, moreover, the criminality of non-nationals was a central theme not only of the political but also the cultural and scientific debate in the countries most involved by (and dependent on) the phenomenon of immigration, such as France and the USA. And it is no surprise that in recent years, with the greater importance and *diffusionism* that have characterized the phenomenon of immigration, this debate has been extended to all the countries of Western Europe. It may further be noted that the theses that have successively come to the fore in this field have gradually gone through various phases, and the concepts formulated in each of them have been different. In brief, and with due apologies for the inevitable reductionism, we could say that a first phase in the debate within the social sciences was one in which the reasons for the criminality of non-nationals were essentially ascribed to biological or racial differences: these, it was alleged, had structurally characterized certain ethnic groups and rendered them inevitably more prone to engage in criminal activities. A second phase was characterized by a shift in the identification of the causal agents from the biological to the cultural elements typical of particular ethnic groups: the cultural differences existing between nationals and non-nationals were alleged to have produced cultural conflicts from which forms of conduct judged criminal, at least by the culture of the host country, all too easily emerged. A third phase was characterized in turn by a shift in explanations to the objective socio-economic conditions of the immigrant, in his rapport with the host society. Criminality appeared, in this perspective, as the more or less probable result of a negative, or at least inadequate, integration or assimilation: the reflection, as it were, of a failed adaptation. The differences between the various ethnic groups now seemed an obsolete theme; or alternatively they were taken into consideration as the cause in turn of the various probabilities of achieving integration rather than as the direct cause of criminal conduct itself.

As for the first of these theses, the hypothesis of a particular propensity to crime within some ethnic groups – a hypothesis which has enjoyed considerable diffusion in popular opinion – the empirical evidence tends rather to discount than support it. It is true, admittedly, that in many European countries it is easy enough to substantiate a particular contribution to crime by non-nationals belonging to some particular ethnic groups. At the same time, non-nationals belonging to other groups show very low levels of criminality in practically all countries. It is clear, therefore, that there is some kind of relation between ethnic group and crime. But this ought not necessarily to be interpreted as a particular *ethnic propensity* to crime on the part of certain groups. At the historical level, it may be pointed out that in the USA some groups have been identified as particularly prone to crime. It is striking, however, that these groups have tended to change over time. This unenviable primacy seems first to have been accorded to the Irish, then to the Italians, then to the Puerto-Ricans, and then to other Latin-American ethnic groups. At the very least, one can say that the race–crime relation is not constant. Already in 1913, after all, when in the USA the idea of an association between race and crime was widespread, it was said: 'Admitting the inferiority of some races – but this is, in truth, for the most part gratuitous assumption and presumption on the part of the "superior" races – who will say that the "inferior" races will not become like the "superior" in the environment of the "superior"?' (Ferrari 1913).

Today, the main ethnic groups involved in immigration are widely represented in all the countries of Western Europe, due to the already underlined diffusionism of migratory flows. Yet the propensity to crime of the same ethnic groups is far from being homogeneous in the various countries. For example, in Belgium the highest index of criminality (in relation to the quantitative size of the ethnic group) is registered for the Tunisian community; in Germany, the highest indices are registered for the Romanian, Lebanese and Polish communities; in Sweden, for the Latin-Americans; in the Netherlands, for the Caribbeans and Moroccans; in Italy, for the Albanians and immigrants from the former Yugoslavia. And so on. Moreover, in the countries of Western Europe, as already in the USA, it may be noted that various ethnic groups succeed each other at the top of the league tables for the highest rate of criminality.

So, rather than any particular propensity to crime of certain ethnic groups, the evidence might suggest that criminality is not a permanent condition, but a contingent phenomenon: in other words, that the high contribution of particular ethnic groups to crime in determined periods might be connected with the changing conditions to which they are subject. We might, in particular, argue that contingent aspects, such as socio-economic marginality, alienation from the host society, lack of opportunities for integration, and the pressure to form criminal associations with other members of the same ethnic group, impact on the levels of criminality of particular ethnic groups. These characteristics, in our view, are especially determined in ethnic groups of recent immigration and – as regards ethnic criminal associations – in groups sufficiently large in numerical terms either not to be dispersed in the host society or at least prone to remain concentrated. In short, we would be dealing with the 'propensity' to criminality of certain ethnic groups in the sense of a particular recourse to illicit activities as a form of *first adaptation*, hopefully to be followed by a shift towards more conformist forms of adaptation.

The hypothesis that immigrants *ex se* are inevitably more prone to crime seems also to be at variance with the empirical data. In the first place, there are great differences in the share that non-nationals have in the official crime figures in the various European countries; moreover, in some countries the contributions to crime of non-national communities seem to be scarcely significant. Now, if the incidence of non-nationals on the crime figures varies from country to country and there are countries in which this incidence is negligible, then the fact *per se* of being an immigrant does not appear to be a sufficient explanation of the contributions that non-nationals make to the crime statistics. This preliminary conclusion, besides, seems to be corroborated by the historical fact that a long series of empirical studies conducted in various countries of Western Europe in the years 1950–60 had come to the conclusion that the contributions made by non-nationals to crime in quantitative terms were not significantly different from those of the indigenous population (see Ch. 1). So, if the current rates of migrant crime registered in many European countries are high, there must be other, probably more complex, explanations than the simplistic equation immigrant = subject-prone-to-criminality. These explanations could regard the *actual* conditions that characterize immigration in the countries of Western Europe, in view of the fact that the rates for criminality of non-nationals were decidedly lower some decades ago.

It is clear that immigration in Western Europe has registered structural changes: (1) there has been, as I said, a form of *diffusionism* of the migratory phenomenon: the countries of origin of influxes of immigrants into Europe are far more than they were in the past, and these influxes have been directed not only at the countries that have traditionally been the goals of immigration in Europe, but virtually at all countries; (2) the phenomenon of immigration has on the whole involved countries of origin characterized by greater socio-economic and cultural disparities than those that gave rise to previous influxes; the share of citizens of Western Europe as a percentage of the overall phenomenon of immigration in this part of the world has declined and simultaneously that of immigrants from Eastern Europe and from the developing world has increased; (3) the reasons that impel a substantial proportion of current emigrants to abandon their homeland seem to have more to do with the internal difficulties (declining living standards, wars, ethnic conflicts, violations of human rights) in their countries of origin than their realistic prospects of finding a place in the societies to which they move; there has been a sharp decline in so-called *guest workers*, i.e. those who go abroad on the basis of a precise prospect of legal insertion in the labour market for a limited period of time; (4) despite their difficulties of integration, the presence of non-nationals in Western Europe has continued to rise significantly in recent years.

It seems reasonable to assume that these structural changes have had an impact on the relation between migration and criminality. In fact, a series of surveys and studies in recent decades has reached the conclusion that the share of non-nationals in the total number of those charged for various offences, as also of the total number of prison inmates in Europe, is far higher than might be expected on the basis of their proportion of the resident population. The share of non-nationals in the prison population, for example, is thought to have undergone continuous growth over the years. And the percentages of non-nationals charged would seem to confirm this trend. However, it is fair to say that some authorities have expressed doubts about these conclusions; and some radically challenge the data themselves, in particular the statistics of criminality registered. It would be as well, therefore, to examine in greater depth the immigrant share of criminality, and to seek to do so in the light of an effectively trans-national investigation.

The studies so far carried out, it is fair to say, have given priority to the elucidation of the problem already underlined here of the share immigrants have in criminality. But they have failed to analyse the relation between the historical evolution of the rates of criminality and the contributions made by immigrants to crime itself. There are explanations for this singular preference, or perhaps presupposition, for the immigrant share in criminality. Not only are the data for the current situation easier to obtain; they are also those most requested both by a public opinion worried by the danger of immigration today, and by mass media fomented by a demagogic agenda. Privileging the figures for the immigrant share of criminality today, rather than an overall analysis of the diachronic evolution of criminality, recalls in some way other dubiously selective evaluations, such as those that privilege the figures for the 'loss' of jobs formerly filled by nationals rather than the figures for the development of the economy of the country to which immigrants also contribute. In this book, our aim is to analyse precisely the problem of the relation between the overall trend of criminality in the various European countries and the presence of immigrants. We are not in fact convinced by the apparently common-sense opinion that prevails at the present time: namely, that the crime rates for immigrants – usually higher than those of nationals – cannot but compound the overall criminality, simply by being added to the home-grown variety.

On the basis of what has been said so far, and in particular the complexity and variations of the phenomena that revolve around the problem of the relation between migration and criminality, it seems to us sensible to start out from the presupposition that various factors have an influence on this relation. In particular, we think that the explanations of the migration–crime relation belong only in part to the *immigrants'* side of the equation and that the *host society* forms a fundamental parameter of the explanatory model. So, the sharp differences in the share of non-nationals in the crime figures in the various countries could be studied from three different perspectives: (1) that of the characteristics – social, economic and cultural – of the host society, which also include the characteristics of the system of social protection, respect for legality, and recognition of the rights of the most vulnerable; (2) that of the aspects relating to the integration of non-nationals, including in this perspective indicators of effective socio-economic and political integration (for example, employment), indicators of marginality (clandestinity), and indirect indicators of the probability of integration, such as the presence of immigrant families (including young children) and the scale of immigrant influxes; (3) and lastly the perspective of how far immigrants are alien or dissimilar from the culture and mores of their host societies, which we may assume will have some impact on their probabilities of adaptation.

As regards the first perspective, that of the *host society*, there is one feature to which, in our view, particular attention should be paid: namely, its attitude, explicit or implicit, to immigration as a phenomenon in itself, to immigrants, and to those who belong to other nations. On this attitude depend, for example, the policies of support for those who are socially and economically weak (a category into which non-nationals all too easily fall), the willingness to hire foreign workers, their discrimination or not in the workplace, whether in social or economic terms, and their feelings or not of being sidelined or alienated in everyday life. In short, on this attitude of the host society depend others of significance for the integration and consequently also for the conformist or deviant behaviour of immigrants themselves. It is worth pointing out here that there is some evidence to show that a social policy that is generous to immigrants 'pays' in terms of the control of criminality.

This propensity, or not, to look favourably on immigration is influenced in a decisive way by the *nationalism* factor and in particular its xenophobic component. This is something that may seem obsolete. Xenophobic nationalism traditionally revolved around a centralized and authoritarian State; around the concept of *blood-and-soil* nationalism; around the idea of a *destiny* that the nation was called to fulfil, and that united the living to the dead and to those yet to be born in a kind of mystical bond; around the conviction, in short, that other nations were not only different but inferior.

Over the last decades, this xenophobic nationalism has been eroded, or discredited, by the memory of the tragedies it has caused, by the growth of important supranational organizations, such as the United Nations and, as far as Western Europe is concerned, especially the European Union, by the globalization of trade, which has reduced the political and economic role of nation states, and, more generally, by the growth of international relations and the far greater direct and indirect knowledge people have of other countries. Today there are those who emphasize the possibility of a society without (or almost without) the nation state at all, of a society forged from a *thousand cities* (Giddens 1998), and of the propagation of a multicultural mentality (Glazer 1997).

From this point of view, Europe is clearly very different from what it was not only before the Second World War but also in the post-war period. Despite all this, however, it is difficult to deny the continuing presence of attitudes at least in part xenophobic. One sign of this is the emergence more or less everywhere in Europe (in France, in Italy, in Austria, in Holland, in Belgium, in Denmark, in Switzerland) of political movements that present a clear component of suspicion of or hostility towards immigrants. And a further grave sign consists of the thousands of episodes of vicious and often unprovoked physical assaults on immigrants reported throughout Europe in recent years.

To justify these xenophobic attitudes it is usual to plead the alleged intolerability of current levels of immigration, and especially its perceived contribution to criminality. Now, hostility towards immigrants may be fuelled by considerations other than those of racism and xenophobia. A society, however 'open' it is, is unable to absorb, without traumas, an *unlimited* and *uncontrolled* influx of immigrants; especially if it is perceived to have characteristics incompatible (in professional and cultural terms) with those of the host society. It is enough to think of the impact that an uncontrolled influx of immigrants may have on the system of guarantees in favour of workers, on the housing market, on the health service and, more widely, on the welfare state. At the same time, some crime rates seem to threaten a society's long-consolidated and characteristic modes of life, and to dig a deep divide between ethnic groups living together in the same territory. The relation between the criminality of immigrants and the hostile reactions of the host society, however, resembles more a serpent biting its tail than a simple unilateral relation of cause and effect.

Current attitudes of hostility towards immigrants have, in our view, different roots than in the past. Among these roots we no longer find the idea of a strong, centralized, and authoritarian nation state, but rather the opposite idea of the priority of the local society. The idea of the nation's historic *destiny* seems to have been abandoned; the concept of blood and soil, *Blut und Boden*, has been consigned to the history books. The characterizing element of current xenophobia seems to be not any mystical concept of nationhood, but that of a world divided between 'us', self-defined as deserving of the prosperity achieved, and 'them', the dispossessed, who are evidently in need and also for this reason considered as undeserving.

The social phenomena that fuel this hostility also seem to be different from those that supported the nationalism of the past. Current hostility to immigrants finds its breeding ground in modernization and, paradoxically, in contemporary democracy. Modernization has broken the equilibria of traditional society, of the network of community support, and of the 'obligatory' but secure paths of existence. It has simultaneously made individuals more isolated in their individual search for satisfaction and more insecure. Globalization of trade may have promoted interaction – the global village – but it has also made protectionist niches more exposed to free competition by those better equipped, or better organized, and also by those made enterprising by poverty and despair. Democracy, in turn, has given political voice to the masses and, within them, inevitably also to the national components that are weaker, more exposed to competition, more insecure in their petty social adjustments and less culturally equipped to understand, still less appreciate, diversity. These new weaknesses of the masses have only in part been intercepted by the traditional political parties; and, by contrast, have been more readily taken on board by new political movements more adept at exploiting popular feelings, including hostility to immigrants. It is, besides, a long-recognized phenomenon (Eysenck 1972) that the so-called working classes, however progressive they are in their attitude to political power, are conservative – or even downright reactionary – on such issues as homosexuality, feminism, nudity, abstract art, capital punishment, attitudes to juvenile delinquency, to hippies and drop-outs, and what scope should be accorded to immigrants.

Current hostility to immigrants has assumed the form of ethnic and cultural discrimination, through which the main assumptions of democracy and human rights are, in daily practice, denied: and yet these same rights, in patent contradiction, are formally enunciated as universal, and declared as inalienable, in the host society and strenuously claimed for themselves by the indigenous population. Just as the *color bar* gave rise to the contradiction between the egalitarianism of its culture and the practice of racial discrimination in the USA a few decades ago, so in contemporary Europe the reaction to immigration is giving rise to new contradictions: between democracy and ethnic discrimination, between parliamentarianism and xenophobic political movements, and not least between freedom of the press and demagogy.

The hostility in question is sufficiently strong to blind many people to the reality of emigration; to make them incapable of recognizing that migrating means uprooting oneself from social, economic and family bonds; confronting the unknown; and coming to terms with uncertainties far worse on average than those that even the most disadvantaged classes of the host society have to cope with. Emigration often means paying enormous sums of money (for those who are not rich) to be able to afford an illegal transit to Europe; it means becoming the victims of unscrupulous merchants of human flesh; risking death, like the untold thousands who fall by the roadside, victims of disease, hunger or privation, or who meet with a watery grave on the routes of clandestine emigration to Europe. Indeed, the nexus between immigration and crime concerns not only the contribution of immigrants to criminality in the host country, as those seem to think who consider the matter exclusively from the viewpoint of the more immediate interests of the native population, but also the criminality of which immigrants themselves are the victims: as clandestines, as *sans-papiers*, exposed to blackmail and the violence of those who illegally manage their transfer; as the easy victims of fraud, theft and violence at the hands of other immigrants; and as the victims of *hate crime*, i.e. the criminality inspired by the ethnic hatred already mentioned above.

On the basis of these considerations, and the persistence of this hostility even towards these immigrants reduced to an extreme condition of destitution and despair, it seems logical to assume that the probabilities of a peaceful and legitimate integration and 'adjustment' of immigrants in host societies in Western Europe depend on the characteristics of these same societies and their citizens at least as much as they depend on the characteristics of the immigrants themselves; and that the probabilities of non-nationals making a disproportionate contribution to crime follows the same logic.

It may be useful to recall, in this regard, that Nicolò Machiavelli had already argued that the real strength of a nation – but today we would say society – is based on the willingness of its citizens to participate in the government of the *cosa pubblica* and more especially to commit themselves to this government by putting on one side their own immediate interests to achieve objectives that represent benefits for everyone. The concept of the priority of *civic values* over self-interest that Machiavelli had derived from his reading of the history of ancient Rome has powerfully come to the fore again in recent decades with a series of studies on *social capital* (Coleman 1988; Putnam 1993, 2000; Cheong *et al.* 2007). The objective of these studies is no longer to explain the greatness of nations, but more prosaic contemporary idols such as overall economic development and prosperity achieved in the various countries and in the various regions of the same country. The factors that ought to determine development and prosperity, however, remain *civil virtues*, represented by trust in others, willingness to cooperate in the pursuit of shared objectives, and solidarity. Trust, transparency, solidarity, and willingness to cooperate, can all be regarded as forms of generosity to others; more precisely they are forms of short-term altruism with a view to the long-term advantage of the wider community. Now, these civil virtues in our view could be even more decisive for the achievement of other objectives: more particularly, to optimize the integration of immigrants and limit the risks of criminality.

For example, a high cost for social protection presupposes generosity towards those most in need, but it is also a way of containing conflicts. A low level of *corruption* and a high level of *respect for rights* may be particularly important not only to permit anyone, even if weak, to obtain what deservedly belongs to him, but also to foster the general climate of trust in and attention to others. A higher level of trust is usually associated in turn with less prejudice towards those who are different and greater consciousness of the *human dimension* of the problem of immigration.

Taking all this into account, we have for the purposes of this book drawn up a plan of theoretical and empirical research. More precisely, we set ourselves the following objectives: (1) reviewing the theses presented since the nineteenth century on the relation between migration and crime and formulating interpretative hypotheses geared to current immigration in Western Europe; (2) tracing the evolution of immigration in Europe in order to define an historical framework in which to place the hypotheses on the relation between migration and crime; (3) checking whether the rates of criminality in the various European countries are correlated with the presence of immigrants in these same countries; and ascertaining whether the variations in the rates of criminality reflect, or are correlated with, the variations of immigrant quotas; (4) providing a quantitative reconstruction of the non-national share of crime in the various countries of Western Europe; (5) gathering data on the socio-economic situation, culture and civic values in the various countries, and on the characteristics of immigration, so as to evaluate the main hypotheses presented on the relation between immigration and criminality.

The empirical research conducted here, despite its exploratory character, has produced results that seem to conform with what has been said so far. In particular, the empirical findings tend to confirm the high percentage of non-nationals in the official figures of criminality in Western Europe. On the other hand, they show that the characteristics of the host society are strongly correlated with the rates of criminality registered for non-nationals in the various countries. The criminality of non-nationals can, it seems, be better understood by making reference both to the characteristics of the host countries and to the characteristics of those who have sought to better their fortunes in them.

Chapter 1

The debate on immigration and criminality
Past and present

1.1 Immigration and criminality: some basic questions

The phenomenon of immigration seems, by its very nature, to be a catalyst of problems, to pose fundamental questions about our society, and to require adaptation and therefore change. It is enough to think of the incorporation of immigrants in the workforce and the adaptation this requires of them; the impact it produces on often inflexible labour markets; the difficult cultural and social adjustment of immigrants to their new country of adoption; and the cultural re-adaptation that their presence requires of the indigenous population itself. All this contains strong and often salutary elements of change and development, both for immigrants and for the society that receives them. Nonetheless, for various reasons, in part psychological, in part social, and in particular as a result of possible xenophobic reactions, a more disturbing, even threatening, aspect emerges from the scenario of migratory phenomena: this aspect is the relation between immigration and criminality.

The character of this relation is widely disputed; considerable differences of view about it exist, not only between politicians, but also between experts, while at a more general level a divergence of view between the expert and the layman can be perceived. The divergences begin with the term 'immigrant' itself. It is not so unambiguous as might be supposed. The term is used to identify, in the various countries, those subjects that belong to categories that only in part coincide. These divergences can be traced, in our view, to cultural and organizational traits peculiar to the various countries; more specifically to different ways of regarding the phenomenon of migration and the relation between immigrants and the host society. In the countries of continental Europe, characterized by the centrality of the State and its bureaucratic apparatus, the semantic value of the term is bound up with the question whether the immigrant has or has not been accorded the same rights as the citizen born and bred in the country in question. The immigrant, seen from this point of view, is, therefore, in essence the *non-national*, i.e. the non-citizen. And so the gathering of information in the countries of continental Western Europe was first of all focused on this dichotomy between national and non-national citizens. Analyses of the criminality of immigrants have also made extensive use of this concept and therefore focused their attention on the criminality of *non-nationals*. The preference given to the concept of nationality/non-nationality has also been reinforced by the fact that immigration to Western Europe was predominantly temporary in the decades following the Second World War: it was the boom period of the guest worker. Seen in this light, the alternative category of the *foreign-born* – a category comprising also those who have assumed the citizenship of the host country – seemed of little interest. A consequence of the preference given to the non-nationals category is that as soon as the immigrant receives the citizenship of his host country he tends to merge with the mass of other citizens, and the information about him becomes correspondingly thin. Not surprisingly, the available information on the children of immigrants, born in the host country and citizens of it, is extremely scarce, in spite of the fact that various studies, especially in North America, drew attention, already in the first half of the twentieth century, to the particular problems of integration and deviance that these subjects posed (see below in this chapter).

The distinction between citizens – whatever be their origin – and non-nationals was adopted by the EU and its statistical studies agency, Eurostat. Some countries, however, seem disinclined to follow this approach. In the United Kingdom, and to a lesser degree in Holland, the colonial past – combined with a lesser state-dominated tradition – seems to re-surface in the tendency to use the concept of ethnicity, or ethnic group, and thus to draw a distinction between whites and others (blacks, Asians), rather than between citizens and non-nationals. In the UK, for example, data relating to the *nationality* of subjects arrested and sentenced by the courts have never been collected, whereas the studies that distinguish them on the basis of their ethnic origin are numerous. This approach has at least the advantage of permitting those who are immigrants, but who have since become citizens of their host country, or who are the children of immigrants, to be easily identified, but it naturally ignores the citizenship variable and its possible repercussions on integration. In the USA – in conformity with its tradition of *light* statehood – the concept of citizenship has not assumed any priority in the analysis of the problems of immigration. The dominant concept has been that of birth in the national territory, a concept that indirectly emphasizes the importance of being born and bred in the country. North American institutions and academics accordingly attach priority to the dichotomy *native/foreign-born* in analysing criminality. Together with the concept of *foreign-born*, considerable emphasis is placed in the USA on ethnicity (whites, blacks, Hispanics, Asians), also as a consequence of the existence in the country of a large population of African-Americans, who although they have been American citizens for centuries continue to be characterized by differentials in terms of their economic level, education, employment and share in criminality.

These contrasts between the categories that can be distinguished within the concept of immigrant have inevitably channelled in different ways the analyses of the whole problem of *immigration and crime*. In spite of this, it may be said that this problem revolves round a basic question: whether the contribution to criminality of immigrants – identified with one or other of the categories described above – is quantitatively and qualitatively different from that of the indigenous population.

The perception of a high rate of criminality among foreigners has often emerged in the Western world, especially in the nations in which the immigration rate has been particularly high, as in France. Already in the years 1860–70, the rate of criminality of foreigners in France was considered far higher than that of native-born French people (roughly five times higher: Tarde 1895); for example, in 1867 alone, the year of the Exposition Universale in Paris, no fewer than 1,544 Italian children were arrested in that city for vagabondage and begging (Du Camp 1870).

In the USA, there was a widespread conviction that immigration had fuelled the growth of crimes of violence against the person, of behaviour contrary to public order and of offences connected with prostitution (US Senate Documents 1911; Laughlin 1922; US National Commission on Law Observance and Enforcement 1931).

Nonetheless, various empirical studies conducted in the twentieth century in countries with a high rate of immigration have denied any higher percentage of criminal activity in the foreign population. The US Senate Report of 1911 found that the percentage of immigrants among the prison population was not higher than the percentage of immigrants in the general population; and, what's more, that immigrants were on average involved in less serious misdemeanours than natives; even if, as regards juvenile delinquents, immigrants were over-represented, while even more pronounced was the over-representation of the children of immigrants among the prison population (US Senate Documents 1911). A few years later, the US National Commission on Law Observance and Enforcement (1931) discovered that, in spite of the evident conditions of disadvantage in social and economic terms in which new arrivals found themselves, the popular image that represented them as prone to crime was unfounded. In effect, the Commission, analysing the figures relating to incriminations, found widely different rates of criminality in the various groups of immigrants; but it had not ascertained any direct relation between immigration and crime; indeed, the overall rate of criminality for foreign-born whites was substantially lower than that of native-born whites (208 contra 347) and a great deal lower than the rate for native-born blacks. In the same years, the US Department of Commerce, Bureau of the Census (1933), no longer found significant differences between children of immigrants and children of natives in terms of prison admissions. Sutherland (1924) summed up his point of view on the relation between immigration and criminality by asserting that it had been reversed. Since 'fresh' immigrants had on average lower rates of criminality than natives, whereas with the passage of time their rates – and especially that of their children – gradually rose and came to resemble more closely those of natives, the inference could be drawn, he argued, that the criminality of immigrants was the effect of their association with natives and with their values; in other words, immigrants did not import criminality but absorbed it from the host society. Several years later, Taft (1936), adopting much the same perspective, not only confirmed the higher rates of criminality of the second generations but pointed out that the percentage of persons who ended up in prison was actually lower in the States in which there was a prevalence of fresh immigrants. Not surprisingly, in the light of these findings, the identification of immigrants as criminals in the USA at the start of the twentieth century was reinterpreted, some decades later, as a *symbolic crusade*, aimed at exorcising the fear determined by the far-reaching changes (urbanization, industrialization) taking place in American society (Gusfield 1963).

Similar findings have been confirmed elsewhere. Thus, in Canada, at the end of the 1960s, the rate of criminality attributed to immigrants (sentenced and imprisoned) was lower than the rate of criminality attributed to natives (Canada, Department of the Solicitor General 1974; Giffen 1976). In Germany, Zimmermann (1966) found a lower rate of criminality in immigrants than in natives. In Switzerland, Neumann (1963) pointed out that the image of foreigners, and in particular of Italians, as responsible for a high level of criminality found no confirmation in the empirical data; and Gillioz (1967), in spite of the considerable presence of foreigners in Switzerland, did not find any consequent increase of the national crime rate. In Belgium, the studies of Liben (1963) and Debuyst (1970) concluded that the level of criminality of immigrant youth was no higher than that of native-born youth. In France, Robert *et al.* (1968) ascertained a rate of criminality among male immigrant youth only slightly higher than natives of the same age group and gender. By contrast, in the UK, both McClintock and Gibson (1961) and Bottoms (1967) found the rate of criminality of Irish immigrants far higher than that of natives. And a few years later, the research of Desdevides (1976) in France reached alarming conclusions about the over-representation of immigrants in the crime statistics at Nantes.

At least by the start of the 1980s, however, the studies on the criminality of non-nationals in Europe seem to indicate the emergence of a new phase. This change in the theoretical debate seems to have come about concurrently with an alteration in the characteristics of immigration to Western Europe. The new waves of immigrants seem to have consisted of individuals who, as we have already mentioned in our Introduction, mainly came from countries more distant from Europe than had been the case in the past. These immigrants were attracted to Europe no longer by the high demand for labour in the European countries, as had been the case before (in the boom years of the *Wirtschaftswunder*), but seem to have been stimulated mainly by their own offer of work (Barbagli 1998). Their arrival in Europe had as a rule in no way been encouraged by European governments, as had been the case when their role as additional manpower had been requested; their presence in Europe, on the contrary, was often characterized by illegality or irregularity. In any case, these new studies conducted on immigration and crime by various scholars in a series of European countries (e.g. Andersson 1984; Junger-Tas 1985; Albrecht 1988; Natale 1988; Junger 1989; Albrecht 1993; Hebberecht 1997; Martens 1997; Tournier 1997; Killias 1997; Barbaret and García-España 1997; Suisse 2001) tended to produce results which were not necessarily homogeneous but which did agree on one basic tendency: they ascertained, that is, a rate of criminality among immigrants that was on average far higher (from two to four times higher) than that of the national population considered. The official data relating to the non-nationals incriminated for various offences show that on average non-nationals are over-represented, in proportion, that is, to their share of the overall population of the country. A similar situation was ascertained for the rate of non-nationals among the prison population in almost all European countries, a rate that was higher than the percentage of non-nationals among the country's total population (see further, Chapter 5).

This trend, which seems to be confirmed throughout Western Europe, is not, however, a universal phenomenon. Nothing similar was ascertained in North America, given that the crime rates of foreign-borns in both the USA and Canada remained lower or at any rate no higher than those of natives (Butcher and Piehl 1997; Reid *et al.* 2005; Rumbaut *et al.* 2006; Hagan *et al.* 2008). At the start of the twenty-first century, the rates of imprisonment in the USA for the critical age group 18–39 years were some five times higher for all natives than those registered for all foreign-borns. The rates for imprisonment for foreign-borns, however, were not homogeneous: they differed greatly depending on ethnic group. In the case of some nationalities of the Hispanic ethnic group, high rates of imprisonment, similar to or higher than those of all natives, were registered. But, in comparison between natives and foreign-borns belonging to the same ethnic group, the foreign-borns invariably showed lower rates of criminality (Rumbaut and Ewin 2007). So it is not surprising that the second generations should continue to have higher crime rates than the first (Morenoff and Astor 2006; Hagan *et al.* 2008).

From these multifarious and often conflicting data, which refer in the main to a rather long time span, the impression was derived that the relation between the phenomena of immigration and crime is ambiguous; that it is not stable in time; and that it may assume different connotations in the various national contexts. Even the hypothesis that non-national communities in Europe currently contribute disproportionately to the scale of criminality needs to be better qualified. It should be pointed out that this hypothesis does not imply that *all* groups of non-nationals present in the various countries of Western Europe are over-represented in the judicial and penitentiary statistics. In fact, in each country of Western Europe there are national groups (or ethnic minorities) that are over-represented, and other national groups (or other ethnic minorities) that are under-represented (Tonry 1997). In other words, the over-representation of non-nationals is the overall result of the sum of the very different rates of criminality in the various groups of non-nationals. For example, in the UK the rates of criminality for Indians and Pakistanis are far lower than those relating to groups coming from the West Indies, and not dissimilar from those of the general population (Smith 1997; see also Radzinowicz and King 1977). In the Netherlands, Turkish and Chinese immigrants present far lower rates that those of other groups coming from North Africa and the Caribbean (Junger-Tas 1997).

Therefore, to consider all groups of immigrants as over-represented in the crime statistics is unfounded. But this is not the only misconception. Let us examine the overall contribution of immigrants to the statistics of national criminality in the various European countries. The above-mentioned studies conducted in recent decades and, even more so, popular opinion, have concurred in considering that this contribution is widely disproportionate if compared with the percentage of immigrants among the resident population. On the basis of all this, the growing presence of immigrants has been perceived as the cause of the growth in crime in Western Europe. But this is a logical short circuit. For any over-representation of immigrants in the crime statistics does not at all imply that, assuming a growth of criminality has been ascertained at least for certain offences, this growth is essentially due to immigrants. This is a fundamental point that has unfortunately been widely ignored in most of the studies cited above. This problem needs to be analysed in greater detail, with the aim of ascertaining whether, and to what extent, the contribution of immigrants to criminality is reflected in the overall trend of crime (see further, Chapter 4).

In any case, while there is some degree of concordance about the fact that high average rates of criminality have been registered for non-nationals in the countries of Western Europe, the reason or the reasons for this phenomenon remain uncertain and contested. A variety of hypotheses, applicable to crime in general, have been used to explain the criminality of immigrants. Some of these seem more significant, or more plausible, today, also in the light of the results produced by empirical studies that have referred to these specific hypotheses.

The hypothesis of deviant forms of behaviour on the part of non-nationals as a consequence of the existence of a *strain*, i.e. of a tension of *anomic type*, has a long history behind it. Already Durkheim in the later nineteenth century had introduced the concept of *anomie* both in general terms and with specific reference to the conduct of non-nationals. At the general level, Durkheim identified *anomie* as a substantial lack of social or moral standards (the Greek term *anomia* means lack of rules), and more specifically as a lack of restraints on individual aspirations. The context in which this took place is characterized by rapid social and especially cultural change, which generates an uncontrolled expansion of the aspirations induced by society (particularly in the industrial and commercial sectors), to which no effective ability to realize them could correspond (Durkheim 1893). More specifically, Durkheim himself (1897), in examining the phenomenon of suicide, ascertained that the frequency of deviant forms of behaviour among immigrants was far higher than among natives.

Formulated in the context of the rapid social and economic transformation of Western Europe in the nineteenth century, the concept of *anomie* and its reference to immigration had no difficulty in being translated into the context of the USA, where both the conditions of rapid change and the continuous influx of immigrants seemed to prepare a fertile terrain for its application. Thus, Thomas and Znaniecki, in their famous research on the immigration of Polish peasants to the USA, were undoubtedly influenced by the concepts formulated by Durkheim. They related the alienation and deviance of immigrants to a situation of *social disorganization*; i.e. to a situation characterized by the diminishing influence of social rules of conduct, as in particular in the case in which 'the old system that controlled more or less effectively the behaviour of members of the group disintegrated so rapidly that the development of a new social system fails to keep step with the process of disintegration' (1918–1920, vol. 5: 165–166).

A few years later, Park, in 1925, described the situation of immigrants in the USA and its relation to the phenomenon of crime. Park noted that, for immigrants of the first generation, the social rituals, customs and moral order that characterized their countries of origin were in some way transferred by immigrants themselves to the host country and continued to subsist for a considerable period, in spite of the influence of North American culture; it played a role of containing any pressure to engage in criminal activity. But this social control disappeared when this system of values weakened and declined, and when attempts were made to replace the social control exercised by *customs* with the lesser restraints of the *written law*: this happened in the case of immigrants of the second generation, i.e. in the case of the children of immigrants. As Park pointed out, the statistical data gathered in the USA in the early years of the century showed that the level of criminality of these children of immigrants was higher than that of longer-standing American citizens. He also emphasized the sharp differences in terms of levels of criminality in the various ethnic communities of immigrants in the USA, and thought it possible to relate these differences to the level of social cohesion and mutual support that characterized the various communities: thus, communities such as that of the Japanese showed simultaneously strong cohesion, mutual support, communication, information, and low levels of crime (Park *et al.* 1925). These arguments of Park seem on the one hand indebted to Durkheim's concepts of cultural integration, cohesion and anomie and, on the other, to suggest the importance of social and economic success (favoured by cohesion and mutual support) as the key to explain the different levels of criminality of the various ethnic communities in the USA. This is a thesis that seems to anticipate the later contributions of Merton.

Park, however, returned to the question a few years later in an article specifically dedicated to the phenomenon of migration. In this article, Park (1928) maintained that the process of migration itself – though one that he himself, rejecting facile racial prejudices (Melossi 2000), considered very rich in positive consequences in terms of social and cultural transformations – inevitably produced a socially pathological type of personality. Park, in reaching this conclusion, had clearly drawn on the contribution made to this question by his mentor Simmel (1908), who had spoken of the foreigner as a social individual characterized at once by *closeness* and *distance*, by the fact of simultaneously confronting the group and being outside it: Park thus described the immigrant as a cultural hybrid, someone who intimately shared the traditions and cultural life of two distinct peoples. So there was a conflict of cultures, but this took place within the immigrant himself: his is a 'divided self' that contains simultaneously the old and the new. 'Moral dichotomy and conflict is probably characteristic of every immigrant during the period of transition, when old habits are being discarded and new ones are not yet formed. It is inevitably a period of inner turmoil and intense self-consciousness' (Park 1928: 893). Park did not tackle here the question of the possible link between this inner conflict and criminal behaviour. He did, however, identify as a consequence of it the emergence of 'spiritual instability, restlessness, and *malaise*'; features that suggest a scenario of anomic type.

The more recent applications of anomic strain theory draw on the theoretical development made to these concepts by Merton (1949); more specifically they refer to the identification of a structural condition of crisis in Western society, in particular in North American society. This crisis is due, argued Merton, to a greater cultural accentuation of the goal of success than the obligation to obey the rules that determine the legitimate means to achieve it. In other words, the dominant culture in North America – influenced in this sense by the values of Protestantism and Calvinism – glorifies personal economic success and propounds it as a moral duty for everyone, and as an objective that is effectively within everyone's reach. At the same time, this culture fails to emphasize with the necessary firmness that only legitimate means should be used to achieve economic success. This structural situation of crisis is associated, in Merton's thought, with the existence of a *gap* between the goal of success, presented as a universal objective, and the peculiar and heterogeneous distribution of the legitimate means to achieve it, which discriminates against the lower classes. The gap is not merely one of inequality, but rather one of *relative deprivation*, perceived as unjust (Cloward and Ohlin 1960). This explains the greater propensity in the lower classes to use illicit means (such as property offences), in substitution of licit ones, to achieve success. Merton maintains that when the differentiation in the access to legitimate means to achieve success coincides with an ethnic differentiation, the rejection of the 'rules of the game' may spread and acquire an endemic character; it may also assume the form of ethnic rebellion. Rebellion – in Merton's theoretical construct – implies the substitution of the goals, and not merely the recourse to alternative means to achieve success. Nonetheless, in real situations, if not in theoretical constructs, it is possible to identify – in our view – attitudes of incomplete or 'developing' rebellion, in which the dominant cultural values are in general despised, with the exception of success, even if it is pursued with illicit means. The hypothesis of anomic strain in Merton's version was not originally conceived to explain the deviant behaviour of immigrants: the references to an ethnically-based differentiation regard the coloured American population, almost always composed of natives, or a traditional colonial background. In neither case are we dealing with immigrants. However, it is obvious enough that this hypothesis offers a useful conceptual tool in analysing the situation of immigrant communities. On average, in fact, the immigrant population finds itself in a condition of deprivation, of being debarred from access to the legitimate means to achieve economic success, however much encouraged to pursue it and share the positive value accorded to it.

Merton's hypothesis of anomic strain was further developed by Cohen (1955), Cloward and Ohlin (1960) and Blau and Blau (1982). They largely concur in suggesting that a greater propensity to crime among underprivileged groups may also be expressed in forms other than the use of illicit means, as an alternative to legitimate ones, to achieve economic success. This greater propensity to crime may also assume the form of a violent reaction to the stress and frustration that result from the perception of their own lack of legitimate opportunities to achieve success, not least because this lack of legitimate opportunities conflicts with society's affirmation of the right of *everyone* to have access to them. In this sense, stress and frustration could become factors of deviant and criminal behaviour that is expressed in forms of aggression, violence and vandalism, i.e. destruction that is not aimed at the achievement of any economic advantage. Blau's research, in particular, supported with empirical data the hypothesis that the level of economic and social inequality is correlated to the level of violent criminality.

Not all that far removed from the anomic strain theory are also the interpretations of crime that underline its role not as a mere means of acquiring wealth, but as a means of rapid upwards social mobility for underprivileged groups, in particular for groups of immigrants and for ethnic minorities (Ianni 1974; Kennet and Martin 1989; cf. Whyte 1943, for a description based on *participant observation*). This social mobility is acquired through a high position in the organization of criminal activities that assume the specific form of *business enterprises*, initially illegal but later destined to be transformed into legal businesses.

So-called *economic rational choice theory* also moves along parallel lines to strain theory. It was originally produced by a group of quantitative economists convinced that crime could best be explained on the basis of rational choices and not on pathologies and deviant impulses. Though not emphasizing the gap between goals dictated by culture and the social opportunities to achieve them, proponents of this theory believe that greater propensity to crime is associated with lesser legitimate opportunities to achieve success. Ehrlich (1974), working on US data, has shown that greater economic inequality (measured by the percentage of persons with an income lower than half the median) is correlated to a greater diffusion of crimes against property.

Due to the clarity of its model and the realism of its basic assumptions, anomic strain theory has represented a privileged point of reference in the social research of the second half of the twentieth century. Empirical corroborations of the criminogenic effects of strain and of 'relative poverty', however, are somewhat uncertain (Paternoster and Mazerolle 1994; Agnew 2001). Various recent surveys of quantitative type, especially conducted in the USA, have cast doubt on the empirical reliability of this theory (Burton *et al.* 1994). In Europe, there have been quantitative results to support the link between 'relative poverty' and crimes against property (Entorf and Spengler 2000, 2002), even if the studies in question were not specifically aimed at ascertaining the conduct of immigrants. In the USA similar results have been published in studies on the violent criminality of immigrants (Lee *et al.* 2001; Stowell 2007).

Overall, the hypothesis of anomic strain, in its various redactions and connotations, has been widely used by several authors who have examined the criminality of non-nationals in Western Europe, such as Basdevant (1983), Killias (1989), Segre (1993), and von Hofer *et al.* (1997). The studies in question, however, are largely qualitative in type.

The theory of *cultural conflict* was, as we have already pointed out, anticipated in the studies of Thomas and Znaniecki, as also in those of Park. It achieves its most complete exposition in the work of Sellin (1938). Departing from a series of considerations on advanced-Western-modern society that do not fail to recall the 'classic' descriptions of anomic situations, Sellin described traditional backward societies as characterized by cultural and social harmony, cooperation, lack of individualism, codes of conduct supported by moral force – since linked to the needs of the community which are clearly felt at the emotional level – and, in short, by the fact of presenting a 'well-knit social fabric'. To all this Sellin contrasted the situation of societies such as that of the USA, where an almost antithetical social model prevails and where the combination of phenomena of socio-cultural differentiation and population mobility generate a 'transformation of culture from a type characterized by homogeneity and integration to one characterized by heterogeneity and lack of integration' (Sellin 1938: IV).

This second type of society inevitably gives rise to situations of cultural conflict. More generally, Sellin identified three different situations that are typical of strong cultural conflict, namely: (1) when different cultural codes come into conflict in the boundary zones, the areas of friction between two different cultural areas; (2) when the normative system of one cultural group is extended to the territory of another group (as happens during processes of colonization, in which the dominant group imposes its own laws by force, and renders illicit some forms of conduct that hitherto had been permissible among the colonized group); and (3) when cultural groups are transplanted within other groups in which their cultural rules are either ignored or rejected.

According to Sellin, crime, in the modern advanced context, is essentially the product of cultural conflicts. To corroborate this thesis empirically, Sellin used the data of the US National Commission on Law Observance and Enforcement (1931) relating to a comparison between the average rates of criminality of subjects born abroad and native subjects, based on crimes registered in a series of North-American cities. Apart from the fairly low overall rate of criminality of foreign-borns – already recalled above – Sellin emphasized that there were great differences between the various ethnic groups; some of them (for example, Greeks and Mexicans) showed rates of criminality far higher than those of natives. Sellin also emphasized that, even in the case of low overall rates of criminality for a particular ethnic group, the rates for some specific offences could be very high (for example, among Italians, who showed an overall rate equivalent to that of natives, the offence of possessing weapons was three times more frequent, and that of wilful bodily harm twice as frequent).

To explain these facts and in particular the differences between the various ethnic groups, Sellin strenuously refused to make any reference to arguments of racial type, in contrast to some North American scholars in previous years (e.g. Laughlin 1922), who had supported the intrinsic threat posed by some ethnic groups. Sellin supported instead an explanatory model based on the hypothesis of cultural conflict. Without having personally conducted any empirical research, Sellin used the results of a series of research projects conducted by others to arrive at some specific conclusions. In particular:

1 Irrespective of belonging to specific cultural groups, the probability of deviant or criminal behaviour is stronger where the social actors move in boundary zones of their respective cultural areas. Sellin here made reference in particular to the research conducted in Chicago by Crook (1934) on the sexual deviance of adolescents; research in which the author, using the concept formulated by Park et al. (1925) of

triangle of conduct (a spatial triangle whose points are formed by the homes of the social actors involved and the site in which the deviant conduct takes place), affirmed that over two-thirds of the deviant behaviour examined took place in 'cultural frontier' zones.

2   First-generation immigrants tend to commit offences in connection with the specific characteristics of their cultures of provenance and with the differences between these cultures and that of the host country. This gives rise to a series of what could be called 'ethnic' crimes, such as the illegal possession of weapons (immigrants from the Mediterranean area, Mexico, etc.); crimes of 'honour' (once again immigrants from the Mediterranean); gambling and prostitution (Asian immigrants); bootlegging (various groups of immigrants).

3   The children of first-generation immigrants tend to shift the focus of their criminal activity from 'ethnic' crimes to offences typical of North American citizens. So, using the data of Stofflet (1935), Sellin showed that Italian immigrants of the second generation committed fewer crimes of violence (homicides, grievous bodily harm), typical of the first generation, and more crimes against property (theft, robbery), typical of the 'average' American criminal. Despite the fact that he was unable to adduce unanimous data to support this conclusion, Sellin, also on the basis of the reflections of other authors, argued that the condition of the children of immigrants was far more vulnerable in terms of their propensity to crime, because they fell into the no-man's land between two cultures: they were unable completely to interiorize the culture of their parents (cf. the theses already presented by Park), and were at the same time unable to adjust fully to North American culture and integrate themselves in it.

After its original formulation in the 1930s, the hypothesis of cultural conflict as the key to explaining the criminal activities of non-nationals has more recently been used, both in the European and in the North American context, by various authors, such as Ferracuti (1968); Robert *et al.* (1968); Ribordy (1970); Cheung (1980); Pogrebin and Poole (1990); Samuel and Faustino-Santos (1991); Yesilgöz (1995); and Kühne (2002). In particular, some authors emphasize the normality of recourse to personal violence in some Balkan cultures (Suisse 2001); others, such as Remotti (1985) and Barbagli (1998), the different perception of theft in gipsy ethnic groups.

In contrast with cultural conflict theory, *social disorganization* theory dismisses cultural differences – and at the same time nationality and ethnicity – as the main factors of criminality. This theory was the product of the School of Sociology in Chicago and is closely bound up with the social situation in that city in the early years of the twentieth century. At that time, Chicago formed an extraordinary social laboratory for the study of the problems of immigration, integration and crime. Over a third of the population of

Chicago then consisted of those who had been born abroad and three-quarters belonged to the category *foreign stock*, comprising those born abroad plus those with at least one parent born abroad (Bursik 2006). Immigration in Chicago was of recent origin, decidedly mobile, and originated from a large variety of countries. In this situation, the objective, or rather the quandary, of local government, social workers and the research community, was how the integration of this huge mass of immigrants could be achieved. Their assimilation through the so-called 'melting pot' was considered the most desirable option.

Social disorganization theory is especially linked with the urban studies conducted by Shaw and McKay (1942), who emphasized the so-called ecological dimension of crime. These studies showed that the rates of criminality of immigrants were influenced by the aspects of disorganization of the quarters of the city in which they lived, aspects such as the rapid turnover of population, its heterogeneity and deracination, rather than by cultural differences and by levels of poverty. In other words, the impact of immigration on crime rates was indirect: it was environmentally conditioned. Immigration conduced to social disorganization, and this in turn increased the crime rate. The high level of criminality was allegedly the consequence of an 'ecological context' incapable of exerting sufficient control on the conduct of residents precisely as a result of social disorganization. Under the influence of the forces of social disintegration resulting from these contexts, the community ceases to exist as an agency of social control and criminal behaviour becomes not only tolerated but even at times accepted (Morris 1958). In a context of generalized social disorganization, individuals belonging to different ethnic groups and different cultures will tend to have similar rates of criminality; whereas persons belonging to the same ethnic and cultural group will present very different rates of criminality if resident in quarters with varying levels of social organization. In this context, poverty is a relevant factor in determining the quarter in which a person lives, but assuming that poverty has a direct link with crime would be mistaken.

After the Second World War, this theory in its wider ramifications inspired some studies in Europe on degraded urban contexts (Morris 1958) and on the role of immigration on disorganization (Wallis and Maliphant 1967). Yet it has been progressively abandoned, also because the phenomenon of mass immigration, like that registered in the USA at the start of the twentieth century, appeared obsolete.

More recently, there has been a revival of ecological studies in the USA, but in a perspective only partially coinciding with the previous one. These new ecological studies revolve around the thesis of so-called 'racial invariance'. They reject the thesis of an ethnic or racial root of crime, and emphasize instead that race and ethnicity represent factors of a particular propensity to crime only in so far as they are associated with specific social contexts (Sampson and Wilson 1995). These contexts are characterized by pronounced anonymity, weak inter-generational bonds, low levels of social participation and consequently lack of shared values: hence cultural disorganization and in particular the spread of subcultural values that may lead to attitudes of cultural indifference or attitudes favourable to criminality.

As may be inferred from what has just been said, this new current of ecological studies is interested not so much in the criminality of immigrants as in that of the slums of North American cities. These inhabitants indeed consist in large part of ethnic minorities, but minorities that are in large part *native*, as in the case of the African-American population. Moreover, precisely because it is aimed at the explanation of the antisocial conduct of the inhabitants of clearly delimited territorial contexts, this current of thought is suited in the main to micro-analyses on a restricted territorial basis; it is not suited to provide an interpretative model of macro type, such as that aimed at providing an explanation of the different levels of criminality between one region and another or between one state and another.

More recently, the so-called *control theory* of Hirschi (1969) starts out from a presupposition opposed to that of anomic strain, and also sharply contrasting with the theory of cultural conflict and with any other approach that suggests a cultural or subcultural root to crime. In explicit polemic with the proponents of anomic strain, control theory considers the condition of strain as a normal experience in the life of individuals, and hence ill-adapted to assume the role of the main causal factor of criminal conduct. Control theory adopts a far less 'extenuating' perspective in elucidating the possible causes of criminal behaviour: these causes are traced back not to negative social factors (poverty, ignorance, underprivilege, etc.), but to rational choices made by the delinquent in the light of his assessment of its costs and benefits. At the same time, in opposition to the theory of cultural conflict (or rather various versions of it), control theory argues that deviants and delinquents are distinguished from other persons not because they have a different system of values, but because they are less subject to social controls. In this sense, according to control theory, anyone may find himself in conditions of strain and have, even under normal circumstances, the potential to commit crime. This potential can only be allayed or reduced by controls: *internal controls*, relating to the interiorization of sound moral values, and the individual's commitment to the pursuit of conformist objectives (such as education); and *external controls*, relating to links with the institutions, with the family, with the neighbourhood, with the working environment, and so on. Where these links are strong, the *cost* of crime for the individual – i.e. the cost in terms of loss of social status, chances for social relations (friendships, rapport with the local community, etc.), opportunities of work and insertion – is high. And since the costs and benefits of any criminal behaviour would normally be calculated in advance by the individual, the vulnerability of the individual to crime grows in proportion as its cost is reduced.

Conceived as a general theory of crime, this theoretical approach has been critically examined, and quantitatively assessed, by various scholars from the viewpoint of its effective empirical relevance. Studies of quantitative type conducted in the USA, and also theoretical analyses, have expressed doubts about this empirical relevance (Agnew 1985; Greenberg 1999; Schulz 2004). Other studies, however, are in favour (Junger-Tas 1992; Paternoster and Mazerolle 1994). What seems certain is that empirical corroboration is complicated by the difficulty of distinguishing factors peculiar to control theory from factors common to other approaches. For example, control theory regards unemployment as a sign of weak social links, whereas strain theory interprets it as an indicator of exclusion from legitimate means, and the theory of social disorganization, as a factor that determines the territorial collocation of the subject, and hence his residence in a socially negative context. Similarly, control theory will interpret low educational level as a sign of lack of internal controls, strain theory as a symptom of social marginalization.

Though it is (as we have said) a general theory of crime, control theory has been used by some authors such as Kaiser (1988), Villmow (1993) and Albrecht (1995) and – in a rare quantitative study – by Junger and Polder (1992) in the more particular perspective of explaining the deviant conduct of immigrants. Immigrants are more exposed to the risks of crime – proponents of control theory allege – since they have not in most cases properly developed social and working relations in the host country, and therefore have not developed those strong links with society (external controls) that act as a curb on delinquency. Control theory has also been used to explain the sharp differences, in terms of rates of criminality, that exist between the various groups of non-nationals or the various ethnic minorities: it has thus been suggested that a cohesive and supportive family context might have been the cause of a far lower level of criminality among Turkish and Chinese immigrants than that of other ethnic groups in Holland (Junger-Tas 1997). The same concept has been used to explain the low rate of criminality among Chinese immigrants in South-East Asia (Shen 2002).

Lastly, in this brief review of the theories useful for contextualizing the relation between immigration and criminality, we should mention the theory of *symbolic interactionism* and its corollary of *labelling*. The approach proposes a decidedly alternative perspective, the possible fall-out of which should at least be taken into consideration. Developed in the 1960s by the second generation of the Chicago School, symbolic interactionism deals in particular with deviant behaviour and is based on the innovative proposition of assuming that what determines such behaviour is not its possible underlying causes (social, economic, temperamental, etc.), but the process of interaction that gives rise to the deviant behaviour itself. As explained in his pioneering study, Becker (1963) argued that the deviant behaviour itself is the cause – within a certain timeframe – of the determination of deviant motivations. Deviant behaviour is described as a process, divided up into innumerable *steps*, which gives rise to the individual's construction of a deviant social role. The deviant role is thus acquired not by heredity, not by upbringing, not by temperament, but through a gradual process whose decisive elements are the recognition and progressive acceptance of this role by the subject himself, within a process of interaction between the subject and the others who form his circle of reference.

The most significant implications of this theory, for purposes of our present investigation, consist in the claim that the role of deviant or criminal is something *latent* in the behaviour of a large number of people. This role, however, emerges, takes on firm contours, and gains in significance, through the action of those – such as the police, judges, etc. – who have the power of defining a form of conduct as deviant or criminal. Becker says that there is a crucial turning point in the construction of a permanent deviant identity: it is the moment not when someone commits a deviant act, but when that person is identified as deviant and labelled as such, i.e. when a *label* is attached to him/her and extended to cover the whole of his/her social identity (Becker 1963; cf. also Erikson 1962). The later analysis of Lemert (1972) distinguishes between a 'primary' and more general deviance – such as might be that linked with the immigrant's 'diversity' – and what he defines as 'secondary' or socially structured deviance, determined by the social reaction and stigmatization of the subject especially by the agencies of control. These concepts are undoubtedly of relevance to our investigation not only in terms of the explanation of the relation between immigration and criminality, but more especially in terms of their implications for the evaluation of the real scale and significance of the contribution of non-nationals to criminality. Reference to the theory of interactionism and in particular labelling is made, either explicitly or implicitly – as we will see below – by those authors who regard the phenomenon of the criminality of non-nationals as something strictly dependent on the discriminatory attitudes of the agencies of social control. Interactionism and especially labelling have further been taken up by a radical criminology – neo-Marxist in derivation and agenda – which on the one hand has interpreted deviance and criminality as a growing manifestation of the development of revolutionary forces, and on the other – without any fear of contradiction – as something essentially trumped up: in other words, the data that register this criminality are dismissed as a mere fabrication of Western governments, of no matter what political complexion. The contradictions seem to increase when – as often happens – attempts are made, as part of a wider radical agenda, to combine this labelling approach with an interpretation of anomic strain that emphasizes the inequitable distribution of legitimate means. So, on the one hand, strain theory is used to present a capitalist society that deprives the most vulnerable and underprivileged immigrants of any legitimate means of success, thus inevitably pressuring them into criminal activities and, on the other hand, labelling is used to explain why to immigrants in particular are attributed those high rates of criminality which their relative deprivation had already abundantly explained.

All the theories presented above were taken into consideration as useful tools for the formulation and realization of the empirical research to which this study is devoted. However, in the course of the research, their potential use was evaluated in the light of a series of findings that led us in the end to privilege some approaches rather than others.

For reasons of method, it is as well to begin by taking into consideration some implications linked to the interactionism and labelling approach. Now, if the theory of interactionism and labelling were to be accepted in its more radical version, the problem of the relation between immigration and criminality would have to be fundamentally challenged at its root and translated into the very different problem of the arbitrary attribution of a criminal identity to non-nationals. This is a hypothesis that finds explicit support in some authors (Gilroy 1982; Quassoli 2000) who refuse, as a matter of principle, or perhaps of prudence, even to take into consideration any quantitative data of the scale of criminality attributed to non-nationals.

We must first ask ourselves how far this reversal of the conceptual framework is justifiable on the basis of present knowledge. It may be suggested, first of all, that the sudden shift in the results of studies on the criminality of non-nationals, which has taken place especially in Western Europe in recent decades, is difficult to attribute to the proposition that the disproportionately high rates of criminality registered for non-nationals are caused by the discriminatory or persecutory attitude shown towards them. For it is difficult to maintain that the non-nationals in Western Europe were not, even before, the victims of prejudice and discrimination; it is especially difficult to maintain that there has been any rapid increase of the level of discrimination towards them and this had led to the attribution of a (presumed) high level of criminality to them. Indeed, if something *has* changed in European culture in recent decades, it is a change in the opposite direction: in the sense of a greater recognition of human rights, including those of immigrants themselves, e.g. also through anti-discrimination laws. Moreover, the hypothesis of discrimination seems incompatible with the already-underlined existence of very different rates of criminality for different groups of non-nationals potentially subjected to similar forms of discrimination. It is not clear, for example, why a discriminatory attitude, assuming it exists, should have led in Holland to a rate of criminality for Turkish and Chinese immigrants that is far lower than that relating to the group of Caribs; or why the rate of criminality of Indians in Great Britain (measured in terms of sentenced and imprisoned offenders) should be similar, indeed slightly lower, than that of the population of European origin and a good deal lower than that of Jamaicans.

However, some of the labelling hypothesis premises are not unsupported by evidence at the level of empirical research. Discriminatory attitudes by the police to non-nationals, and more generally to members of ethnic minorities, have been corroborated by many empirical studies (Landau and Nathan 1983; Carr-Hill 1987; Crow 1987; De Valkeneer 1987; Junger 1989; Skogan 1990; Casman *et al.* 1992): for example, Casman's research, which may be considered in some sense as typical, shows that many police officers, convinced that non-nationals pose a significant problem for public order, focus their attention on them and subject them to arbitrary controls.

Research conducted in the USA shows, moreover, that police officers are all too easily influenced by the socio-economic level of the offender as also by the characteristics of the quarter in which the incident they are investigating took place (Hollinger 1984; Smith and Klein 1984; Flowers 1990). This implies an attitude generally unfavourable, if not discriminatory, to non-nationals and more generally to the members of minority communities.

Should we therefore assume that the police, in their attitude to non-nationals, act by applying the model of thought made famous by Captain Renault who, in the film *Casablanca* (directed by Michael Curtiz, 1942), inevitably gives the order 'Round up the usual suspects'? It should be pointed out that a significant number of studies have shown that the arrests made by the law enforcement agencies are primarily the consequence of the effectively criminal behaviour of those arrested, and not of ethnic prejudices towards them (Walker 1987; Junger 1990; Aalberts 1990; Junger-Tas 1997). Moreover, a negative attitude of the police to the members of some ethnic groups (and the more frequent controls resulting from it) could be 'justified by the previous results' (Smith 1997). In other words, the police would be inclined to subject the members of these groups to more rigorous controls on the basis of the fact that they have shown a higher statistical propensity to crime; precisely as happens when the police tend to flag down a jalopy with several male youths on board rather than an immaculate limousine with an elderly lady on board. This hypothesis, if well founded, would imply a certain accentuation of the over-representation of particular ethnic groups in the statistics of criminality; but it would also imply that this over-representation is first of all the consequence of an objectively greater contribution to criminality by part of these groups. Similar conclusions have been reached by studies conducted in Sweden (Martens and Holmberg 2005).

In any case, the impact on the statistics of crime by these prejudicial attitudes of the law enforcement agencies is not necessarily great. Valuable information on this question is provided by surveys on the victims of crime, which represent an excellent source to control the involvement of non-nationals or members of minorities in the phenomenon of crime, and hence indirectly to check the reliability of official data. It seems clear, indeed, that there cannot be in general any good reason to claim, in the course of such surveys, that one has been injured by a coloured man or robbed by someone who had difficulty in speaking the national language, if this were not true. Now, the data of the National Crime Victimization Survey in the USA show that there is a strong convergence between the percentage of the perpetrators of crimes identified by their victims as members of ethnic minorities and the percentage of the same ethnic subjects in the statistics of arrests by the law enforcement agencies reported by the Uniform Crime Report (LaFree and Russell 1993; US Department of Justice 2006). In England and Wales, too, official investigations have shown that the distribution of perpetrators of crimes by broad ethnic groups (whites, blacks, Asians), as identified by the victims, corresponds to the distribution by ethnic groups of those arrested by the police (UK Home Office 1989). Similar findings also come from Switzerland (Suisse 2001).

All this would seem to indicate that the presumed presence of stereotypes in the culture of the law enforcement agencies and of prejudices in their attitudes is realistic; but at the same time that the high rates of criminality registered in some groups of non-nationals (or in some ethnic minorities) are effectively the result of their greater involvement in penally chargeable offences.

It is even more important to note that the great majority of registered offences (in many cases 90 per cent or over) are reported by the public and not by the police (Albrecht 1993). This goes not only for the overall total of offences but also in general for specific kinds of offence, with some exceptions (for example, drug offences, offences relating to public order). Now, a discriminatory attitude by the public as regards the identity of the perpetrators of offences reported – and especially a discriminatory attitude *against* non-nationals – is in general repudiated by empirical surveys. Several analyses have shown that the ethnic identity of the perpetrator of the offence reported gives rise to insignificant differences in the percentages of crimes reported to the police by citizens (Hindelang 1978; Killias 1988; Shah and Pease 1992; Hart and Rennison 2003; even though some exceptions to this rule could be cited, in particular in the case of the owners of large commercial businesses, who seem more inclined to report non-national than national thieves (shoplifters) to the police: Killias 1988; Barbagli 1994).

In any case, the impact on criminal statistics of any improbable discrimination against non-nationals by the public (in general) would at least in part be compensated by a specific fact. A large proportion of the crimes committed by non-nationals have other non-nationals as their victims (Liben 1963; Sessar 1981; Albrecht 1987; Kammhuber 1997), and, more generally, the criminality of ethnic minorities is in large part expressed within the minority itself (Smith 1997; Junger-Tas 1997; US Department of Justice 2006). Now, it is well known that the propensity of people to go to the police to report illegal actions is in inverse proportion to their social and cultural marginality, their sense of impotence, their fear of retaliation, and in particular their situation of being illegally present in the host country. It is undeniable that a large proportion of non-nationals is characterized by one or more of these conditions; the propensity of non-nationals to report crimes to the police is likely to be even lower if the perpetrator of the crime belongs to the same ethnic group as its victim (Stevens and Willis 1979; Kidd and Chayet 1984; Pitsela 1986; Clancy *et al.* 2001; Horowitz 2001). All this ought to lead to the criminality of non-nationals being underestimated in the official statistics.

A discriminatory attitude to non-nationals, voluntary or involuntary, on the other hand, is far more supported by firm evidence as regards sentences and in particular the use of preventive detention. More specifically, various empirical studies have shown that more extensive use of preventive detention is made in the case of non-nationals or members of minority groups in Europe (Malewska-Peyre 1982; Hanak *et al.* 1984; Carr-Hill 1987; Tournier and Robert 1991; Hood 1992; Barbaret and García-España 1997; Barbagli 1998; Holmberg and Kyvsgaard 2003; see also Wacquant 2005). This situation may be attributable in the first place to the often poor economic condition of non-nationals, which hamper their chance of obtaining a good legal defence. In the second instance, it may be attributable to some basic characteristics of the condition of many non-nationals, such as having no fixed address, no permanent job, poor grasp of the national language, limited familiarity with the territory and lack of integration in it, including lack of relations with both public and private institutions, and being unprovided in many cases with the requisite documents or even identity papers. All these characteristics are an obstacle to the granting, first, of bail and then of alternative measures to detention, both in terms of preventive detention and incarceration following sentencing by the courts (Solivetti 1993). So it is no surprise that, as several studies have shown, non-nationals have greater probabilities of being sentenced to terms of imprisonment (Petersilia 1985; Crow 1987; Junger 1989; Tournier and Robert 1991; Tournier 1997).

Nonetheless, the greater recourse to detention in dealing with immigrants, and with non-nationals in particular, does not mean that their share in the prison population has been skewed to such an extent that it cannot be considered an indicator of their actual contribution to the officially registered crime figures. It cannot be a coincidence that in the USA, where the studies on immigration and crime agree in concluding that the contribution of immigrants to crime is lower or at least not higher than that of natives, the share of immigrants in the prison population is lower than that of natives. Butcher and Piehl (1997), working on census data, have calculated that the probability of being imprisoned for male foreign-borns aged between 18 and 40 is lower than that of their age group who were born in the USA. There's no reason to doubt that, in Europe too, if the contribution of immigrants to crime were lower than that of natives, the share of immigrants in the prison population would also be lower.

To sum up, the approach of symbolic interactionism and of labelling does not seem to throw into serious doubt the validity of an analysis of the criminality of immigrants based on the official figures for such criminality.

In particular, the figures relating to crimes reported to the police seem those least influenced, or liable to be influenced, by any discriminatory attitudes. Greater caution is needed in interpreting the figures for those sentenced and those detained. Here there could in effect be an over-representation of the non-national population as a consequence of the judicial and penal policies that disadvantage them more than they do nationals. However, it is possible to foresee and contain this danger of a distortion in the interpretation of the basic phenomenon. First, the situation of those detained can be compared with that of those reported to the police, which, as we have seen, seems less exposed to possible distortion. Second, the indicators of the *presences* in prison, rather than those of *admissions*, can be analysed. Prison admission indicators are more responsive to brief periods of imprisonment, in other words, the measures more frequently taken against immigrants, since their condition (as we have said) largely precludes alternative measures in their case. Third, the data relating to prison inmates may be used to conduct a comparative analysis of the various countries on the basis of the share of non-nationals in their prison population, so that any discriminatory factors that determined the greater use of custodial sentences to the detriment of non-nationals may be absorbed in the framework of a more comprehensive analysis of the basic social, cultural and organizational conditions that negatively influence the integration of non-nationals and increase their probability of 'having problems' with the law.

The applicability of cultural conflict theory to the situation studied here seems to have more in its favour. First, it may be noted that this theory finds some support in the very different rates of criminality ascertained in the various groups of non-nationals in Western Europe. On this basis, it might be affirmed that the contribution of non-nationals to criminality is in short the result of profound cultural differences between them and the host society. At the same time, however, it should be recalled that it is not necessarily the same groups that present the highest rates of criminality in the various countries (see our Introduction).

That the various non-national groups present such different rates of criminality is in any case an ambivalent factor and one that lends itself well to completely different interpretations. It may be used, as we have already noted, to support the validity of *control theory* as a sufficient explanation of the phenomena of crime among immigrant communities. In this sense, groups of non-nationals, extremely well-integrated within their own communities, would guarantee a strong control. Moreover, the fact that rates of criminality are so very different for the various non-national groups is not only compatible with, but a perfect illustration of, *anomic strain* theory. For in this case one would expect different rates of criminality within the various groups of non-nationals as a consequence of their varying levels of integration in the host society and especially their varying levels of access to the legitimate means for achieving success.

In any case, the fact that current immigration in Europe mainly consists of those coming from distant lands (see Section 3.3 in Chapter 3), from countries that are very different in cultural, economic, religious, ethical and institutional terms, and not least in terms of family and sexual models, makes the hypothesis of cultural conflict plausible. One would expect that these differences *would* give rise to conflicts of values in specific fields such as family life, personal consumption of drugs, and relations between the sexes (it's enough to think of the very different conception of the role and the rights and duties of women in many of the countries that are fuelling emigration to Europe). At the same time, however, one would expect that the contribution made by non-nationals to criminality would remain limited to specific crimes linked to situations of greater cultural conflict, and hence to specific offences: violence within the family, some sexual offences, corruption, extortion/graft, personal consumption of some specific drugs, linked to particular 'cultures', and so on. Cultural conflict may less easily be cited as a causal agent to explain offences apparently far more prosaic and far less 'cultural' in nature, such as theft or robbery. Moreover, while reference to cultural conflict may seem appropriate to explain the peculiar contribution of non-nationals to certain categories of crime in general, it may seem far less suitable to explain certain specific cases within these categories. For example, drug offences could be placed in relation to particular cultures in which there is a tradition of drug use. But what would we say if we were to discover that the drug offences imputed to non-nationals concern not so much the possession of drugs for personal use as their trafficking on an international scale or within a context of organized delinquency that has little to do with traditional cultures? Equally, if a particular frequency of offences that fall into the category of transgressions against sexual morality is attributed to non-nationals, the reference to cultural conflict seems – as we have already suggested – appropriate; but it is difficult to continue to support such theses if, on closer inspection, one discovers that the transgressions against sexual morality frequently imputed to non-nationals include not only rape – which could be interpreted as an extreme consequence of conflicts over the meanings attributed in the various cultures to sexual mores – but also the exploitation of prostitution: an offence less easily attributable to cultural differences, at least in the sense of belonging to a pre-modern traditional culture.

Now, some data from specific studies on the criminal behaviour of non-nationals in Europe seem to suggest precisely the somewhat 'uncultural' character of the offences attributed to them: offences that are especially concentrated, to a higher degree than what happens for the citizens of the host country, in the prosaic category *against property* (Solivetti and D'Onofrio 1998). If all this were to be confirmed, the scope for any reference to cultural conflict theory would inevitably be reduced.

As regards *control* theory, it may be noted that it is essentially focused on the idea of the deviant/delinquent as a human being whose propensity to antisocial conduct is based on evaluations that imply calculation and rationality. Control theory in effect revives the concept of *choice* – a legacy of classical Enlightenment criminology – on the basis of an evaluation of costs and benefits, though, in contrast to earlier conceptions, it shifts attention from costs in terms of simple penal sanctions to costs in terms of loss of social and economic links within the circle of reference. The emphasis on the evaluation of costs and benefits and on the rationality implicit also in criminal activities, however, makes control theory not only antithetical to such theories as culture conflict and anomic strain, but also unsuited to explain all those forms of criminal or deviant behaviour that can be gathered under the label of deeds dictated by impulse or passion. These are forms of behaviour that seem instead to find a fairly satisfactory explanation, at least in theory, in the light of hypotheses of culture conflict; and that are also taken into consideration – as we have pointed out – by anomic strain theory as reaction to the frustrations of relative deprivation. What is the share of these criminal acts dictated by impulse or passion out of the total of the phenomenon of crime? It is difficult to say. Such acts ought, one might assume, to be concentrated among offences committed against the person or against the family, morality and public decency. Nonetheless, it is probable that many offences labelled as having been dictated by impulse or passion – crimes of passion in short – are a good deal more 'rational' than they might seem at first sight: we may recall the type of uxoricide, apparently impulsive but in actual fact long and meticulously prepared, described by Pietro Germi in his film *Divorzio all'italiana* (1961). On the other hand, if we accept the point of view of Pareto (1916), according to whom human beings rarely behave according to reason, but usually strive to make others believe they are rational, we would then be encouraged to think that these criminal acts dictated by impulse or passion are more numerous than are usually thought. In any case, it is clear that social control theory has always had difficulty in explaining this type of antisocial conduct.

Besides, when one tries to apply control theory to the criminality of non-nationals there are other aspects that arouse doubts. First of all, one would expect those who emigrate to be characterized by a relatively high level of aspirations – in particular by the determination to improve their own economic and social condition – and also by a willingness to make sacrifices, and endure hardship, to achieve this end. This would seem to imply an interiorization of conventional objectives and values; and this, in the light of control theory, ought to form a solid defence against any propensity to crime. Second, it may be noted that the non-nationals present in Europe are in large part the result of recent waves of immigration, especially in some countries in southern Europe (e.g. Spain, Italy, and Greece). The rapidity of the influx of immigrants, and the fact that it is of recent occurrence, presumably have had an effect on the level of the mechanisms of *external* control. For the difficulties that already characterize, under normal circumstances, the social and economic integration of non-nationals can only be aggravated when the influx of immigrants is so recent, so large and expanding so fast. And the lack of satisfactory and legitimate social relations available to them might imply that the cost of crime, represented by the loss of these relations, would be reduced; and that recourse to crime would simultaneously appear more attractive. However, this assumption is offset by another consideration: for the fact that a large part of the migration towards the countries of Western Europe is very recent ought to have had the effect of maintaining *internal* controls, which would not have had time to loosen, and thus ought to compensate for the lack of *external* controls. A low level of both external and internal controls is predictable mainly in the case of immigrants not of the first, but of the second generation. It may be presumed that the 'firmly established' values that their fathers had brought with them from their societies of origin, which are very often of traditional type or in any case less advanced and more integrated than those of the host society, no longer exist, or have been irreparably eroded, in the case of second-generation immigrants. The non-nationals we are dealing with here, however, are usually immigrants of the first generation. In fact, in most countries of Western Europe, the children of immigrants born in the host country become citizens of it. The data currently at our disposal for the criminality of non-nationals thus relate in large part to immigrants of the first generation. And it is preeminently for them that the arguments presented above hold good.

Given these doubts, it seems appropriate to devote particular attention to the *anomic strain* theory in its various declensions. Therefore, without ignoring the contributions made by other approaches, we shall analyse the question whether comparatively disadvantaged conditions of socio-economic insertion may be accompanied by, or correlated to, a higher non-national share in the figures for criminality. Yet, if the hypothesis of anomic strain may seem relatively more productive, it also presents aspects that are hard to reconcile with the situation that currently characterizes non-nationals in Europe.

For, even if we assume that the dominant culture in the countries of Western Europe proposes 'universal' objectives of success (i.e. objectives that are valid for all the members of that culture), it is not clear that these objectives are also valid for non-nationals, who could set themselves somewhat different objectives, as a consequence of the fact of belonging to what is in effect a minority. If we bear in mind the enormous disparity in incomes (and wages) that exists between Western Europe and the countries whence come the majority of non-nationals today (see our Introduction), it is realistic to assume that the objectives of non-nationals, especially during the initial years of their presence in the host country, are likely to be more limited than those of the indigenous population. The objectives of non-nationals seem normally to revolve around such aspects as the achievement of a minimum level of material well-being, finding a job, not necessarily skilled, finding accommodation, however modest, and so on. More than the obstacles on the way to reaching the 'universal' economic success flagged up as the common goal for the citizens who belong to the national culture, it seems to us that in the case of non-nationals we ought to bear in mind the obstacles they encounter on the more modest way to a minimum of adaptation and well-being. In any case the attainment of this minimum level of adaptation and well-being is conditioned by the social policies applied to newly arrived immigrants, forms of social protection, a climate of transparency, legality and fairness of treatment that have little to do with the propagation of ideals of economic success and the emphasis placed on them. In short, the analyses on the criminality of non-nationals ought in our view to consider such aspects as what chances they have of obtaining social protection, respect for basic rights, a minimum of economic well-being and a perhaps not insignificant share of the national wealth, rather than ask ourselves what chances they have of making the ascent to full economic and social success.

In the second place, we should bear in mind that the attainment of a minimum level of material prosperity is not necessarily the supreme problem that impedes the adaptation of immigrants. A host society that is insensible or blind to the problems of immigrants, unable or disinterested in realizing the ideals of justice, lacking an impartial and transparent legal system, ready to exploit the weaknesses of those who have only recently arrived, and corrupted by widespread illegality, will, in more than one respect, form a negative context for immigrants (as also for its own citizens themselves). This context will not only have repercussions on the chance of non-nationals to gain a foothold in the labour market and achieve economic well-being, but will even more probably reduce their chances of social adjustment. The two aspects do not necessarily coincide. As the history of emigration teaches us, the host society may easily maintain an attitude towards non-nationals of discrimination, inequity and the negation of rights, while at the same time giving them scope to find work (and hence a degree of economic prosperity), so long as this is to the advantage of the indigenous population. In this case, even the attainment of a (relative) economic success may not represent grounds for real satisfaction. From all this, which we could sum up in the concept of *social injustice*, it would be reasonable to expect a sense of frustration to be created in non-nationals: in short, the kind of dissatisfaction expressed in the well-known song *Lacreme napulitane* (*Neapolitan Tears*) (Bovio and Buongiovanni 1925) which deals precisely with the situation of emigrants:

> *Mo' tengo quacche dollaro, e mme pare*
> *ca nun so' stato maje tanto pezzente!*

> (Now that I have some dollars, it seems to me
> that I've never been such a loser!)

The negative attitude of the host society will also be translated into the disaffection of immigrants: their unwillingness to share in the culture and institutions of the host country, with which they feel no rapport, and toward which they have no reason to feel respect. Respect for the penal code cannot easily be separated from respect for the country that produced it. And if immigrants are placed in a condition in which there is little reason to foster this respect, the consequences seem obvious. The perception of living in a society in which illegality and injustice is common cannot but encourage deviant or explicitly criminal behaviour. So the condition of immigrants in this case is not one of *relative deprivation* or lack of social mobility, but rather one of living in a society that encourages and reproduces deviance and criminality. And the difference does not seem negligible.

If all this is plausible, it follows that to predict the probabilities of deviant and criminal forms of behaviour we would have to take into account not only the aspects relating to poverty, inequality and relative deprivation, but also the aspects relating to the cultural prejudices of the host society against non-nationals or its active discrimination against them. If the prejudices against non-nationals don't seem to be the direct cause of their over-representation among those charged and detained, as the theory of labelling would have us believe, an attitude to them characterized by discrimination, and by lack of justice and fairness to the most vulnerable, might well contribute to a climate unfavourable to integration, and hence to a greater propensity to criminality. These are aspects that have not been considered (or only marginally so) by the main sociological models for explaining the criminality of immigrants.

Chapter 2

The research project

2.1 Objectives and methods of research

In light of the theoretical foundations discussed in the previous chapter, the primary objective we posed in this research project was to ascertain whether there is any relation between the presence of non-nationals and the dimension and variation of crime in the various countries of Western Europe. Second, we wished to control whether the contribution of the non-national population to the official crime figures varies with the socio-economic and cultural characteristics of the host countries and with the problems and difficulties of integration faced by the non-national population within them.

The book's approach is decidedly a cross-national one. A few fine studies using a comparative approach to the problem of migration and crime have been published over the past few years: in particular, those edited by Tonry (1997), and by Marshall (1997). However, these collections of papers by various authors presented the situation of migration and crime in a relatively limited group of Western countries (nine). Each country's situation was thoroughly analysed by a different author, by means of an in-depth study. This approach, unsurprisingly, was accompanied by a low level of homogeneity between the individual studies, each devoted to a different country; no attempt was made to carry out an analysis on the entire group of countries taken into consideration. In the present book, by contrast, we shall test a different approach. We shall examine migration and crime by presenting the situation regarding all the West European countries and by trying, as far as is possible, to use homogeneous parameters for all of them. The aim is to draw a picture based on theory as well as on quantitative variables for all these countries. On the other hand, no in-depth national study for any of these countries will be carried out. At the outset, it has to be admitted that the approach adopted in this book does present some serious obstacles, not least those relating to the difficulties in finding homogeneous parameters. As a consequence, the present study will necessarily be exploratory in nature.

The study we present is clearly of macro-sociological type. This type of approach is obligatory for a study of the relation between the presence of immigrants and the variation of criminality in the various countries. As regards the conditions that are associated with the criminality of immigrants, a micro approach, based on the data relating to the individual or to individual families, would have permitted us to follow more immediately the influence of individual differences, of socio-economic and cultural type, on individual lifestyles, including criminal ones. But a micro approach of this type would have at the same time presented major weaknesses from our point of view. By focusing on the individual dimension, it would have complicated an evaluation of the impact of all the structural aspects, the so-called *externalities*, in other words the *social forces*: all those aspects that belong to society more than they do to the individual. More particularly, it would have made it difficult to follow a perspective based on comparison between countries, given that the differences between countries consist in large measure precisely of structural aspects, of social forces. Moreover, a micro approach would have required individual data relating to representative samples of population (national and non-national) and gathered by the same methods in all countries. The fact is that data of this type are not available. Hence, of necessity, but also out of conviction, we have adopted a macro-sociological approach. The variables used will in general consist of *aggregate data* which sum up the level and variation of criminality, the presence of non-nationals, the socio-economic and cultural conditions of the host countries and the factors that characterize the integration of the non-national population in the various countries. The data in question often represent, in the case of quantitative characteristics, *average* values: for example, the average income per person of the national population. In the case of qualitative characteristics, such as gender, country of origin or level of education, the variables will consist of the percentage share of the characteristic in question: for example, the percentage of non-nationals with educational level no higher than that of lower secondary school (third year of secondary school) out of the total non-national population.

The reader should be warned at the outset that, in our quest for conditions that might influence the criminality of non-nationals, we have avoided as far as possible any reference to composite, ill-defined and largely unquantifiable aspects – such as complex legislative provisions on immigration in the various countries, though these have progressively become more homogeneous as a result of common European policies. Instead we have focused on more circumscribed and measurable aspects – e.g. the mean disposable income of the less privileged classes, rather than 'poverty'; the number of newspapers sold, rather than 'culture' – using these aspects at the same time as indicators of more general conditions. These data will then be transformed into indices to permit sound comparisons to be made between country and country.

Unfortunately, in such international comparative research as that presented here, it is rare to have at one's disposal the homogeneous data that one would wish. In our case, we have succeeded in finding or elaborating a good number of variables relating to the characteristics of the host societies. It immediately became apparent, on the other hand, that the data relating to the non-nationals present in the various countries are limited. We keenly felt the lack of data on such aspects as non-nationals' knowledge of the language of the host country, on their professional activities, on the time spent in their host country, religion, previous experiences (as well as previous criminal records): data that would have been useful for gaining a better understanding of any relation between immigrants and criminality in the host country. Information of this type is sometimes available for particular countries, but, due to lack of homogeneity, is not useful for a comparative analysis. Account should be taken of this.

2.2 The countries covered by the research

The research project covered 18 countries in Western Europe. The choice of these countries was based on the assumption that Western Europe presents a fairly homogeneous set of parameters, in geographical, economic, legal, institutional and other terms. On the one hand, this homogeneity makes it an area on the whole favoured by immigration; and, on the other hand, forms a favourable condition for a comparative assessment within it, given that a comparison between the characteristics of migratory phenomena in countries that profoundly differ from each other, such as Belgium and Rwanda, would make little sense. At the same time, Western Europe presents significant internal differences that may be taken into consideration as a cause, in turn, of significant consequences in terms of the acceptance and integration of non-nationals, and in the last analysis as an aspect associated with a varying contribution of non-nationals to the official crime figures.

The choice fell in particular on countries forming part of the European Union (those of the – pre-2004 – 15-member Europe: Belgium, Denmark, Germany, Greece, Spain, France, Ireland, Italy, Luxembourg, Holland, Austria, Portugal, Finland, Sweden and the UK) and member states of EFTA (European Free Trade Association): Liechtenstein, Iceland, Norway and Switzerland. The inclusion of the EFTA States was prompted both by the fact that they present characteristics similar to the countries of the EU and have a series of economic and political accords with it, and by the availability of official data (Eurostat, for example, cites, together with the data for the countries of the EU, also those for the EFTA States). Liechtenstein, however, was not taken into consideration since the main European sources of statistical information do not make available sufficient data on it. Sometimes, referring to the 18 countries included in our comparative study, we have for the sake of convenience spoken in general of EU countries, despite the fact that the EFTA countries cannot be included among the member states of the European Union. In the presentation of the data, the countries are cited with the abbreviations used by Eurostat: B (Belgium), DK (Denmark), D (Germany), EL (Greece), E (Spain), F (France), IRL (Ireland), I (Italy), L (Luxembourg), NL (Netherlands), A (Austria), P (Portugal), FIN (Finland), S (Sweden), UK (United Kingdom), ISL (Iceland), NOR (Norway), and CH (Switzerland).

Altogether, the 18 countries considered represent, with some approximation, the whole political and geographical area of Western Europe: only those countries with very limited population, such as Liechtenstein, San Marino, Andorra, and Monaco, are excluded; the data available for these states, in any case, are unsuitable for an international comparison.

2.3 The non-national populations covered by the research: some preliminary remarks

The research has tried to identify not only the characteristics of the host country, but also those of its non-national communities, consisting of those who don't have citizenship of the host country. In this regard, some preliminary remarks should be made. Many foreigners, long resident in a given country, even if not citizens of it, are not perceived, nor do they perceive themselves, as immigrants. By contrast, immigrants with citizenship of the host country, as well as the naturalized children of immigrants, though they do not fall into the category of non-nationals, may possess all the distinctive hallmarks of the immigrant and hence be considered as *nationals* involved in the problem of the link between immigration and criminality. Of necessity, more precisely due to the fact that proper information – in terms of quantity, quality and homogeneity of data – is not available for naturalized immigrants and more generally on the substantial aspects of the concept of *immigrant*, we are unable to examine these distinctions more closely in this study. We will therefore use, as the main criterion for the definition of the non-national population to which this study is devoted, the formal aspect of *not being citizens* of the host country.

It should be emphasized that the timeframe and procedures for non-nationals to become citizens of the host country vary from country to country in Europe. This has repercussions both on the number of individuals considered non-nationals present in the various countries, and on their chances of becoming naturalized, and hence fully integrated, in the host country. As a consequence, it also impacts on the probability of their propensity towards deviant or criminal behaviour. That said, the information relating to the timescales, procedures and difficulties that non-nationals encounter in their attempts to acquire citizenship of the host country may only in limited terms be translated into indices useful for the comparative evaluations that form the basis of this study. It is information mainly of qualitative type, which more often than not is ill-suited to being transformed into more precise data of quantitative type. It should be pointed out, however, that the transition from the status of non-national to that of citizen of the host country depends not only on what is said above, but also on a precise and conscious choice of the immigrant in question, which in turn will depend on many other factors, to which we shall presently return.

Chapter 3

National and non-national population in Western Europe

3.1 Population of Western Europe and its evolution in time

The resident population in the countries of Western Europe amounted to about 300 million in 1950. It had grown to 400 million by 2005 (see Table 3.1).

The growth of the population of Western Europe between 1950 and 2005 may at first sight seem considerable. In comparative terms, however, it is very limited. Indeed, it represents by far the lowest growth of those registered in the various geopolitical regions of the world during the same period. For, while the countries of Western Europe increased their overall population by roughly 32 per cent (with a compound annual growth rate of only 5 per thousand) between 1950 and the start of the twenty-first century, the world population grew by 140 per cent (with an annual growth of 17 per thousand) during the same period. The population of Eastern Europe grew by 36 per cent (annual growth of 6 per thousand) during this period; North America by over 90 per cent (12 per thousand); the whole of Africa by c. 300 per cent (26 per thousand); North Africa and Latin America each by c. 250 per cent (22 per thousand); the whole of Asia by 180 per cent (19 per thousand); and Western Asia by over 300 per cent (26 per thousand). Figure 3.1 gives some idea of the diversity of these varying levels of population increase.

The limited demographic growth of Western Europe in the second half of the twentieth century thus contrasts with the far more rapid growth of the regions geographically closest to it; especially those of North Africa, Africa in general and Western Asia. This fact, as already mentioned in our introduction, is of crucial importance to understanding the scenarios of immigration to Western Europe. Overall, it may be recalled that the population of Western Europe historically is thought to have formed approximately a fifth of the world population. The share of the European population had grown as a percentage of world population in the nineteenth century. But thereafter Europe's population shrank (in comparative terms) and already by 1950 represented only some 12 per cent of the world population. By the start of the twenty-first century its share had been halved in comparison with 1950, and formed only c. 6 per cent of the world population.

Table 3.1 Total resident population in the countries of Western Europe – absolute values in thousands, at 31/12 – Years: 1950–2005

States	1950	1960	1970	1980	1985	1990	1995	2000	2005
B	8,639	9,178	9,651	9,863	9,859	9,987	10,143	10,263	10,511
DK	4,271	4,594	4,951	5,124	5,116	5,147	5,251	5,349	5,427
D	68,376	73,087	78,070	78,396	77,661	79,753	81,818	82,260	82,438
EL	7,566	8,367	8,805	9,701	9,949	10,200	10,465	10,565	11,125
E	28,009	30,583	33,918	37,636	38,470	38,875	39,242	40,122	43,758
F	41,829	45,904	51,016	54,029	55,411	56,893	58,256	59,039	62,999
IRL	2,969	2,822	2,971	3,433	3,541	3,521	3,616	3,826	4,209
I	47,104	50,374	53,958	56,479	56,598	56,744	57,333	57,844	58,752
L	296	315	340	365	367	384	413	440	460
NL	10,114	11,556	13,119	14,209	14,529	15,010	15,494	15,987	16,334
A	6,935	7,065	7,479	7,553	7,582	7,769	8,055	8,121	8,266
P	8,405	8,889	8,663	9,819	10,014	9,873	9,921	10,263	10,570
FIN	4,009	4,462	4,598	4,788	4,911	4,999	5,117	5,181	5,256
S	7,014	7,498	8,081	8,318	8,358	8,591	8,838	8,883	9,048
UK	50,616	52,590	55,780	56,341	56,768	57,681	58,694	59,863	60,393
ISL	143	178	205	229	242	256	268	283	300
NOR	3,265	3,595	3,888	4,092	4,159	4,250	4,370	4,503	4,640
CH	4,694	5,360	6,193	6,335	6,485	6,751	7,062	7,204	7,459
Total	304,254	326,417	351,686	366,710	370,020	376,684	384,356	389,995	401,945

Source: Eurostat 1996, 1997, 2002, 2007, UN 2001.

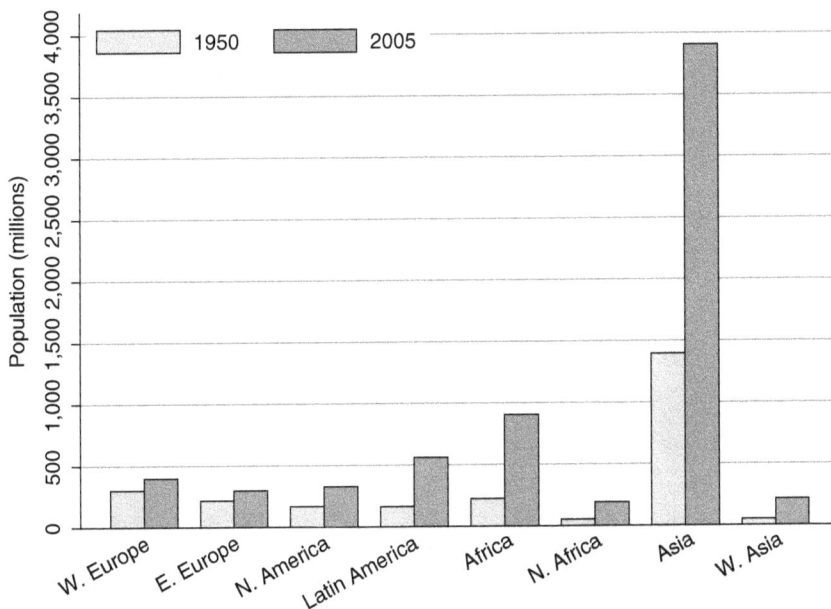

Figure 3.1 Comparative evolution of the population of Western Europe and other regions of the world – Years: 1950 and 2005.

We can better follow the evolution of the population of Western Europe from 1950 onwards by means of Table 3.2, which shows the annual variation of population.

In the 1950s and 1960s, the overall increases are relatively larger, even if very far from those registered in other regions of the world. But by 1970 the annual increase begins to drop rapidly, until it reaches a low point in 1985. In the following years there is a slight recovery, followed by a further decline. Since the 1980s the population of Western Europe has in general registered very limited mean levels of growth, albeit with some oscillations.

The demographic situation as a whole is clearer if we bear in mind that the variation of a population is determined not only by endogenous population variation (natural balance, i.e. the difference between the number of live births and deaths), but also by the differential between population inflows and outflows to and from the territory in question (migratory balance).

Now, natural population variation in the countries of Western Europe (Table 3.3) shows that there was a substantial natural increase (in comparison with the ensuing period) in the years 1950–60. But by 1970 a diminution of the increase can be noted. This became more accentuated in the

Table 3.2 Annual variation of population per 1,000 inhabitants in the countries of Western Europe – Years: 1950–2005

States	1950–55	1960	1970	1980	1985	1990	1995	2000	2005
B	5.2	5.4	−1.0	0.8	0.1	3.9	1.2	2.4	6.3
DK	7.7	7.7	6.9	0.3	1.0	2.2	6.8	3.6	3.0
D	5.6	7.5	−2.6	2.8	−0.6	8.1	3.4	1.2	−0.8
EL	10.3	7.9	2.8	11.5	3.0	7.8	2.1	1.0	3.8
E	8.4	9.4	15.6	5.8	3.3	1.8	1.6	9.7	16.7
F	7.9	9.6	9.6	5.5	4.6	5.6	4.1	4.9	7.7
IRL	−3.3	−4.9	9.4	11.7	−1.0	4.0	6.2	13.0	24.3
I	6.0	6.9	5.1	1.6	0.2	0.9	1.1	2.8	4.9
L	6.0	5.9	4.0	3.8	2.7	13.4	15.1	8.7	9.9
NL	12.2	12.1	12.4	8.3	5.2	7.9	4.5	7.7	1.8
A	0.3	4.9	3.2	1.0	1.0	10.3	1.9	2.3	7.2
P	4.8	7.2	−4.0	10.8	0.6	−4.7	0.9	6.3	3.8
FIN	11.0	7.5	−3.5	3.4	3.4	4.8	3.5	1.9	3.6
S	7.0	3.6	9.5	1.8	1.9	7.4	2.4	2.4	4.0
UK	2.3	8.1	4.2	1.0	3.0	3.9	3.5	4.0	5.5
ISL	20.0	20.7	4.9	10.7	6.6	8.2	3.7	15.3	21.5
NOR	9.7	7.6	6.5	3.3	3.2	3.9	4.9	5.5	7.3
CH	11.8	12.1	3.9	5.0	4.5	11.5	6.2	5.5	5.9
Total	6.1	7.0	4.7	3.7	1.9	4.8	3.0	4.1	5.6

Source: Eurostat 1996, 1997, 2002, 2007, UN 2001.

following years, with the result that the population increases registered were very modest. In the second half of the 1990s, overall levels of increase lower than 1 per thousand (i.e. 0.1 per cent) were registered. We can therefore speak of an essentially stable population, in terms of its natural variation.

National situations of course vary considerably. Between 1950 and 1970, the Mediterranean countries had relatively high rates of natural population increase. So too did some countries in Northern Europe, such as Iceland, Ireland, the Netherlands, Norway and Finland. Germany, on the contrary, already showed by the 1970s a situation of stable population, in terms of natural variation. In the following years Germany entered a phase of negative variations. Italy followed suit in this trend of negative variation at the start of the 1990s. In the second half of the 1990s Sweden and Greece also embarked on a phase of negative variation. Austria oscillated round the zero mark in terms of natural population increase. At the start of the new century, only Iceland and Ireland, among the countries of Western Europe, still maintained relatively significant rates of increase.

Table 3.3 Annual natural variation of the population per 1,000 inhabitants in the countries of Western Europe – Years: 1950–2005

States	1950–55	1960	1970	1980	1985	1990	1995	2000	2005
B	4.5	4.5	2.4	1.1	0.3	1.9	0.9	1.1	1.4
DK	8.9	7.1	4.6	0.3	–0.9	0.5	1.3	1.7	1.7
D	4.9	5.3	0.9	–1.1	–1.5	–0.2	–1.5	–0.9	–1.8
EL	12.3	11.6	8.1	6.3	2.4	0.8	0.1	–0.2	0.2
E	10.1	12.3	11.2	7.5	3.7	1.8	0.4	0.9	1.8
F	6.7	6.5	6.0	4.7	3.9	4.2	3.4	4.0	4.4
IRL	8.8	9.9	10.4	11.9	8.2	6.2	4.6	6.1	8.2
I	8.5	8.6	7.1	1.5	0.5	0.5	–0.5	–0.3	–0.6
L	3.0	4.2	0.8	0.2	0.2	3.0	4.0	4.3	3.8
NL	14.6	13.2	9.9	4.7	3.8	4.6	3.5	4.2	3.2
A	2.8	5.2	1.8	–0.2	–0.3	1.0	0.9	0.2	0.4
P	16.9	13.4	10.1	6.5	3.3	1.3	0.3	1.4	0.2
FIN	13.1	9.6	4.4	3.9	3.0	3.1	2.7	1.4	1.9
S	5.7	3.6	3.7	0.6	0.5	3.4	1.1	–0.3	1.1
UK	4.2	6.0	4.5	1.7	1.4	2.7	1.5	1.2	2.3
ISL	20.4	21.3	12.5	13.1	9.1	12.0	8.8	8.5	8.3
NOR	10.6	8.2	6.7	2.4	1.6	3.5	3.5	3.4	3.4
CH	7.2	7.9	6.8	2.3	2.3	3.0	2.7	2.2	1.6
Total	7.2	7.6	5.4	2.5	1.4	1.9	0.7	1.1	1.2

The net migratory balance (Table 3.4) shows an overall situation that is consistent with these demographic premises. At the start of the period, all the Mediterranean countries, and also Ireland, Finland, Iceland, Norway and the Netherlands – in other words, all the countries with large natural population increase – had a negative net migratory balance; they were characterized, that is, by a net outflow of population. It is well known, in fact, that large numbers of Europeans chose emigration as a way of seeking their fortunes in the years following the Second World War, in an impoverished Europe characterized by sharp unemployment and huge masses of refugees (Caselli 2001). Between 1950 and 1970, the net migratory balance of Italy, Spain, Portugal and Greece was negative, with a total outflow of 6 million people (Macura 1994). In the same years, Italy alone had a negative migratory balance of 2.5 million people (Rosoli 1978). In the countries of Northern Europe, too, emigration during those years represented a large-scale phenomenon. This mass emigration, as regards the countries of Southern Europe,

Table 3.4 Net migratory balance (adjustments included), by year, per 1,000 inhabitants, in the countries of Western Europe – Years: 1950–2005

States	1950–55	1960	1970	1980	1985	1990	1995	2000	2005
B	0.7	0.9	−3.4	−0.2	−0.1	2.0	0.4	1.3	4.9
DK	−1.2	0.7	2.4	0.1	1.9	1.7	5.5	1.9	1.2
D	0.7	2.2	−3.5	3.9	0.9	8.3	4.9	2.0	1.0
EL	−2.0	−3.7	−5.3	5.2	0.6	7.0	2.0	1.2	3.6
E	−1.7	−2.2	4.4	−1.7	−0.5	0.0	1.2	8.8	14.9
F	1.2	3.1	3.6	0.8	0.7	1.4	0.7	0.9	3.3
IRL	−12.1	−14.8	−0.9	−0.2	−9.3	−2.2	1.6	6.9	16.1
I	−2.5	−1.6	−2.0	0.1	−0.4	0.4	1.7	3.1	5.5
L	3.0	1.7	3.2	3.7	2.5	10.3	11.2	4.3	6.0
NL	−2.4	−1.1	2.5	3.6	1.4	3.3	1.0	3.6	−1.4
A	−2.5	−0.3	1.4	1.2	1.3	9.3	0.9	2.1	6.9
P	−12.1	−6.3	−14.0	4.3	−2.7	−6.1	0.5	4.9	3.6
FIN	−2.1	−2.1	−7.9	−0.5	0.5	1.7	0.8	0.5	1.7
S	1.3	−0.1	5.8	1.2	1.3	4.1	1.3	2.8	3.0
UK	−1.9	2.1	−0.3	−0.7	1.6	1.2	2.0	2.8	3.2
ISL	−0.4	−0.6	−7.6	−2.7	−2.5	−3.9	−5.1	6.8	13.2
NOR	−0.9	−0.6	−0.2	0.9	1.6	0.4	1.5	2.2	4.0
CH	4.6	4.2	−2.9	2.7	2.1	8.4	3.5	3.3	4.3
Total	−1.1	0.4	−0.6	1.2	0.5	2.9	2.2	3.0	4.4

was in the main directed both at the countries at the heart of Europe (France, Germany, Switzerland and Belgium) and at countries outside Europe (USA, Canada, Australia, Latin America). As regards the countries of Northern Europe, emigration was mainly directed at non-European countries.

By the 1970s, this movement of emigration had been exhausted, also as a result of the negative consequences of the petroleum crisis on the world economy in 1973. In the following decade, quite the reverse situation was registered. As may be ascertained from Table 3.4, France, Germany, Luxembourg, Switzerland and Sweden are the countries in which the phenomenon of a decidedly positive net migratory balance was registered ahead of other countries. From the end of the 1970s the phenomenon became generalized. While natural population growth was reduced to the point of insignificance, or even registered a negative variation, the net migratory balance became significantly positive as a result of new influxes of immigrants. And this phenomenon was progressively extended, also involving those countries of the Mediterranean in which the migratory balance had previously been so negative.

So, the evidence shows that, since the end of the 1980s, the growth of the influx of immigrants into the countries of Western Europe was the main factor for the albeit modest total population increase of the region. As far as national situations are concerned, in Germany the negative natural balance was thus compensated by the markedly positive migratory balance; the same compensatory mechanism was registered, in an even more pronounced way, in Italy. In Luxembourg, the migratory balance has always exceeded natural population growth, reaching values higher than 10‰ in the 1990s. Similar situations have been registered in Denmark and Sweden. By contrast, the contribution of natural population growth continued to prevail over the contribution of influxes of migrants in some countries: in particular in Finland, the Netherlands and France.

3.2 Immigration and the presence of non-nationals in Europe: what has changed?

Flows of migrants towards Western Europe determined the formation, within each country, of populations of individuals with nationalities different from that of the country in which they live: these are the *non-nationals*, according to the terminology adopted by Eurostat. Non-nationals are equivalent to *foreigners* – understood in the strict sense – in other words, those present in a country different from the one to which (by birth and nationality) they belong.

The study of the dimensions and variations of non-national population may draw on the data collected by two main cross-European statistical sources: Eurostat (the statistical office of the EU, an agency of the European Commission) and the OECD (Organization for Economic Co-operation and Development). The OECD and in particular its International Migration Outlook agency (Sopemi) gathers and publishes a large number of qualitative and quantitative data on migratory phenomena in all its member countries: the data are gathered by an international migration watchdog, Sopemi, which has no authority to impose homogeneous procedures for the collection of data at the national level. Eurostat especially furnishes quantitative data relating to the member countries of the EU, member countries of EFTA, other European countries, the USA and Canada, and Japan. Eurostat has an official character and hence has greater leverage in influencing individual states in adopting measures to achieve homogeneity in data collection. Despite that, significant obstacles remain in achieving such homogeneity. As regards the data relating to non-national communities, the registration of migratory phenomena depends on the initiative and resources of the individual countries and especially on the system of registration adopted. Different data-gathering methods in fact exist; they primarily differ on the basis of the existence or not of a registry for the systematic gathering of personal data. The use of personal data banks (which is the main source for data gathering in a series of countries such as Belgium, Denmark, Finland, Sweden, Norway and Switzerland) permits, at least in theory, a constantly updated picture of the entire population resident in the country. In its tracking of the non-national population it relies in the main on applications for residence and the issue of related certificates; recourse may also be made to other sources of information on the presence of foreigners in the country, such as the residence permits issued by the police. As regards the countries that don't use personal data banks, information on non-nationals is based on other procedures. For example, in France and in Austria the data on emigration have been primarily drawn from censuses; but this does not permit a precise year-by-year picture of the variations of the migratory phenomenon. In other countries (Germany, Italy, Netherlands) the data are based on the information obtained at frontier posts (*entry/exit forms*). In other countries again (Ireland, UK), the data are extrapolated from sample surveys. In sum, the different procedures for estimating the foreign population may give rise to evaluations that do not always coincide with the data published by the various international data-gathering agencies, also due to time lags in the publication of the final data. Moreover, it is clear that these sources of data can only furnish estimations of irregular, or clandestine, immigration, which has a greater impact in some countries than in others.

Lastly, it should be pointed out that the less recent data inevitably suffer from the fact that the systematic surveying of immigration/emigration by Eurostat and the OECD did not begin until 1985. The data available for previous years are scarce and fragmentary. It has thus been necessary, for purposes of this study, to draw on other sources. It is clear, however, that the comparability of data on migration in Europe prior to the 1980s presents margins of uncertainty, but these ought not to prejudice the overall significance of the picture.

Having clarified these limitations, we can observe that the data at our disposal (Table 3.5) clearly show the impact that the migratory phenomenon has assumed in European countries in recent years. The overall data permit us to ascertain two phenomena of great importance. First, the non-national population in Europe shows an ever growing trend and a quantitatively significant growth; some periods of deceleration of growth can be identified, in the early 1980s and in the second half of the 1990s, but the variation for the entire period is huge: *c.* 600 per cent. Second, the percentage share of the non-national population out of the total population is progressively growing (Table 3.6).

The most recent data show that the countries in which the foreign presence is quantitatively most substantial are Germany, France and the UK; they are followed by Italy and Spain. The share of the non-national population out of the total resident population is also important, however (Table 3.6). The situation relating to the individual countries is highly

Table 3.5 Non-national population resident in the countries of Western Europe – Absolute values in thousands, at 31/12 – Years: 1950–2005

States	1950	1960	1970	1980	1985	1990	1995	2000	2005
B	368	453	696	861	847	904	910	862	901
DK			90	102	117	161	223	259	270
D	532	686	3,054	4,453	4,379	5,342	7,174	7,297	6,756
EL	31	55	63	70	119	184	263	570	891
E	93	68	148	183	242	408	500	896	2,739
F	1,737	2,170	2,621	3,680	3,638	3,559	3,374	3,263	3,500
IRL				83	78	85	96	127	259
I	47	63	121	299	423	781	991	1,388	2,671
L	29	42	63	96	98	110	138	165	182
NL	104	118	252	521	552	692	725	668	691
A	323	102	212	291	304	456	724	758	802
P	21	30	32	63	66	78	168	267	432
FIN	11	5	6	13	17	27	69	91	114
S	124	191	408	422	389	484	532	477	480
UK	392	810	1,227	1,650	1,845	1,805	1,992	2,342	3,035
ISL			3	3	3	5	5	9	14
NOR	16	25	76	82	101	143	161	184	222
CH	285	585	1,080	915	961	1,127	1,331	1,384	1,512
Total	4,113	5,403	10,151	13,704	14,179	16,350	19,267	21,006	25,470

Source: Eurostat 1995, 1996, 2000, 2000a, 2002, 2007, 2008. Sopemi 1991, 1993 and following years.

NB: For the 1950–1980 data, given the lack of more systematic surveys, reference has been made to various censuses, as also to Penninx 1984, Haskey 1992, Fassmann and Münz 1994, Caselli 2001, and Strozza 2002. The data refer to the year indicated in the table headings, or, in its absence, the most approximate year for which data are available. The data for the UK and Ireland are derived from the Labour Force Survey. As far as the UK is concerned, prior to 1985, the data on non-nationals excluded those coming from the Commonwealth countries, Ireland and the West Indies; so the data in question underestimate the presence of non-nationals. Again as far as the UK is concerned, the data relating to 1960 and 1970 have been obtained by interpolation. The data for Greece after 1990 have been recalculated on the basis of the regularization in 1998 and the census in 2001. The data for Portugal in 2000 were recalculated on the basis of the regularization in 2001. France: data interpolated on the basis of the censuses of 1982, 1990 and 1999.

differentiated and markedly dissimilar to that furnished by Table 3.5, since the absolute values for the foreign presence need to be related to, i.e. expressed as a percentage of, the overall population. Luxembourg presents by far the highest percentage of non-nationals; it is followed by Switzerland; then by Austria, Belgium and Germany. Other countries are characterized by a relatively limited share of non-nationals: namely, Finland, Portugal, Iceland and Italy.

Table 3.6 Percentage of non-nationals out of the total population resident in the countries of Western Europe, at 31/12 – Years: 1950–2005

States	1950	1960	1970	1980	1985	1990	1995	2000	2005
B	4.3	4.9	7.2	8.7	8.6	9.1	9.0	8.4	8.6
DK		1.8	2.0	2.3	3.1	4.2	4.8	5.0	
D	0.8	0.9	3.9	5.7	5.6	6.7	8.8	8.9	8.2
EL	0.4	0.7	0.7	0.7	1.2	1.8	2.5	5.4	8.0
E	0.3	0.2	0.4	0.5	0.6	1.0	1.3	2.2	6.3
F	4.2	4.7	5.1	6.8	6.6	6.3	5.8	5.5	5.7
IRL			2.4	2.2	2.4	2.7	3.3	6.2	
I	0.1	0.1	0.2	0.5	0.7	1.4	1.7	2.4	4.5
L	9.8	13.3	18.5	26.2	26.7	28.6	33.4	37.5	39.6
NL	1.0	1.0	1.9	3.7	3.8	4.6	4.7	4.2	4.2
A	4.7	1.4	2.8	3.9	4.0	5.9	9.0	9.3	9.7
P	0.2	0.3	0.4	0.6	0.7	0.8	1.7	2.6	4.1
FIN	0.3	0.1	0.1	0.3	0.3	0.5	1.3	1.8	2.2
S	1.8	2.5	5.0	5.1	4.7	5.6	6.0	5.4	5.3
UK	0.8	1.5	2.2	2.9	3.3	3.1	3.4	3.9	5.0
ISL		1.4	1.4	1.3	1.9	1.9	3.1	4.6	
NOR	0.5	0.7	2.0	2.0	2.4	3.4	3.7	4.1	4.8
CH	6.1	10.9	17.4	14.4	14.8	16.7	18.8	19.2	20.3
Total	1.4	1.7	2.9	3.8	3.8	4.3	5.0	5.4	6.4
Aver. val.	2.3	2.9	4.2	4.9	5.0	5.7	6.7	7.3	8.5

Chart 3.1, which uses the same data as Table 3.6, though shown by means of graduated symbols, permits an immediate perception of the dissimilar situations in the various countries with regard to the percentages of non-nationals out of the total of their respective populations.

Despite the limited information on the foreign-born – available only for the more recent years (Sopemi 2006) – over 36 million foreign-borns, equivalent to 9 per cent of the resident population, were ascertained for Western Europe as a whole at the start of the twenty-first century; the average value for the 18 main countries was higher, *c.* 11 per cent. The percentage of foreign-borns out of the total resident population, however, is still lower than that registered in the USA (12 per cent in 2004); whereas the average percentage of the 18 European countries – to which this study is specifically devoted – is already higher than the average percentage of the 51 states of the USA (8 per cent). Indeed, the percentage of foreign-borns out of the total resident population in many European countries (France, Greece, Holland, Ireland, Belgium, Sweden, Germany and Austria) ranges between 10 and

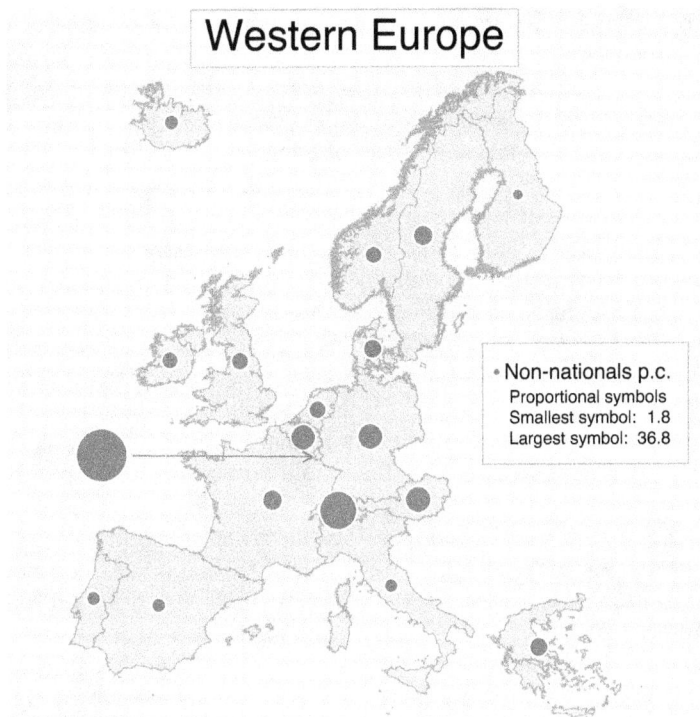

Chart 3.1 Percentage of non-nationals out of the total population resident in the countries of Western Europe – Average for the years 1995–2005.

13 per cent. It is no surprise that in Switzerland and Luxembourg that percentage reaches a far higher figure.

If we examine the situation in a diachronic perspective, rather than the situation today, we can identify quite distinct phases in the trend of the non-national population in Western Europe. First, the presence of non-nationals in the period between 1950 and 1960 is on the whole modest. In particular it is low in the Mediterranean countries, characterized by marked emigration during this period. Some more affluent and developed countries of Central and Northern Europe, Switzerland, Luxembourg, France, Belgium and to a lesser degree Sweden, form an exception to the general rule (Caselli 2001). In the situation of economic and social difficulties in post-war Europe, these countries drew waves of immigration especially from the countries of Southern Europe. This is a migratory process propelled by *pull factors*, in other words, the sharp demand for manpower and the low rate of unemployment in the countries to which these immigrants were attracted. As we have already pointed out, some of the countries of destination, such as France, already had a tradition of a significant presence of non-nationals going back to the period before the war. It should be noted, at the same time, that the two main colonial powers in the region, France and Great Britain, received large numbers of emigrants from their colonies and former colonies. France in particular maintained, until the crisis in the 1970s, a policy in favour of accepting quasi-French citizens from her former colonies (Hollifield 1994). The UK adopted a far more restrictive policy, which also included an attitude unfavourable to coloured immigrants, whose integration was thought to pose difficulties. But, despite such restrictions, large groups of immigrants from the West Indies, India, and Pakistan settled in the country between the 1950s and 1960s, and were added to the numerous, traditional Irish immigrants (Layton-Henry 1994). Holland too received large numbers of immigrants from its former colonies. This was the first emergence of a new phenomenon that would powerfully develop only a few years later.

There was a strong acceleration of the migratory phenomenon as a whole in the 1960s. As may be noted from Tables 3.5 and 3.6, non-nationals doubled in number between 1960 and 1970. The basic situation remained substantially that already described. The countries to which this inflow was directed were the same as in the previous decade; the most significant new features was the boom of non-nationals in Germany, drawn by the rapid process of economic development then underway (the *Wirtschaftswunder*) and by the need for extra manpower, also to compensate for the huge numbers of the working population that had been killed during the war (Golini 2000). From that time onwards, Germany vied with France, and later overtook it, as the main magnet of immigration in Europe. Other traditional countries of immigration, such as Switzerland and Luxembourg, exceeded Germany, however, in terms of non-national population as percentage of the total population. The main countries of origin of these non-nationals remained those of the southernmost countries of Western Europe, such as Italy and Spain, to which were added Yugoslavia, Turkey and Algeria (Fassmann and Münz 1994). The non-nationals consisted in the main of migrant *workers*, also known under the telling name of *guest workers*: their object was not to find a permanent home, but to spend a *pro tempore* period of residence in the host countries, which evaluated them on the basis of the same parameter. These migrant workers were mainly employed in big factories in the industrial sector (Strozza 2002).

This first phase of post-war emigration to Europe, the so-called phase of the 'thirty glorious years' (Garson and Loizillon 2003), ended abruptly with the petroleum crisis in 1973. The consequent economic crisis, that involved Western Europe together with the Western hemisphere as a whole, caused a sudden reduction in labour demand in those European countries that had most attracted migrants hitherto. A series of restrictions imposed on migrant workers was also a consequence of the crisis. Many permits were not renewed and efforts made to limit new arrivals. Governments also provided incentives to encourage the repatriation of a part of non-nationals. This second, more repressive phase, which clearly marked a turning-point, was gradually extended to all the countries of Western Europe; and the policy of the following decades – guided and harmonized by the interventions of the EU – would be characterized by far tougher immigration controls and various forms of quota system to regulate immigration according to country of origin. Such policies opened up a clear divide between the rights to immigration of the nationals of other EU countries and the rights of all others, in particular those from the 'less developed' countries; these would later in many cases be denied even tourist visas, out of the fear lest, once they had arrived in their country of destination, they would settle there as clandestine immigrants.

The deterioration of overall economic conditions in the 1970s led to the visible emergence of tensions of various kinds, notably to the latent conflict between migrant workers and the lowest ranks of native-born blue-collar workers (Fassmann and Münz 1994). In particular, conflicts with a clear ethnic character between immigrants and natives erupted in France and England. In Switzerland, a mass movement developed that openly expressed xenophobic attitudes, and fielded its own parliamentary candidates, on the basis of programmes dominated by an agenda of open hostility to immigrants.

In spite of this new phase in the development of the migratory phenomenon in Europe, however, there was no arrest of the influx of migrants or of the presence of non-nationals in the 1970s. The new policies of containment and control partially reduced the influx of migrant workers and also generated some reflux in terms of the return of foreign workers to their countries of origin, but at the same time the process of family reunification for those that remained gained in momentum; also as a result of this movement, the birth rate of non-nationals in Western Europe grew sharply. The structure of the non-national population consequently underwent change; instead of migrant workers, preponderantly male, now the non-national population consisted of more nuclear families; and non-national women were added to men on the labour market. Some of the non-nationals received the citizenship of their host country. These naturalizations led to some of the immigrants disappearing from the statistics of non-nationals. But all this increased the local *network* of compatriots to which new immigrants, even if illegal, could look to find support, receive advice, find work, and obtain assistance (Cornelius *et al.* 1994). In effect, the new restrictive policies were in part circumvented by a new and growing phenomenon: that of the entry of clandestine or irregular immigrants (e.g. through the prolongation of short-term visits initially authorized for purposes of tourism) (Sopemi 2000). As an effect of all this, the presence of non-nationals increased, rather than decreased, in the late 1970s (see Tables 3.5 and 3.6).

A third phase of immigration to Europe began in the early 1980s. Its characteristics were in part merely a form of stabilization and reinforcement of the trends that had already emerged after the crisis in 1973. It is thus characterized by a greater number of family reunifications; and a growing presence of the female component among the non-nationals. At the same time a growth was registered in the number of the underage children of non-nationals, as well as a growth in naturalizations, and in the scale and impact of clandestine or irregular immigration. Alongside these phenomena, others, decidedly new, emerged. They would help to define this period as a new phase in the dynamics of migration to Western Europe. These new phenomena included, first, the fact that the flow of migrants inside Europe, and especially those from the Mediterranean countries, was sharply reduced. At the same time, immigration both from European countries not forming part of Western Europe and from non-European countries grew. This new influx was no longer propelled by the traditional *pull factors*, since economic growth in Western Europe was less than what it had been in the period before the 1970s economic crisis, and unemployment was high (Melotti 1993), even if altogether the prosperity of Western Europe continued to seem fabulous in comparison with the situation in the less developed countries. Other *pull factors*, however, emerged in Europe, such as the opportunities to study that drew students from less privileged countries, and also continuing opportunities to find work in Europe, even if humble and not infrequently in conditions of marginality. Job vacancies were also supported by the fact that the high overall prosperity of the indigenous inhabitants of Western Europe led to their progressive disaffection from those jobs that were more demeaning and less attractive in social and economic terms (Strozza 2002). More in general, immigration to Western Europe in recent decades has found opportunities for work in the parallel development of a hidden economy, a black market in jobs, or 'off-the-books' employment, which ensures flexibility and low costs to the economy, especially in the services sector but also in that of small businesses and agriculture. This use of immigrant manpower in the hidden economy seems particularly developed in such countries as Spain, Italy, Greece and Belgium (Cornelius *et al.* 1994).

Behind the migration of this new phase, however, we especially find *push factors*. In particular, these factors include strong demographic growth combined with low economic growth in the Third World; human rights violations, ethnic conflicts and political persecutions, again in the Third World; and the disintegration of the Communist political systems in Eastern Europe between the late 1980s and the early 1990s. A sign of the impact of these *push factors* is the enormous expansion of entries into Western Europe following application for political asylum: from the start to the end of the 1990s these entries amounted to approximately 4 million. But also the economic situation in many so-called developing countries represented in itself a powerful push factor. When, as has been the case in recent years, conditions in the country of origin are such that any kind of activity, however precarious, however illegal, in whatever country of Western Europe promises earnings at least ten times higher, then it is understandable why the uncertain fate of emigration seems preferable to the negative certainty of remaining at home.

Altogether, these phenomena can be summed up in the concept of the *diffusionism* of the dynamics of migration towards Europe. One significant consequence is a change in the various areas of origin of emigration to Europe; but equally significant is the change in the countries of destination. As for the former change, there has been a strong growth of migrant inflows from European countries not forming part of Western Europe (typical is the boom of immigration from the countries of the former Communist bloc). As for the latter change, there has been a rapid and massive development of immigration towards the countries of Southern Europe, i.e. towards those countries that until recently had been zones not of immigration but of emigration. As may be noted from Table 3.6, the percentage of non-nationals in Portugal, Spain, Italy and Greece at the start of the twenty-first century was far higher than what it had been in 1980. Also as a result of this boom of immigration to the countries of Southern Europe, the overall percentage of non-nationals in the countries of Western Europe almost doubled between 1980 and 2005.

It is particularly in this new immigration to the countries of Southern Europe that a fundamental role has been played by the component consisting of immigrants from Eastern Europe and especially from Third World countries (see further, Section 3.3). And, what is more, a high rate of irregularity is associated with this component: a factor that aggravates the already significant difficulties of achieving the integration of immigrants characterized on the whole by greater cultural, social and economic disparity from the indigenous population. The scale of the presence of clandestine or irregular immigrants in Western Europe was estimated as not less than 10 per cent of the non-national population in the 1990s. To subject this irregular or clandestine component to greater controls, the European countries most affected by the phenomenon have adopted a series of provisions aimed at re-absorbing this component in the number of regular non-nationals. First France, then Spain, Italy, Portugal, Greece, and even Belgium, have since the 1980s implemented a series of procedures aimed at the regularization of the non-nationals present in their territory. In some cases these regularizations have involved a relatively small number of irregular immigrants in relation to the size of the regular non-national population; in other cases, as in Greece, Portugal and Italy in the years round the turn of the new millennium, the number of immigrants regularized in this way was on the whole very high.

Not surprisingly, in the light of these developments, political movements whose common denominator was a firm antagonism to immigration were formed and grew in influence, albeit with variable success, in many countries of Western Europe in the 1990s. The measures adopted by these movements ranged from strongly restrictive and selective attitudes to immigrants to frankly xenophobic political formulae. These political movements, which in some measure reproduce the anti-immigration movement that had already made inroads in Switzerland in the 1970s, independently emerged in countries widely different in tradition, culture and outlook: for example, in Germany, in Holland, in Italy, in France, in Austria, and in Belgium. All of them have a pronounced nationalistic character and are mainly targeted at the lower middle and working classes of the indigenous population. These movements seem to confirm the intuition of Gellner (1983), who had predicted that the growing participation of the masses in politics would lead in Western democracies to the emergence of new forms of nationalism: forms based on the vulnerability of these masses to the changes taking place in the social and economic situation, and in particular the greater fluidity and instability of their positions in an ever more *open* society.

In this general climate, we have witnessed, especially in Germany, in the UK and in France, thousands of episodes of sometimes grave physical assaults on immigrants. These episodes, which at least at the official level have been condemned by virtually all political forces, have led, also under EU pressure, to the introduction in all the countries of Europe of new laws to combat the various manifestations of ethnic hatred (so-called *hate crime*).

3.3 Immigrant influxes and the origin of non-nationals

The number of resident non-nationals in the various countries and their share of the population are not the only parameters of the migratory phenomenon. Other significant information can be deduced from data relating to the inflow of new immigrants on entry into the country. The situation does not correspond to that of non-nationals resident in the various countries. Overall inflows may vary independently in time on the basis of the general dynamics of migratory phenomena: for example, on the basis of the sequence of phases of the migratory phenomenon in Western Europe we have already distinguished earlier in this chapter. High inflows tend to augment the non-national population, but not all new arrivals are transformed into lasting presences. Inflows are influenced by the more or less seasonal character of non-national presences, but also by the objective conditions existing within the country, the difficulties that non-nationals encounter on arrival and, subsequently, the overall attraction that the host country exerts on them. For all these reasons, the data relating to inflows are of interest for any study on the problems of integration and on the difficulties that non-nationals face.

Unfortunately, the data for the period prior to the late 1980s are incomplete. The data for the subsequent period are also indicative, and also suffer from the difficulties encountered in the calculation of the clandestine and irregular immigration component. Figure 3.2 attempts, in diagrammatic form, to sum up the trend of inflows of the non-national population in Western Europe (in absolute figures), compared with that of the USA, in the period from 1989 to 2005. The inflows show at first a relatively stable trend, which begins to rise significantly at the end of the 1990s. The phase of inflow stability coincides with the deceleration of the growth of the non-national population in Western Europe, registered in the second half of the 1990s (see Table 3.5).

This undulating trend should not, however, make us overlook a fundamental datum, already underlined: namely, the overall dimension of this inflow. In the 1990s the inflow amounts on average to *c.* 1,700,000 entries a year; and from 2001, to 2,500,000. This is an inflow far higher than that registered in other areas of the world (in particular the USA, Figure 3.2).

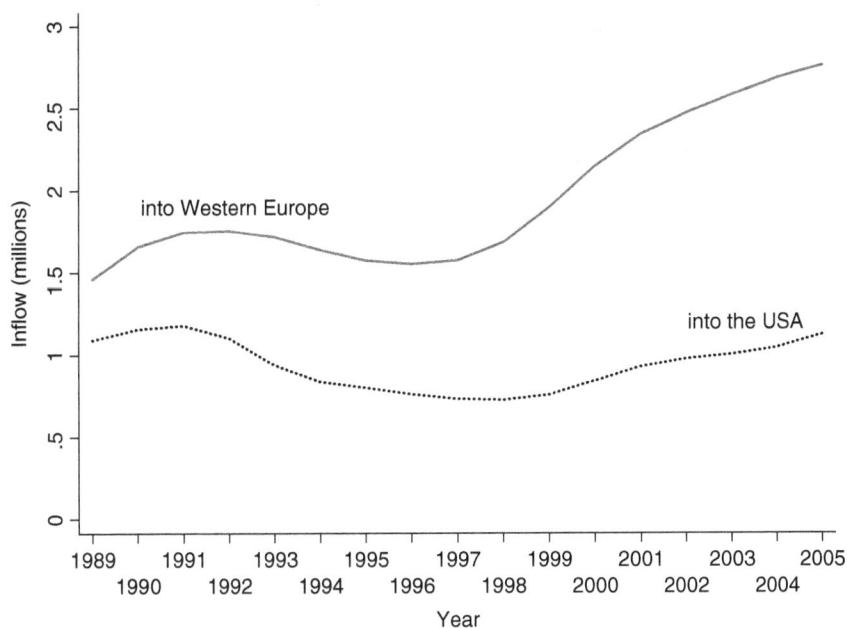

Figure 3.2 Inflows of non-nationals with residence or work permits in the countries of Western Europe and the USA (permanent inflow) – absolute values – Years: 1989–2005.

Sources: Eurostat 1996, 2008; Sopemi 1991, 1993 and following years; Kanellopoulos and Gregou 2006; Salt 2007.

NB: Here and in the other line charts, time series data smoothed by means of technique 4253H (running median smoother plus Hanning linear smoother).

The inflow figures for the USA are not only lower but also without the growth registered in Europe over the last few years. The current inflow into Europe is, moreover, far higher than that registered in this region during the previous boom of immigration, in other words, in the period prior to the economic crisis in the 1970s.

As regards the situation in the various countries, Germany takes first place in terms of the scale of the influx, which fluctuated between 600,000 and one million entries in the period (1989–2005); Spain, the UK and Italy follow, at some remove. Spain and Italy, however, are characterized by sharply growing inflows.

One significant aspect of immigration in Europe consists of the fact that the origin of immigrants differs in the various host countries. In our presentation of the theoretical aspects, we pointed out that the studies of the early decades of the twentieth century tended to attribute great importance to the ethnic differences between immigrants; more recent studies, by contrast, tend to privilege other concepts, such as integration. On the other hand, even those who refuse to emphasize the impact of ethnic differences *per se* will have difficulty in denying the fact that the origin of non-nationals is reflected in their cultural attitudes and even more clearly in their economic and professional conditions and, more generally, in their degree of integration in the host country. The question deserves some further analysis.

The data on the origin of non-nationals are in large measure extrapolated from census results. For this reason, the data are especially available for the years at the start of each decade (when censuses are normally conducted). Now, if we subdivide non-nationals into *EU nationals, European non-EU nationals*, and *non-Europeans* (Table 3.7), it emerges that in 2000 the group of EU nationals was in percentage terms somewhat higher than the other two groups, if we take as our parameter the average percentages for all countries. On the other hand, the group of *EU nationals* has a percentage almost identical to the other two if we use as the basis of our calculation the overall non-national population of Western Europe as a whole.

Table 3.7 shows that the distribution of the three groups of provenance in the individual countries is highly differentiated: and it is this fact that might have had most significance in explaining differences in integration. In 2000, Luxembourg had the highest percentage of *EU-nationals*, c. 90 per cent; followed by Ireland, Belgium and Switzerland; low percentages may be noted in Austria, Italy and Greece. *Non-EU European nationals* (and hence non-nationals coming from the countries of the former Soviet bloc, Yugoslavia, Albania and Turkey) form roughly a third of the total non-national population in Western Europe. For reasons evidently of geographical vicinity, they are most present in percentage terms in Austria, Greece, Germany and Finland. *Non-Europeans*, lastly, have a strong presence in percentage terms in the countries of Southern Europe, and specifically in

Table 3.7 Percentages of EU nationals (citizens of pre-2004 EU member states + EFTA), non-EU Europeans, and non-Europeans, out of the total of the non-national population in the countries of Western Europe – Annual percentages for 1980, 1990, 2000 (or the closest year for which data are available)

States	1980			1990			2000		
	EU (+EFTA)	Non-EU Europeans	Non-Europeans	EU (+EFTA)	Non-EU Europeans	Non-Europeans	EU (+EFTA)	Non-EU Europeans	Non-Europeans
B	69	9	22	63	11	26	67	11	22
DK	44	30	26	34	31	35	29	34	37
D	38	51	11	30	54	16	26	56	18
EL	34	33	33	35	21	44	6	76	18
E	51	1	48	49	1	50	41	3	56
F	44	7	49	37	9	54	38	10	52
IRL	76	1	23	77	1	22	74	6	20
I	46	9	45	25	13	62	13	26	61
L	94	4	2	91	6	3	87	8	5
NL	33	32	35	25	33	42	34	23	43
A	22	70	8	16	75	9	16	75	9
P	31	2	67	28	1	71	28	1	71
FIN	59	16	25	36	36	28	20	50	30
S	71	18	11	49	21	30	45	24	31
UK	48	4	48	42	6	52	39	8	53

Continued

Table 3.7 (Cont.)

States	1980			1990			2000		
	EU (+EFTA)	Non-EU Europeans	Non-Europeans	EU (+EFTA)	Non-EU Europeans	Non-Europeans	EU (+EFTA)	Non-EU Europeans	Non-Europeans
ISL	67	2	31	55	14	31	40	30	30
NOR	54	11	35	40	10	50	47	19	34
CH	80	14	6	69	22	9	58	31	11
Total	47	24	29	38	29	33	34	33	33
Aver. val.	53	18	29	45	20	35	39	28	33

Sources: Various national censuses (Greece, Ireland, Italy, Luxembourg, Austria, Portugal, Finland, Sweden, Iceland, Switzerland). Eurostat 1988, 1994a, 1995, 1996, 2000a, 2002, 2002a; Sopemi 1991,1993 and following years; Conseil de l'Europe 1984; Bonifazi 1998.

NB: Immigrants of Turkish nationality have been calculated among non-EU European nationals. For Ireland 1980 and 1990, the distinction between non-EU European nationals and non-Europeans, in the absence of separate data distinguishing these groups, has been calculated on the basis of the 1981 and 1991 censuses, though these distinguish the population only by country of birth. For Ireland 2000, the same distinction between non-EU European nationals and non-Europeans has been calculated on the basis of the 2002 census, which this time distinguished the population by nationality. For Greece, Luxembourg and Austria all the distinctions for 2000 were calculated on the basis of the 2001 censuses.

Portugal, Italy, Spain, and France; but also in the UK, where the phenomenon seems to have been influenced more by the country's colonial history than by geographical factors. A comparatively low level of non-Europeans, by contrast, characterizes Luxembourg, Austria and Switzerland.

The most recent trend (2000), in comparison with the situation in 1980 and in 1990 (Table 3.7), seems of particular interest. We may note in particular the overall reduction of the percentage of EU nationals and the concurrent growth of non-EU nationals and non-Europeans. The progressive reduction of EU nationals, however, is in percentage but not in absolute terms, in view of the overall growth of the non-national population during the period. Non-Europeans sharply increased in the 1980s, while their percentage remained stable in the 1990s (though their number continued to grow in terms of absolute values). The percentage of non-EU nationals, on the other hand, showed a constant trend of growth in the 1980s and 1990s.

The growth of non-EU nationals and non-Europeans forms part of the already discussed phenomenon of *diffusionism* that characterized what we have described as the third phase of immigration in Europe, from the 1980s onwards. The decline in the percentage of EU nationals was particularly marked in such countries as Greece, Italy and Finland. The highest percentage of non-EU Europeans in 2000, together with the highest increases of this group in comparison with the situation in 1980, were registered in Greece, Finland and Iceland; in Austria and Germany, on the other hand, the high percentage of non-EU European immigrants seems to have remained stable in time.

Table 3.8 enables us to observe in greater detail the breakdown of the origin of the non-national population in Western Europe at the close of the twentieth century. In percentage terms, out of the total non-national population in Europe, the area *Rest of Europe* (represented essentially by Turkish immigrants) now represents some 14 per cent: as a percentage it has been surpassed in more recent years by *Africa*, and especially by *Central and Eastern Europe*, following the explosion of immigration from the former Soviet bloc. *Asia* follows with a percentage of 11 per cent. The percentages of *North* and *Latin America* and, even more so, of *Oceania*, are comparatively marginal.

In terms of the individual host countries, foreigners coming from *Central and Eastern Europe* are in percentage terms more numerous in Greece, Austria and Finland; in other words in the countries bordering on this geographical area. Immigrants from the *Rest of Europe* are in percentage terms more numerous in Germany and Austria. *African* communities are in percentage terms strongest in Portugal and France, where they represent just under half of all non-nationals; they also form large percentages of the non-national population in Italy, in Holland and in Spain. *American* communities are in percentage terms most significant in Portugal and Spain, where

Table 3.8 Non-nationals (subdivided by main areas of origin) as percentages of the total non-national population in the countries of Western Europe – Year: 2000

States	EU (+ EFTA)	Central & Eastern Europe	Rest of Europe	Africa	North America	Latin America	Asia	Oceania
B	67	3	8	18	2	1	2	0
DK	29	19	15	10	3	1	22	0
D	26	27	28	4	2	1	11	0
EL	6	73	3	2	3	0	11	1
E	41	3	0	27	2	19	8	0
F	38	4	6	44	1	1	6	0
IRL	74	4	2	6	7	1	6	1
I	13	26	1	32	2	8	19	0
L	87	8	0	2	1	1	2	0
NL	34	6	17	26	3	3	11	1
A	16	57	18	2	1	1	5	0
P	28	1	0	47	5	14	4	0
FIN	20	48	2	9	3	1	16	1
S	45	21	3	6	2	4	18	0
UK	39	5	3	13	6	5	25	4
ISL	40	29	3	3	9	3	15	1
NOR	47	18	2	6	5	3	19	0
CH	58	26	6	3	1	2	5	0
Total	34	20	14	15	2	3	11	1

the legacy, also cultural, of the colonial system remains strong. *Asian* communities show a more homogeneous distribution than the others, though their share of the non-national population is greatest in the UK and in Denmark. Immigrants from *Oceania* (in substance, from Australia and New Zealand) assume some significance in percentage terms in the United Kingdom.

Chapter 4

Criminality in the countries of Western Europe

4.1. Criminality and social control

Analysis of the diffusion of crime in a particular territory has always posed problems: problems of method, problems of the nature, or deficiency, of the source material, problems of interpretation. The available data usually consist of the official crime figures, registered by the agencies of social control (police and judiciary). These figures usually refer to the number of recorded offences, the number of charged subjects, the number of sentenced offenders, and the number of prison admissions and prison inmates (or prison population). The correspondence between these figures and the real extent of criminality is, however, conditioned first of all by the phenomenon of the *dark figure*: in other words, the existence of crimes that remain unreported, and hence unknown, to the law enforcement agencies. The size of the *dark figure*, in comparison with the figures of official criminality, is considerable, even if it is difficult to assess its real scale. For example, if we compare the official figures and those reported by the victims in the British Crime Surveys in the late 1990s, we can deduce that less than half of all cases were reported to the police, and even less were incorporated in the official statistics (Downes and Rock 2003). The differences, understandably, are greater in the case of sexual offences, fraud, petty theft, and financial criminality (Radzinowicz and King 1977). Scholars like Quetelet and Guerry, who were among the first to devote attention to the systematic study of the data for criminality in the mid-nineteenth century, had already posed the problem whether this unknown dimension of crime would compromise the possibility of conducting *any* scientific analysis of the criminal phenomenon. They had come to the conclusion that the *dark figure* represents an almost constant dimension (except in periods of serious social unrest, such as wars, revolutions, etc.): so the problem could be considered largely irrelevant. Today we know that not only certain crimes more easily than others end up in the *dark figure* (e.g. crimes of rape, physical assaults); but also that the share of the *dark figure* as a percentage of total crime may vary in space and time. One factor of this variance consists of the overall commitment made by the law enforcement agencies to 'discover' particular crimes, especially so-called crimes 'without victim' (drug trafficking, prostitution, corruption). The commitment made by the law enforcement agencies, in turn, is the result of two very different components: one is simply the sum of the personal dedication of individual law enforcement agents; the other consists of the directives in terms of social control issued by governments; these directives may encourage the action of the police in a particular sector, e.g. illegal drugs, to the detriment of another sector, for instance that of corruption and financial offences.

How great an impact the 'commitment of the law enforcement agencies' factor has on the *dark figure* is open to question. It is, however, limited by the fact, already recalled, that there is a victim in the majority of criminal events: and it is on the victim that is usually placed the onus for informing the law enforcement agencies, by means of a formal signed statement made to the police when reporting the crime. But here too various factors influence the propensity of victims, and society as a whole, to report crimes and hence the size of the *dark figure*. These factors – social, psychological, financial – include social habits, or social taboos, which may influence people's propensity to report certain crimes, such as maltreatment (violence, sexual abuse, rape) in the family; the spread of insurance (which may encourage individuals to report certain offences for economic reasons); confidence in the police and a perception of the moral duty to support the system of justice by reporting crimes; the level of personal prosperity, which may lead people to attach importance to the economic damage they have suffered, and so on.

In the case of an international comparative study, like the present one, the problem of the *dark figure* is particularly critical, given that different countries could present somewhat different rates for officially unrecorded crimes. So, the above-mentioned factors, which influence the dimension of the *dark figure*, could give rise to heterogeneity in the distribution of the *dark figure* of crimes. This, in turn, would reduce the value of the analyses conducted on the available data, which refer, as we have explained, to officially known and recorded offences. It should be noted, moreover, that the procedures for the registration of offences vary from country to country: in those countries in which penal action is obligatory, the judiciary and the police are bound by law to record and pursue any crime that is brought to their knowledge (even if all this holds good only in theory); in those countries in which penal action is not obligatory, this does not happen.

To overcome the problem of the unknown dimension of crime, attempts have been made in recent years to draw on alternative sources for ascertaining the diffusion of criminality: in particular, so-called victim surveys – in practice, surveys on crimes suffered, based on the statements of their victims among representative population samples. In other cases, recourse has been had to the statements, in general anonymous, made by subjects in population samples, aimed at ascertaining the number and quality of the criminal acts they admit to having committed. The data furnished by these alternative sources, however, are not suitable for a comparative study like the present one, due to their lack of homogeneity. Despite that, the information derived from these surveys has enabled some basic points to be ascertained: (1) the percentage of crimes reported to the police by the victims tends over time to remain proportionate to the crimes that have actually been suffered – in other words, the *dark figure* tends to be constant; (2) for those crimes that involve major economic damage or that are intrinsically grave, the cross-national propensity to report the crimes suffered is fairly similar, at least in the countries of Western Europe; (3) even if the data of the official statistics are always lower than those of the victim surveys, cross-national analyses show there is a correlation between them, when specific and grave offences are considered, and hence there is no reason to delegitimize the official data (Aebi *et al.* 2002; Killias *et al.* 2007; for the results of victim surveys, see for example EUICS 2007; UK Home Office 2008; Netherlands 2008a). In short, the official statistics do better than some critics have alleged, and the intuitions of Quetelet and Guerry on the constant relation between manifest and hidden criminality have been belatedly vindicated.

The problem of the relation between effective criminality and the official crime figures can thus, I believe, be downplayed. Recourse can also be had to particular calculation procedures to correct any built-in disparity and make it even less influential. More precisely, as far as our study is concerned, analysis can be concentrated not on the rates of criminality of non-nationals, but on the relation between this criminality and the overall crime rates registered in the various countries (for further information on this procedure, see the following pages). In this way the dimension of the criminality committed by non-nationals can more correctly be placed in the context of the society in which it takes place, and the problem of whether the *dark figure* impacts differently, and to different degrees, in the various countries, can be better controlled.

Yet, when we deal with the diffusion of the criminal phenomenon within a particular subpopulation, such as that of non-nationals, we do need to take into account the hypothetical variability of the *dark figure* and the question whether its impact on this subpopulation is different from that on the population of *nationals*. As already underlined, the law enforcement agencies could be encouraged by public opinion, by politicians or also by their own cultural attitudes, or prejudices, to keep these minorities under closer surveillance and to pursue any offences they commit with greater diligence. This could lead to a reduction of the *dark figure* for the offences committed by these minorities and hence make their share of criminality seem higher than it actually is. The possibility of a reduction of the *dark figure* for the crimes committed by non-nationals, and its lesser share in criminality as a whole, represents a specific aspect that can be subsumed in the more general problem of whether there is any built-in discrimination in the surveys of criminal forms of behaviour within the non-national population – a problem we have already touched on at some length. The theory of a lesser incidence of the *dark figure* in the case of non-nationals can be countered by a series of arguments and research findings, already discussed in Chapter 1. Here we will limit ourselves to recalling a finding that is difficult to rebut: namely, that the high rate of crime attributed to non-nationals is precisely the direct consequence of their high involvement in activities or incidents *de facto* considered criminal.

It may be noted, however, that non-nationals could be involved mainly in certain particular types of offence (drug trafficking, robberies, violations of emigration laws, etc.) which would thus present a high *visibility* in comparison with other offences. Among these latter we could include so-called white-collar crime, the visibility of which is low and the incidence of its *dark figure* correspondingly high. The criminality of immigrants, therefore, could be characterized by a lesser share of the *dark figure* for objective reasons, irrespective of any discriminatory attitudes of the police towards them. All this could lead to a greater probability of immigrants being identified, detained, charged, sentenced and imprisoned. This, in turn, would tend to increase the rates of criminality of non-nationals proportionately more than it does those of nationals. This conclusion, however, can be countered by two different considerations, which we already touched on in Chapter 1, with regard to the relation between non-nationals and crime. First, specific research on the criminality of non-nationals (and of ethnic minorities) shows that they present a high level of criminality, if compared with nationals, for a huge range of crimes, and hence not just for particular offences (Solivetti and D'Onofrio 1998; see also the data on non-nationals reported, presented in Chapter 5). Second, non-nationals tend to commit crimes (homicides, grievous bodily harm, rape, fraud, drug trafficking, etc.) which often have as their victims other non-nationals, and often persons belonging to the same national group as the perpetrator himself. And in these social contexts, there is, by tradition, and for a variety of reasons, as we have already emphasized, a low propensity to report the crimes committed to the law enforcement agencies: this implies a built-in tendency for the *dark figure* to be increased and at the same time for the level of criminality of non-nationals to be underestimated.

There also exists another more general aspect that has nothing to do with the *dark figure* or the visibility of crimes, but that in the last analysis could have similar effects. This aspect is the *philosophy of the penal code*, or the determination of what forms of behaviour should be prosecuted as penal offences: an aspect much loved by radical criminologists. To illustrate the point, it is clear that if the authorities – legislators, governments, parliaments, public prosecutors – decide to pursue with grave penal sanctions certain dubious activities of the banks that are now placed in a kind of legal limbo between what is lawful and what is not, or to prosecute the politicians or senior civil servants responsible for the maladministration of public funds, the share of nationals in the total crime figures would inevitably increase, while that of non-nationals would simultaneously decrease; for non-nationals are, almost by definition, excluded from public office. This is something we should bear in mind. We would also have to admit that the kind of analyses we are conducting here cannot ignore what the penal codes 'label' as crime, even if this does not mean we necessarily agree with the political decisions that led to certain forms of conduct being considered a crime in the first place. Besides, if some revolutionaries in the past have branded property as theft, it seems more difficult to find legislations that have considered theft as a right. Forms of behaviour like those involved in standard crimes, such as robbery, murder, rape and violence, are punishable under the penal code practically everywhere. And it is significant, in this regard, that the so-called lower classes, on average, express judgements of these offences in a far more forthright and punitive fashion than those expressed by certain self-appointed defenders of these classes. The reason is no doubt because it is just these 'lower classes' that have to pay a steep price as the victims of the criminality that others merely pontificate about.

Besides, how can we study criminal phenomena by disregarding the penal codes in force and the official statistics for the crimes codified in them? Attempts to do so do not seem to have had much success, as Cloward and Ohlin (1960, Chapter 1) point out, given that criminal phenomena are distinguished from other forms of conduct precisely because they are identified as such by the agencies officially put in place for their control.

There are, however, other difficulties to which some preliminary remarks should at least be devoted. These difficulties have to do with the homogeneity, and hence the comparability, of the data at our disposal. The data relating to prison inmates and recorded offenders suffer from the disparities that exist between the various countries in terms of the criminalization of specific forms of behaviour, the sanctions provided and the procedures followed in criminal trials (Tonry 1997). The statistics of charged offenders may present significant differences between one country and another, due to the types of misdemeanours that are or are not included in them. In particular, certain types of very common infringements of the law, such as traffic offences, or irregularities in the issuing of cheques, may be treated in very different ways in the various countries: for example, they may be excluded altogether from the statistics of recorded offences since considered administrative infringements. Equally, the distribution of prison inmates in the various countries according to the main offence attributed to them may present some differences due to the heterogeneity of the sanctions provided and in particular the greater or lesser propensity to have recourse to custodial sentences for individual violations. Comparisons with countries belonging to other geographical and cultural contexts show, however, that all these differences are less marked in Western Europe than elsewhere. Yet they cannot be ignored. To reduce the danger of comparisons between dissimilar sets of data, it is therefore preferable to relate the crime data of non-nationals to the overall dimension of the criminal phenomenon in their respective countries.

Another fundamental premise needs to be made: namely, that to calculate the share of criminality among non-nationals, we need to relate the data in question to the data on the presence of non-nationals on the territory of the various countries. Now, the data on resident non-nationals exclude from consideration those non-nationals who are temporarily present for purposes of tourism. This, however, does not represent a significant obstacle, due to the brevity of the presence of tourists and their low contribution to criminality. More significant is the fact that the data on the presence of non-nationals tend, by their very nature, to be underestimated, because they exclude a percentage of clandestine or irregular immigrants. We will see below how this problem can be kept under control. It should never be forgotten, however, that evaluations of the scale of clandestine or irregular immigration, though they can make use of sophisticated indirect systems of measurement (cf. Jandle 2003), retain all the same their character as estimates. It is sensible, therefore, to continue to privilege the official figures for immigration.

4.2. Immigrants and criminality in Western Europe: easy stereotypes, difficult realities

Having clarified these limitations, we may now begin to examine the nature of the relation between immigration and crime in Western Europe in recent decades. Are the two phenomena in fact associated? If we were to place ourselves in the shoes of the man on the street, and share the fears so widespread at the popular level, we would answer that question with an unqualified yes. We would expect to find a clear association between the number of immigrants and the level of criminality in the various countries in Europe: in other words, the more immigrants there are, the higher the crime rate. But is that the case?

Let us first take into consideration the most classic of the crimes of violence, the one that has always aroused the greatest fears: intentional homicide or wilful murder (for the standard definition adopted by the main source of our data, the *European Sourcebook of Crime and Criminal Justice Statistics*, see Council of Europe 1999, 2003, 2006). Due to its gravity, intentional homicide is the crime to which particular attention is devoted both by the law enforcement agencies and by those responsible for compiling the national statistics. It is, moreover, a crime that is difficult to conceal. For all these reasons the *dark figure* for this crime is low. Intentional homicide indeed is the offence that presents the best characteristics for an international comparison. Homicide rates vary significantly between Western European countries (Figure 4.1). This remains the case even if attempted murders are excluded; five of the eighteen countries included in this study – Norway, Denmark, Belgium, Holland, Greece – have excluded cases of 'assault leading to death' from the figures for intentional homicide: but it is generally recognized that these differences do not alter in substance the sense of the figures reported (Council of Europe 2003). We may note that such countries as Luxembourg, Switzerland, Germany and Austria, which are at the top of the classification of the countries with the highest percentage of non-nationals, present a medium-to-low homicide rate. Quite the opposite is the case of Finland: relatively low share of non-nationals among the resident population, and the highest homicide rate in Western Europe. The regression line shows that the relation between non-nationals present in the various countries and the homicide rate is decidedly negative: altogether, higher shares of non-nationals among the total population can be associated with lower homicide rates.

A situation not altogether dissimilar emerges in the case of robberies (Figure 4.1). Here, the countries with the highest robbery rates include Spain, Belgium, France, Portugal, and the UK: countries very different from each other in terms of the share of non-nationals in their respective populations. By contrast, countries with a high share of non-nationals, such as Luxembourg, Switzerland, Germany and Austria, present a rather low robbery rate.

The third of the classic 'major crimes of violence' is rape. It should be premised that rape is a crime that by its very nature may lead the victim not to report the fact to the authorities, for fear lest it enters the public domain. For this reason, rape, in contrast to intentional homicide, is considered a crime with a high incidence of the *dark figure*. Moreover, deviations from the standard definition of rape in individual European countries (Council of Europe 1999, 2003, 2006) are probably more substantial than those for other offences. Consequently, statistical data for this crime need to be treated with extreme caution. The results, however, present a situation in substance similar to that of the previous crimes: and this is in favour of the reliability of the analysis. Figure 4.1 shows in fact that the countries with the highest rates of rape – Sweden and Belgium – present no more than an average share of non-nationals among their resident population; countries like Switzerland and Luxembourg present rates similar to those of Spain, Portugal and Italy, though the percentages of non-nationals among their population are enormously higher than these latter.

In short, in all the cases of major crimes of violence, the relation between the rate of criminality registered in the country and the share of non-nationals among its resident population is negative, even if statistically non-significant.

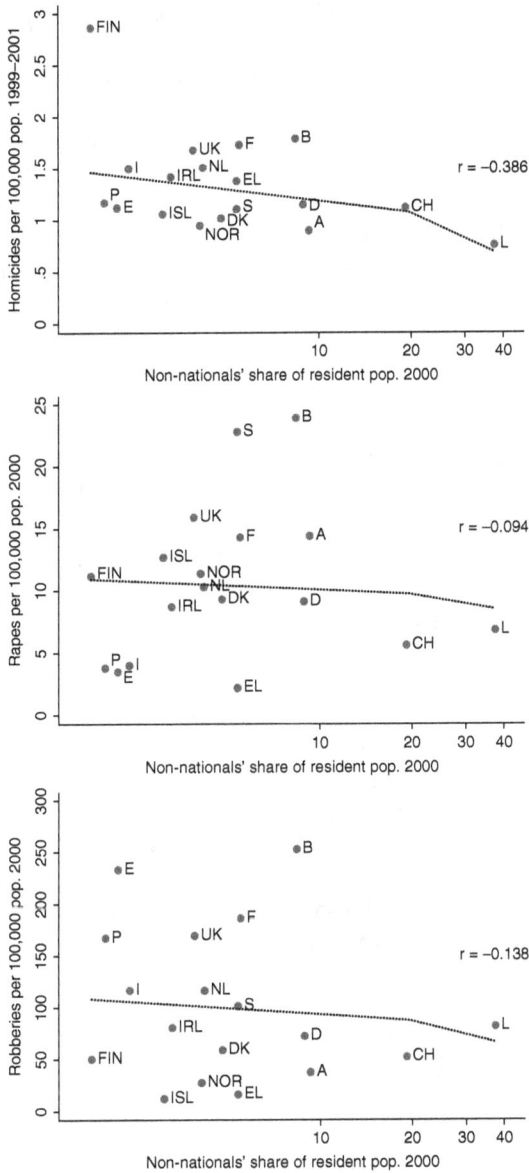

Figure 4.1 Western Europe: distribution of the percentages of non-nationals and of the rates for intentional homicides (excluding attempted homicides), rapes and robberies in the various countries: linear regression fit lines and coefficients.

Sources: Council of Europe 1999, 2003, 2006.

NB: Homicide: Belgium, Denmark, Greece and The Netherlands exclude assault leading to death. Rapes: Denmark, Greece and England and Wales exclude acts without penetration. Robbery: Denmark, Greece and Sweden exclude bag-snatching.
The x axes have logarithmic scales.

This ought to suffice to exclude any facile and direct connections between immigration and criminality.

It may be of interest to compare the situation we have just described, relating to the countries of Western Europe, with the situation in the USA. The cases analyzed cover all the States of the Union, excluding the District of Columbia, which has anomalous characteristics in terms of territory, urbanization, ethnic population mix, income and its distribution. Since – as we have already explained – the USA continues to privilege the gathering of data relating to foreign-borns rather than to resident non-nationals, we have adopted this parameter. The average percentage of foreign-borns in the States of the Union is virtually identical with the average percentage of non-nationals registered in the countries of Western Europe at the turn of millennium (7.3 per cent). The two percentages refer, however, to phenomena that do not coincide, as we have already explained: foreign-borns may, or may not, have become American citizens. The foreign-borns indicator, therefore, is less valid as a measure of social and cultural marginality. That said, let's see how the distribution of homicide rates in the various States of the Union is shown in Figure 4.2. The high average rate of homicides is immediately striking: it is roughly four times higher than the mean registered in the countries of Western Europe. No less evident is the fact that there is no relation between the percentage of foreign-borns and homicides. Most of the States with high homicide rates – in particular Louisiana, Mississippi, Alabama and Tennessee – present a low share of foreign-borns among their resident population.

A fairly similar situation emerges as regards the rates for rape in the USA. The average rate for this offence is also comparatively high: three times higher than the average for Western Europe. At the same time, there is no correlation between the number of foreign-borns and the rate of rape. States like New Jersey and New York, for example, which have very high percentages of foreign-borns, present the lowest rates of rape. Arkansas, which presents by far the highest rate for rape, is one of the States with a low percentage of foreign-borns.

As regards robberies, on the other hand, the situation is different. The mean rate for all the States of the Union is similar to that registered in Western Europe. The relation between percentage presence of foreign-borns and robbery rate, in turn, is positive and significant. It's an association recognized by North American researchers (Reid et al. 2005; Martinez 2006). But it is also an association behind which lie more complex phenomena than might appear at first sight, for the States in which the highest robbery rates are registered present particular characteristics which go beyond the percentage presence of foreign-borns. The distribution of robbery rates in the various States of the Union is in fact strongly associated with other indicators, relating to the social and economic situation of the States themselves. If we use some of these indicators, such as the percentages of coloured population

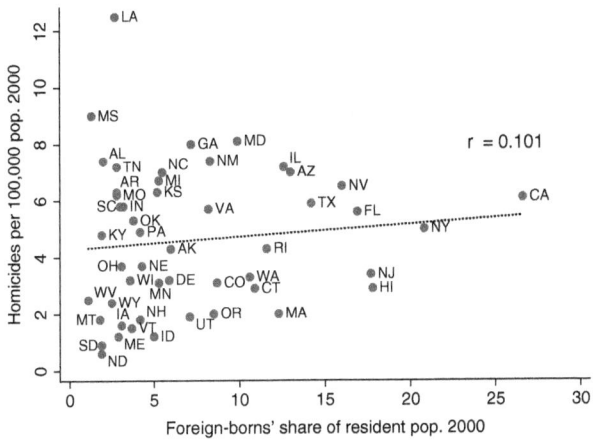

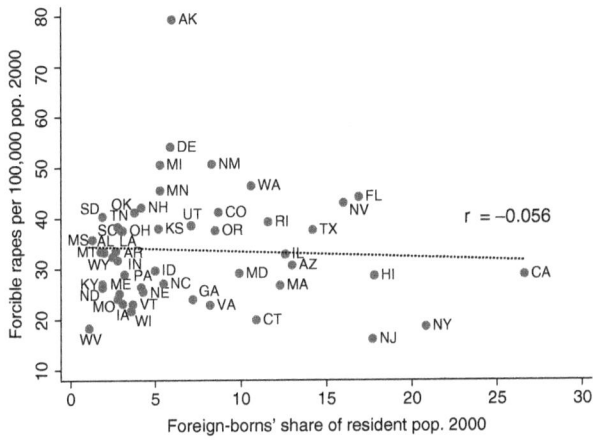

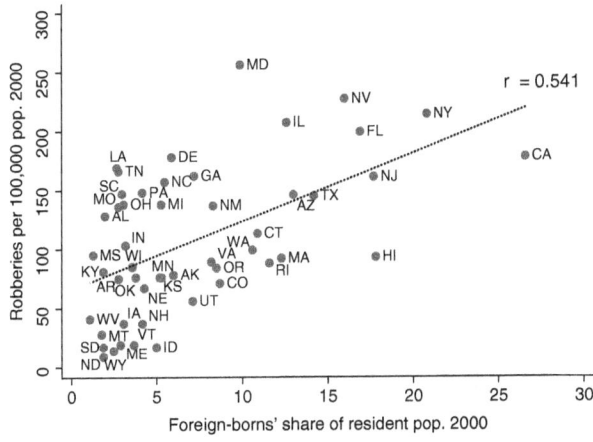

Figure 4.2 USA: distribution of the percentages of foreign-borns and of the rates of homicides, including non-negligent manslaughter, rapes and robberies in the various States of the Union: linear regression fit lines and coefficients.

Source: US 2007.

and of population living in metropolitan areas, and the unemployment rate, in a linear regression model, we find that their association with the robbery rate is far higher than that shown by the percentage of foreign-borns ($r = 0.875$ instead of $r = 0.541$); but more especially we discover that these indicators make the contribution of the foreign-borns variable statistically non-significant (Appendix I).

In sum, the US data show that the rates for the major crimes of violence in the various States of the Union are more closely associated with the basic characteristics of these States than with the percentage presence of immigrants – just as seems to be the case in the countries of Western Europe.

To analyse further the relation between immigration and crime, we can control the evolution of rates of criminality in a diachronic perspective, in the light of variations in the percentage of non-nationals in the resident population. To this end, let us put to one side the aspect of the diffusion of the most serious crimes in the various countries – a diffusion that, as we have seen, can vary greatly from country to country – and concentrate instead on the variations registered in the rates of criminality in relation to variations in the percentage of non-nationals.

This analysis of diachronic variations in the rates of criminality in the various countries also has the advantage of resting on more solid comparative foundations. Our previous comparative analysis of the relation between the percentages of non-nationals and rates of criminality could have been influenced, i.e. skewed, by factors we have already discussed, capable of affecting the crime rates, such as differences in the investigative capacity of the police forces or the propensity in the various countries to report crimes. Though the impact of these factors, as we have argued, ought to be less than some have feared – and especially so in the USA, which is a Union of more homogeneous States than are the member states of the EU – it is as well not to ignore them. An analysis of the diachronic variations of the rates of criminality, by contrast, does not pose the above-mentioned dangers, given that these variations are calculated within each country. We may presume that any short-term variations due to non-criminal factors (e.g. greater attention by the law enforcement agencies to particular offences) within the same country are less relevant than those due to variations in the same factors between country and country. One problem that should be taken into account in these longitudinal analyses is, however, the question whether there has been any change in the definition of a crime during the period in question. Changes of this type have indeed taken place in Europe in recent years. As we shall see more clearly in due course, however, it does not seem that these changes could have substantially altered the overall results obtained. An analysis of the diachronic variations of the percentages of non-nationals and the rates of criminality is, however, subject to the condition that the phenomena in question may really have varied in time.

A rapid examination of the phenomena being considered here confirms, indeed, that there has been such a variation. If we take into consideration the period 1990–2003, for which the rates of criminality of all the countries of Europe are available, as registered by the *European Sourcebook of Crime and Criminal Justice Statistics* (Council of Europe 1999, 2003, 2006), we find a substantial variation of these rates; nor can there be any doubt that the presence of non-nationals has also registered a considerable variation, more precisely an increase, during the same period. We can therefore proceed.

The picture that emerges, however, seems, right from the start, different from what many would expect. As regards so-called *common crimes* (thefts, burglaries, physical assaults/bodily harm, robberies), recent surveys on the victims of such crimes conducted in Western Europe show that there has been a prevalent decline in their number – with the exception of Belgium and Ireland – and that the current level of criminality has reverted to pre-1990 levels (EUICS 2007). The same has happened in the USA, in Canada, in Australia and in the other industrialized countries. So it is clear that the data of victims surveys do not coincide with the trend of the presence of immigrants, which is growing in virtually all the countries cited. It may be asked whether the same downward trend is also shown by the official registration of criminality, and in particular what has happened with regard to the crimes of major gravity.

Let us now look at the rates of major offences officially registered in Europe. If we assume that the level of criminality is proportionate to the number of non-nationals, it follows that, where their percentage of the total population has grown, a corresponding increase of criminality ought also to be registered. Yet, as far as the countries of Western Europe are concerned, the situation shown in Figure 4.3 does not coincide with this hypothesis.

First, we may observe that, on average, there has been no overall increase in the rates for intentional homicides in recent years: some European countries have registered an increase, but many others a decrease. Some of the countries that have registered a significant increase (Belgium, Sweden) have in any case had minimal variations in their share of the non-national population. Other countries that have had sharp increases in their share of non-national population (Italy, Finland, Luxembourg, Portugal), on the other hand, have registered essential stability, or even a drop, in their homicide rates. So, on the whole, there is no significant relation between variation of non-national population and variation of homicides, as shown by the regression line, which suggests indeed a slight diminution of the homicide rate in relation to the growth of non-nationals (Figure 4.3). The situation as regards robberies and rapes is different. For rape, there has been an increase in most of the countries in recent years; robbery rates tended to increase, though with exceptions (e.g. that of Spain, Italy, Ireland and Finland). In any case, even for robberies and rapes, there is no positive relation between variation

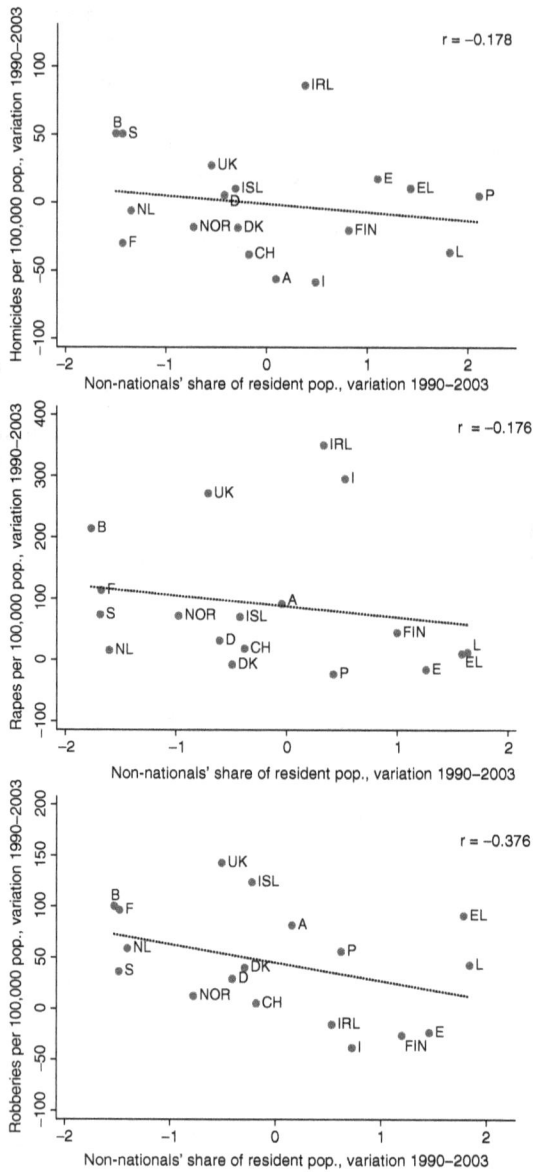

Figure 4.3 Western Europe: distribution of the variations in the percentages of non-nationals and in the rates of intentional homicides (excluding attempted homicides), rapes and robberies in the various countries: linear regression fit lines and coefficients.

Sources: Council of Europe 1999, 2003, 2006.

NB: Homicides: for Denmark, Iceland and Luxembourg, data smoothing, prompted by strong annual variations. Rapes: Belgium, data for the period 1994–2003; Portugal, 1993–2003; Norway, 1991–2003. Robberies: Belgium, 1995–2003; Portugal, 1993–2003; Norway, 1991–2003; Denmark, Greece and Sweden exclude bag-snatching. Since both the percentage variation and the variation in absolute values of the non-nationals' share are relevant, we have combined them into a single variable by means of principal components analysis.

of the percentage of non-nationals and variation of the rates of criminality. As regards robberies, there is on the contrary a neat tendency for their rates to decrease as the percentage of non-nationals simultaneously increases, though the relation is statistically non-significant.

It should further be noted that, as regards rapes, there was, in the period we have examined, a significant extension of the definition of rape in Ireland (1990), England and Wales (1994), Italy (1996), Spain (1996, 1999), Finland (1998), and Germany (1998). These countries, with the exception of Spain, have registered an increase of the recorded cases of rape, and four of them – Ireland, Italy, Finland and Spain – also registered sharp increases in terms of non-national population. It may be concluded that – if this extension of the definition of rape had not taken place – the relation between variation of non-national population and variation of cases of rape would have been even more negative.

Let us now compare the situation in the USA, for which we have at our disposal more extensive historical series of data. Figure 4.4 shows that the registered increases for foreign-borns are not associated with any increases in the rates of major crimes. More precisely, there is a negative – even if statistically non-significant – relation between the variations of foreign-borns in the various States and the variations of homicides; a negative and significant relation as regards rapes; and a positive – but non-significant – relation for robberies; but even this latter relation becomes negative if we exclude the State of North Carolina, which clearly represents an anomaly.

The fact that there has been no association between the variations of the shares of non-nationals (shares that have been increasing almost everywhere) and the trends in the rates of criminality is clearly an important piece of evidence. And the confirmation of this fact by the US data provides further support for our findings. But all this is of little help to us in trying to understand what effectively happened.

As regards some European countries, we have at our disposal more extensive series of data and more detailed information on the contribution of non-nationals to criminality. We can therefore analyse more extensively the relation between variation of non-national population and variation of criminality in each of them.

Figure 4.5 shows the evolution of intentional homicides and of the non-national population in France, in the period 1985–2005. As has already emerged in Chapter 3, the non-European component is high among the immigrant population in France, also as a legacy of the colonial past. But the EU component among the non-national population is also sizeable; the overall share of the non-national population shows an essentially stable trend. The figures for the historical series of data on homicides also include attempted homicides, and hence are higher than those for intentional homicides (excluding attempted homicides) presented in Figure 4.1. The trend of homicides grew slightly until the early 1990s and then underwent a

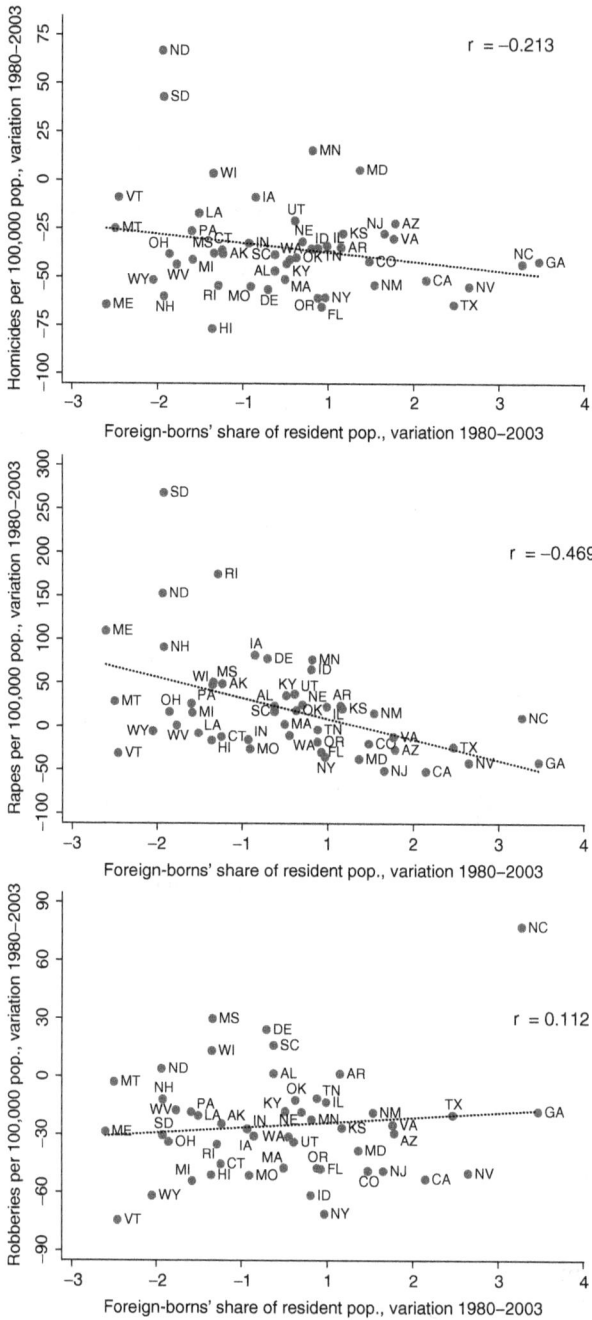

Figure 4.4 USA: distribution of the variations in the percentages of foreign-borns and in the rates of homicides (including non-negligent manslaughter), rapes and robberies in the various States of the Union: linear regression fit lines and coefficients.

Sources: US 2007 and previous years.

NB: To measure the variation of foreign-borns, the same procedure as that described for the countries of Europe was used.

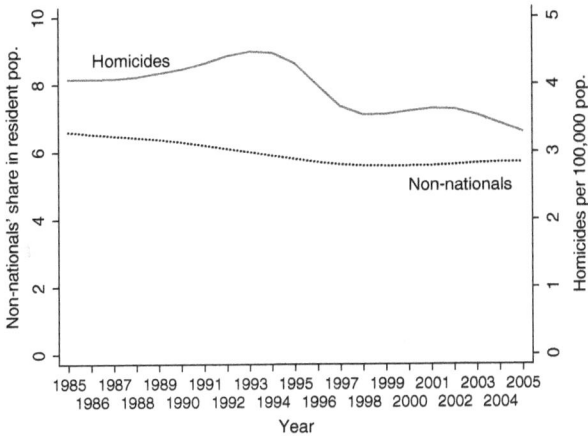

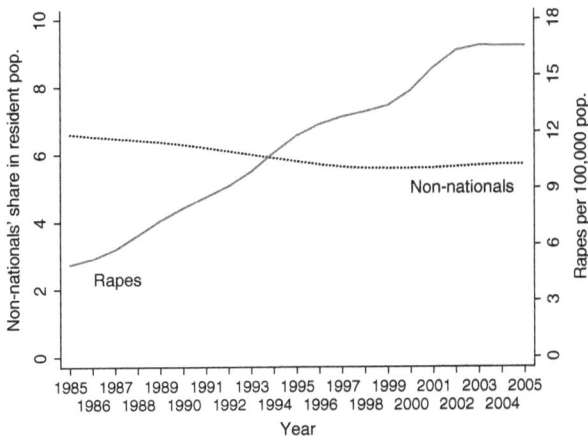

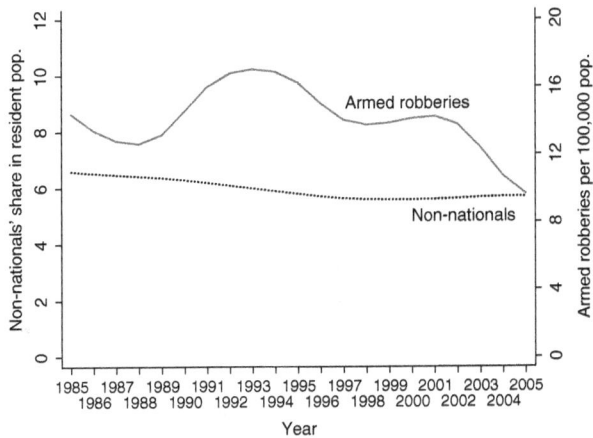

Figure 4.5 France: variation of the percentage of non-nationals among the resident population and of the rates of intentional homicides (including attempted homicides), rapes and *rapines à main armée* (armed robberies).

Sources: France 2006 and previous years.

pronounced downward curve. The percentage of non-nationals among those charged for murder in France remains rather stable in time, in contrast to what happened in other countries. This percentage was around 15 per cent of the total charged offenders during the period in question. The percentage of cases solved (*taux d'élucidation*) is high, *c.* 80 per cent: and this suggests that the effective percentage value of the involvement of non-nationals in this crime ought not to be altered by the cases of crimes attributed to persons unknown.

The evolution of the rate of rapes in France is very different from that of homicides. There has been a sharp and continuous growth of this offence in France during the period under examination: at the end of the period the cases of rape had tripled in number. Yet while the levels reached by this offence are high, the contribution of non-nationals to the total of those charged for it has remained low, and even more recently their share of those charged does not exceed 15 per cent. It may therefore be affirmed that the continual growth registered for this offence in France is in the main associated with a greater contribution of nationals.

A trend similar to that of homicides is that registered by the rates for robbery in France. The data available for the period 1985–2005 are those relating to the sole category of armed robberies. A tendency can be noted for the rates to decline from the early 1990s onward, as in the case of homicides. The involvement of non-nationals in cases of armed robberies is maintained at a relatively low level (*c.* 10 per cent). In conclusion, the trend in France of the rates of criminality for some of the major crimes of violence (intentional homicides, armed robberies) is characterized either by essential stability or by a decline, whereas cases of rape registered a sharp increase. However, the involvement of non-nationals in major crimes seems limited and presents no significant variations; the same goes for the variation in the share of non-nationals among the resident population. This does not remove the fact that there has been, and remains, in France a high level of popular apprehension about the role of non-nationals in the criminal phenomenon: their share among those charged for some less serious but nonetheless alarming offences is high. In particular, non-nationals constitute roughly a half of all those charged for *vol à la tire*, i.e. pickpockets.

The case of the United Kingdom, as regards the evolution of criminality and non-nationals, is interesting, also because it is in part similar to, in part dissimilar from, the case of France. The two countries are similar in terms of the composition of their non-national population: in the UK, too, the non-European component, at least in part attributable to the colonial past, is considerable; the EU component is also large, while the component of non-EU European non-nationals is small. In the United Kingdom, however, the share of non-nationals is growing rapidly.

At first sight, the homicide rate seems not only to have grown significantly but also to be growing *pari passu* with the growth of the non-national share of the resident population (Figure 4.6). To better understand what has happened, however, some other remarks on the homicide rate in the UK should be added. As we will see more clearly below, data on the contribution of non-nationals to criminality in Great Britain are meagre. Recent police estimates suggest, however, that the non-national share of the total number of those charged for wilful murder (intentional homicide) is of the order of 20 per cent (figures are based on cases for England and Wales, which represent 9/10 of the total). Given that the percentage of cases solved (the clearing rate) is very high for murder (90 per cent), it is realistic to assume that the cases attributed to persons unknown ought not to influence the figures relating to the contribution of non-nationals. No data are available on the non-national share of murders in the years at the start of the period taken into examination here, but it is realistic to assume it was minor though not negligible. So, assuming that the contribution of non-nationals was equivalent, at most, to 20 per cent of the total, while the growth of the murder rate was of the order of 45 per cent in the period 1985–2005, we can conclude that the pronounced increase of murders cannot be adequately explained by

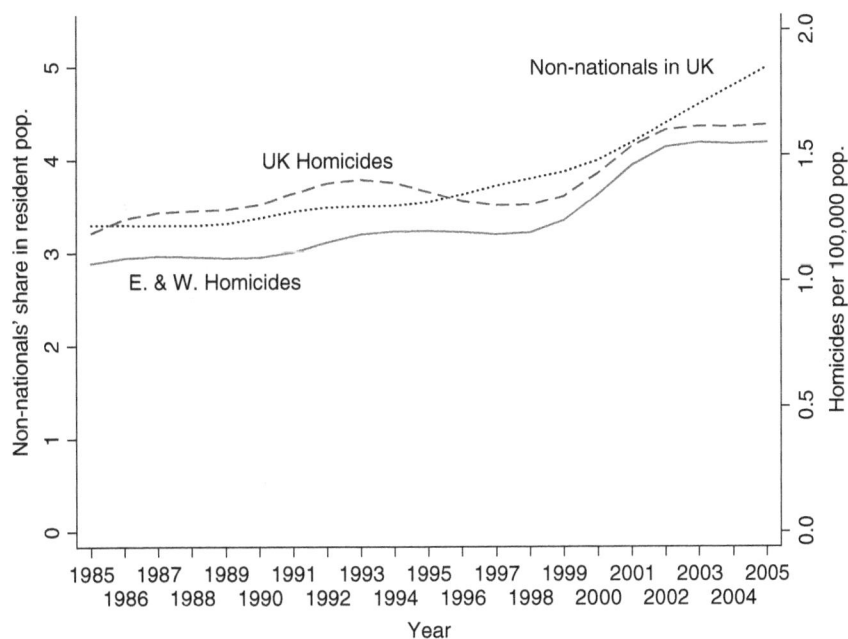

Figure 4.6 United Kingdom (England and Wales): variation of the percentage of non-nationals among the resident population and of the rate of intentional homicides (currently recorded).

Source: Povey 2005.

a growth of the contribution of non-nationals. The increase of the murder rate in England and Wales is more realistically attributable to a growth of cases involving nationals, compounded by a growth of cases involving non-nationals.

The case of Italy is significantly different from that of France or that of the UK. In Italy, the growth of the non-national share of the resident population has been very sharp in recent decades. The composition of the immigrant population is strongly skewed in favour of non-Europeans, even more so than in France and the UK; but in contrast to the situation in these latter countries, the EU component of non-nationals is low. The rate of intentional homicides (excluding attempted murders) at first grew significantly in the 1980s; then it began to fall in a very pronounced way. The share of non-nationals among the total number of those charged for intentional homicides was *c.* 3 per cent at the beginning of the period under review here, but 22 per cent at its end. So the increase of the non-national share in homicide has been very sharp, even more so than the increase of the share of non-nationals among the resident population. The non-national percentage of the total number charged for murder is clearly much higher than the non-national percentage of the resident population. It should be noted, however, that the sharp increase of the non-national share of the resident population, as registered also after the start of the 1990s, was accompanied not by a further increase but by a decided reduction of the homicide rate. The evidence suggests therefore that, since the start of the 1990s, there has been a partial substitution of charged nationals by charged non-nationals, but in the overall context of a downwards trend of the homicide rate.

As regards robberies, we find ourselves faced with a more complex trend in Italy. If we include cases of bag-snatching among robberies, as the majority of European countries do, then the trend registered in Italy in the period 1985–2005 is decreasing, as may also be deduced from Figure 4.3 which showed the situation in all Western European countries. The situation seems similar to that registered for homicides, again in Italy. The percentage of non-nationals among those charged for bag-snatching in Italy grew by *c.* 30 per cent in the period under review, while at the same time there has been an overall decrease of this offence: so there has been a partial substitution of nationals by non-nationals. The trend of robberies proper in Italy is the reverse of that of bag-snatching and is therefore growing. As shown by Figure 4.7, the trend of the cases of robbery seems to be closely mirrored by the trend of the non-national share of the resident population.

The share of non-nationals among those charged for robbery in Italy has soared: it has progressively grown from less than 5 per cent to almost 40 per cent. The growth of the rate of robberies proper (excluding bag-snatching) in Italy would therefore seem to be substantially due to the growth of the share of non-nationals among the (presumed) perpetrators of this offence.

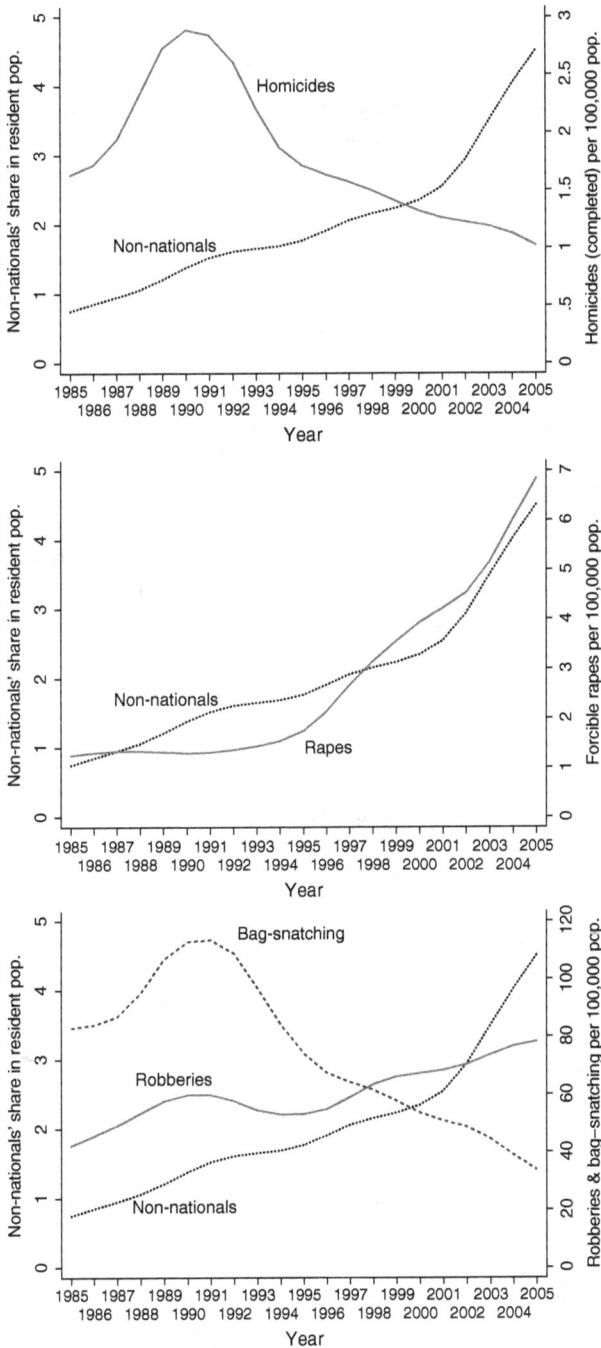

Figure 4.7 Italy: variation of the percentage of non-nationals among the resident population and of the rates of intentional homicides (excluding attempted homicides), rapes, robberies and bag-snatching.

Source: Italy 1985 ff.

As far as rape in Italy is concerned, there has been a huge increase that puts even that for robberies in the shade: the rate of rape per population has quintupled and its growth seems interwoven with that of the non-national population. Though it is fair to say that a contribution to the growth in the number of cases of rape in Italy was also made by the new law of 1996, which introduced some changes in the definition of this offence, and in particular widened the applicability of the concept of rape, Figure 4.7 shows that rape continued to grow even several years after the new law came into force. The share of non-nationals out of the total number charged for rape has registered a very sharp increase, rising from *c*. 3 per cent to over a third of the total. But this admittedly huge increase of the non-national share in absolute terms cannot adequately explain the growth of the trend of rape, which is far higher. What in effect seems to have happened is that the cases of rape attributed to nationals have risen sharply, reaching a figure at the end of the period almost double that at its start. In other words, there has been in Italy both a growth of the involvement in rape of non-nationals – who are strongly overrepresented as far as this offence is concerned – and a growth of the involvement of nationals, though combined with a decrease in their share. On the other hand, since the crime of rape presents a relatively limited number of cases attributed to persons unknown, the analysis of the involvement of nationals and non-nationals in this offence rests on fairly firm foundations.

The homicide trend in Switzerland is extremely interesting, also in the light of the fact that it is the European country that has the highest share of non-nationals in its population, after Luxembourg. However, this high percentage of non-nationals should be qualified by the fact that immigration in Switzerland preponderantly consists of citizens of other EU countries; the share of non-Europeans in the non-national population is particularly small. It may be noted, first, that the homicide rate per population remained at a level that is one of the lowest in Europe in the period being examined here, in spite of the high percentage of non-nationals. After having peaked in the early 1990s, the homicide rate in Switzerland began to decline, while the percentage of non-nationals among the resident population continued to grow. The involvement of non-nationals in this crime is nonetheless significant and growing. During the period under review, the percentage of non-nationals involved in this major crime rose from approximately a third of the total to *c*. 60 per cent. We are therefore faced – in the case of intentional homicides – with a situation where non-nationals substituted citizens of the host country as perpetrators of this crime.

A very similar trend is ascertained for robberies in Switzerland. In the second half of the 1980s, the robbery rate seemed to mirror the growth of non-nationals, then it began to fall, and at the end of the period showed values similar to those at the start. By contrast, the share of non-nationals among those charged for robbery – which has already been high at the start of the period – grew further, rising to over 60 per cent.

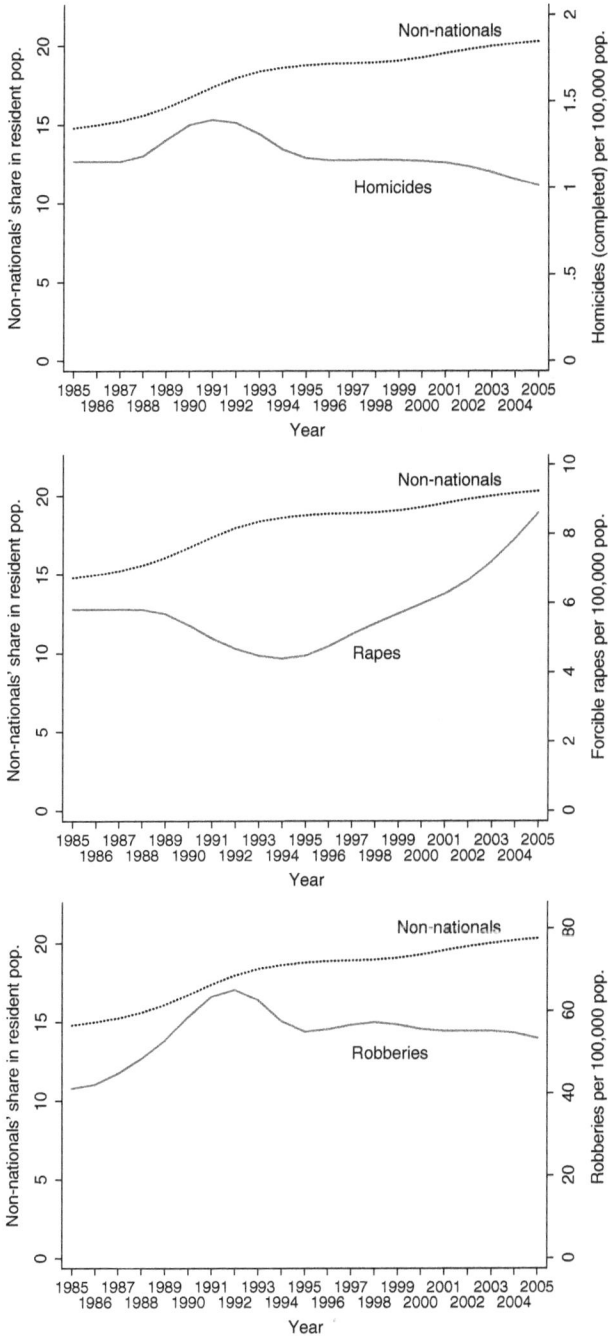

Figure 4.8 Switzerland: variation of the percentage of non-nationals among the resident population and of the rates of intentional homicides (excluding attempted homicides), rapes and robberies.

Sources: Suisse 1985 ff.; and data supplied by the Office Fédéral de la Statistique.

A different trend characterized rape in Switzerland. Its rate declined down to the early 1990s. It then grew rapidly, and even doubled its values. And while the number of nationals charged for this offence remained substantially the same during the whole of this period, that of non-nationals has tripled, and their share grew from approximately one-third to two-thirds of the total. The trends of these three kinds of criminal activity in Switzerland are shown in Figure 4.8.

The case of Germany permits us to throw further light on the relation between immigration and criminality. Like Switzerland, this is a country with a relatively small percentage of non-European non-nationals, while the non-EU component, composed in large part of immigrants from Turkey, is very high.

In Germany, the homicide rate peaked with the reunification of the two Germanies in 1990. But since then a sharp decline has been registered, much as happened in Switzerland and in Italy during the same period. But the resemblance to Italy is only superficial. In Germany, in fact, the decline in the homicide rate was accompanied by substantial stability not only of the non-national percentage of the resident population, but also of the non-national share of the total of those charged for homicide. At the start of the period (1985), the non-national share of the total of those charged was 25 per cent; it grew to 30–35 per cent in the years following reunification and has once again dropped below 30 per cent in more recent years. The situation registered for homicides is substantially reproduced by the trend in rapes. The rate of these offences shows limited variations during the whole period, including the years immediately following reunification. The percentage of non-nationals has also registered little variation: it was just under 30 per cent at the start of the period, and just over 30 per cent at its end.

The overall trend in the relation between non-nationals and crime in Germany can be summed up by the trend in the percentage of non-nationals among suspects of criminal activities (Figure 4.9). This percentage showed a clear trend to growth in the period 1985–95, in combination with a more limited growth in the presence of non-nationals. Thereafter, there was a pronounced decline, as a result of which the percentages of non-nationals among those charged fell back to values similar to those at the start of the period, in spite of their higher percentage among the resident population. The overall trend in the relation between non-nationals and criminality in Germany gives the impression of a situation under control.

The situation in Sweden seems somewhat different from that of Germany. Sweden, in contrast to Germany, maintained an immigration policy unfavourable to the presence of guest-workers. It encouraged a stabilization of immigrants on its own territory through their full integration and has also absorbed a large number of refugees, more than 300,000 since the 1980s.

Consequently, the share of non-nationals has not varied much in Sweden in the course of recent decades, while the share of foreign-borns has sharply grown; it includes – as we know – also those immigrants who had already obtained citizenship of the host country (Figure 4.10). The EU component

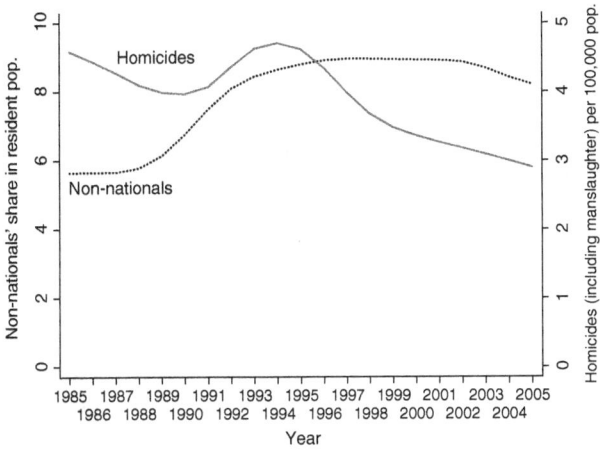

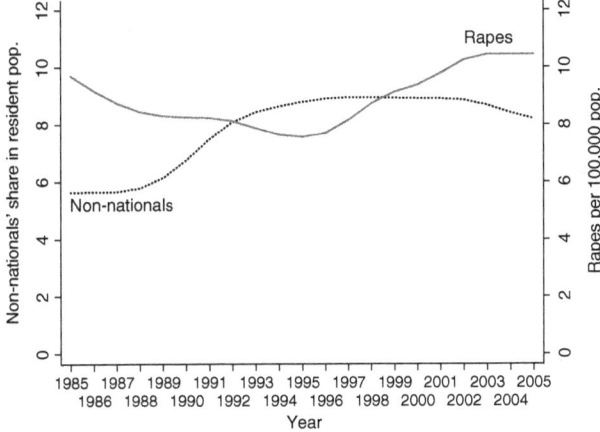

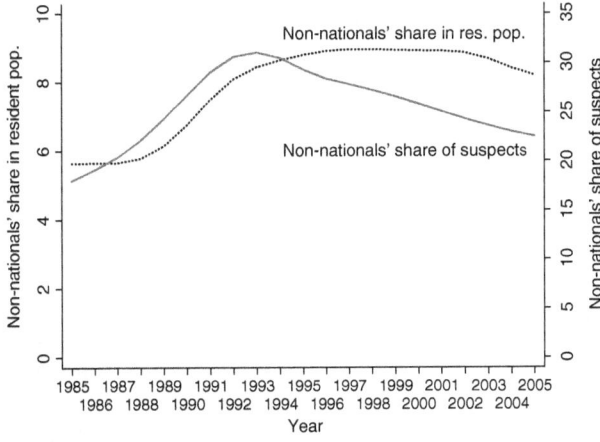

Figure 4.9 Germany: variation of the percentage of non-nationals among the resident population and among those charged for penal offences (suspects), and of the rates of intentional homicides (including manslaughter) and rapes.

Sources: Germany 2007a; and data supplied by the Bundeskriminalamt.

is preponderant among the immigrant population in Sweden; but the non-European component is also large (see Chapter 3). In spite of the growth of the share of foreign-borns, the overall crime rate per population has remained fairly constant in time, suggesting a situation under control (Figure 4.10). The information on the involvement of immigrants in criminal activities was gathered more systematically in Sweden with regard to foreign-borns and only on an occasional basis with regard to non-nationals.

The Swedish data show that the share of foreign-borns is around a quarter of the total number of those charged for all offences: in other words, the foreign-born involvement in charged offences is some 2.5 times higher than their share of the resident population. The share of foreign-borns out of the total of those charged, however, is thought to have grown only slightly and hence in no very alarming fashion (Martens and Holmberg 2005).

This interpretation of the situation in Sweden, however, is not realistic in terms of some specific crimes. In contrast to the total crime rate, the rate of intentional homicides shows a pronounced tendency to growth. By the end of the 1990s the share of non-nationals out of the total of those charged for intentional homicide was similar to that in Germany (just under 30 per cent). The share of foreign-borns among those charged for this crime was even higher, exceeding 40 per cent.

The situation relating to rape is no better. As shown by Figure 4.10, there has been a sharp growth of crimes of rape in Sweden. Indeed, the Swedish rates for this crime are among the highest in Europe. The growth of rape seems to have proceeded for many years *pari passu* with the growth of the share of foreign-borns in the resident population, and more recently has increased its pace. However, it is fair to assume that the reform of the law, which extended the criminal scope of 'sexual violence' in 1998, influenced the registered growth of rape in Sweden (von Hofer 2000), as indeed happened during the same period in other countries, such as Italy. Despite that, the growth of the rate of this offence is not limited to the period immediately subsequent to the reform of the law. In any case, the fact remains that the share of immigrants among those recorded for this crime is high and growing. The share of non-nationals was equivalent to approximately a third of the total number of those charged for rape at the end of the 1990s. The share of foreign-borns was even higher and grew until it had reached approximately half of the total number of those charged for this offence – in other words, a percentage approximately four times higher than the share of foreign-borns in the resident population – predictably arousing anxieties in Sweden. The growth over time of the incidence of rape in Sweden is, however, greater than that of the percentage of foreign-borns among those charged: a fact that suggests there has been a growth in absolute values also of the contribution of Swedish nationals to this offence.

The situation in the Netherlands is in part similar to that in Sweden: the share of non-nationals has remained fairly constant in time; the number of

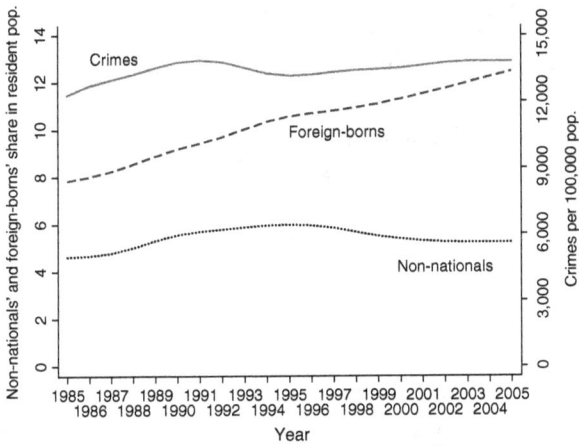

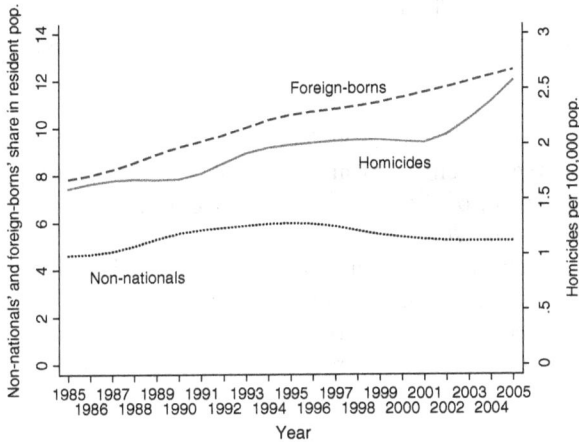

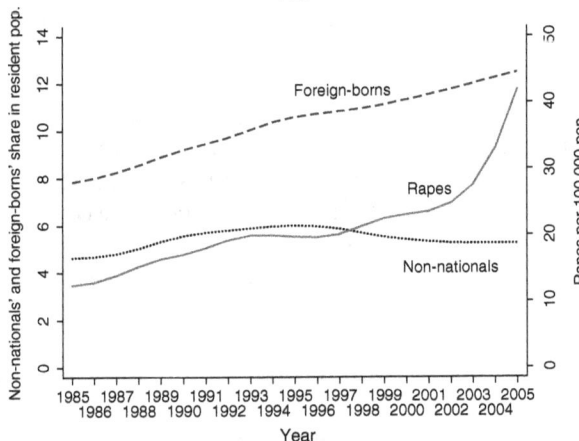

Figure 4.10 Sweden: variation of the percentages of non-nationals and of foreign-borns among the resident population and of the rates of total crimes, intentional homicides and rapes.

Source: Sweden 2007.

foreign-borns has substantially increased. The immigrant population here is, however, predominantly formed of non-Europeans, largely as a consequence of Holland's colonial legacy in the East Indies and in the Caribbean. The share of illegal immigrants is estimated to be large and is at least in part linked to the fame, or the notoriety, of the Netherlands as a country unusually tolerant of deviance, prostitution – militant feminists have branded Holland 'a pimp state' – and in particular the trafficking of small quantities of soft drugs. This tolerance, however, has turned sour during more recent years, with the result that the Netherlands has become one of the European countries with the highest rate of detainees per population (see further, Chapter 5). The perception of immigration as a source of criminality has not been absent from this change in attitude, and the penal policy resulting from it. Particularly high-profile crimes of vendetta, in which immigrants have been implicated, have concurred to increase the sense of jeopardy associated with immigration.

A significant quantity of sociological/statistical studies on immigration and crime has been produced in the Netherlands: yet the data relating to the non-national category remain meagre, at least in terms of charged offenders; the target population of these studies usually consists of those classified as *allochthones* (the *allochthonous* being contrasted with the *autochthonous* population). Allochthones are, in turn, divided into allochthones of the first generation – the category corresponding to foreign-borns – and allochthones of the second generation; information on these latter permits further light to be thrown on a situation on which scarce data exist in Europe.

The preference given to the allochthonous category in Holland makes comparisons with other countries more difficult. It should be recalled, however, that criminality is concentrated in the young adult's age group, which forms, among all immigrant adults of the first generation, the age group in which non-nationals, i.e. those who have not yet obtained citizenship of the host country, are concentrated. So, we can assume that the criminality of the first generations of allochthones largely coincides with that of non-nationals.

Figure 4.11 shows that the trend of the crimes of rape and robbery in the Netherlands in recent decades seems to follow the curve of foreign-borns. A rather different curve is presented for homicides, the rates of which at the end of the period are much the same as they were at the start. For all three major crimes, the rates register a decrease in more recent years, despite the growth in the percentage of foreign-borns.

The percentage of foreign-borns reported for any crime in the Netherlands is *c.* 2.5 times that of nationals; the percentage of non-Western foreign-borns is even higher, and the maximum is reached with the non-Western second generation, *c.* 4-5 times over-represented in comparison with nationals. Altogether, foreign-borns represent roughly a quarter of the total of those charged. But if we look at some particular types of crime, the over-representation of immigrants increases. The share of foreign-borns charged

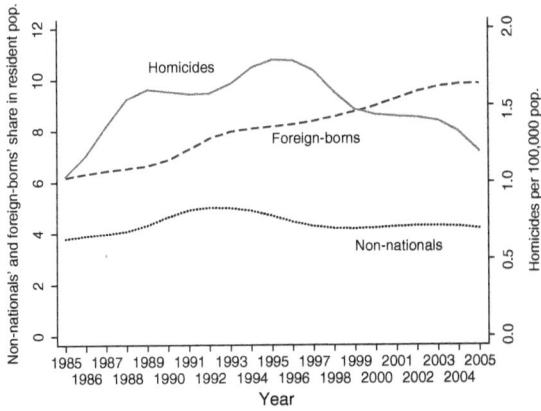

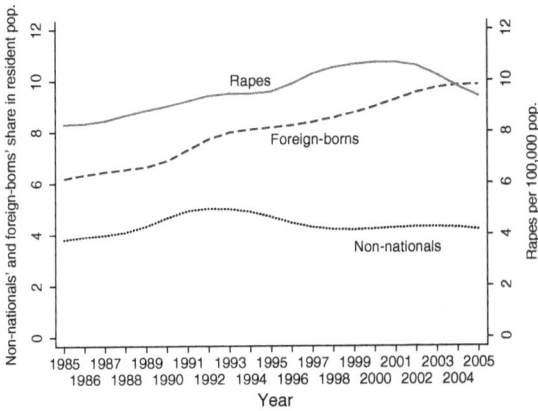

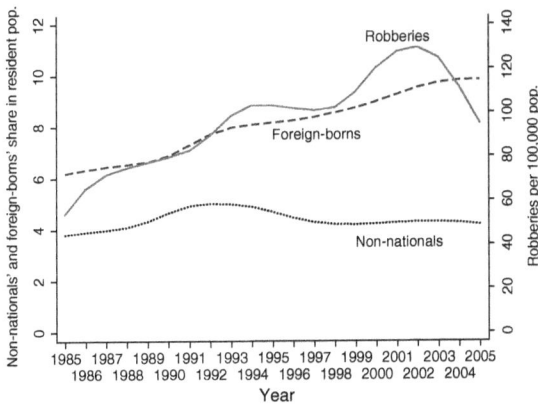

Figure 4.11 The Netherlands: variation of the percentages of non-nationals and foreign-borns among the resident population and of the rates of intentional homicides, rapes and robberies.

Sources: Netherlands (The) 2008b; and data supplied by the Ministerie van Justitie (Research and Documentation Centre).

for crimes against property is *c.* 40 per cent of the total charged for this offence; for crimes of violence, their percentage is approximately a third of the total.

The case of Finland presents a situation characterized by a rapid growth of the percentage of non-nationals among the total resident population. So, the situation of Finland in this respect is similar to that in Italy and Spain.

In the case of Finland, however, non-nationals preponderantly consist of non-EU immigrants from the countries of Eastern Europe rather than of non-Europeans. Despite the sharp growth of the non-national population since the early 1990s, i.e. from the collapse of the Eastern bloc, the homicide rate – though high – has tended to fall since 2000 (Figure 4.12). The share of non-nationals among those recorded for homicide has risen to a level roughly twice as high as that of non-nationals among the resident population. Non-nationals, however, represent a small percentage of the total number of those registered for homicide.

We can therefore conclude that the growth of the non-national population in Finland has had limited repercussions on the trend in the homicide rate. Finland, as we have already pointed out, is the Western European country with the highest homicide rates, but – as already shown by Figure 4.1 – these rates are *not* associated with the presence of non-nationals, which is modest. Moreover, even the trend of homicide rates during our period does not seem significantly to depend on non-nationals.

The situation relating to rape in Finland also seems to follow a trend of its own. The rate of this crime has doubled in the period under review (Figure 4.12). The share of non-nationals among those charged for this crime is 8–10 times their share of the resident population. So there are grounds for assuming that the growth of non-nationals has substantially contributed to the growth in the number of indicted cases of rape in Finland, even if there has been a concurrent growth in the component consisting of Finnish citizens.

As regards robberies in Finland, the trend seems similar to that of homicides but different from that of rape. As in the case of homicides, the rate of robberies reached its peak in the early 1990s and started to drop ten years later. The share of non-nationals among those charged for robbery is *c.* 4–5 times their share of the resident population. The trend deducible from this is a substitution of nationals by non-nationals.

The situation in Spain, if compared with that of Finland – which it resembles in the surging growth of its non-national population – permits us to trace the different outcomes in terms of the evolution of the rates for the major crimes. Against the background of a situation in which the non-national population in Spain grew rapidly, rising from *c.* 1 per cent to 6 per cent of the resident population in the space of 20 years, it is striking that the rates for intentional homicide and rape do not present any significant variations (Figure 4.13).

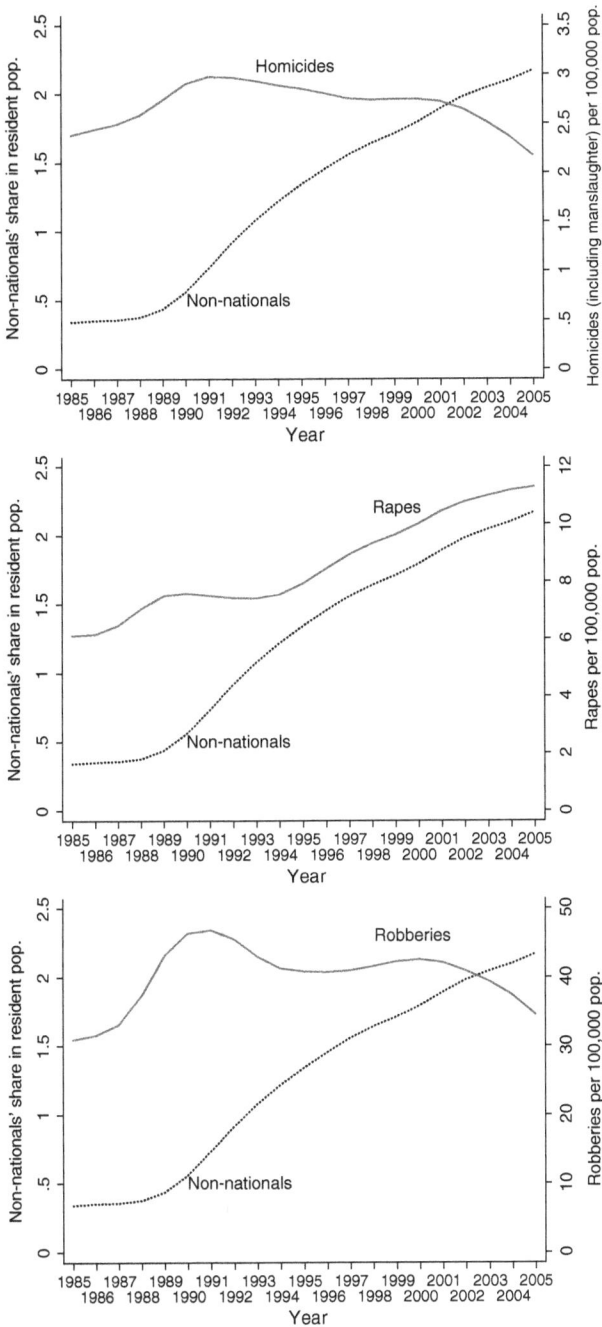

Figure 4.12 Finland: variation of the percentage of non-nationals among the resident population and of the rates of intentional homicides (including manslaughter), rapes and robberies.

Sources: Finland 2004; and data supplied by Statistics Finland.

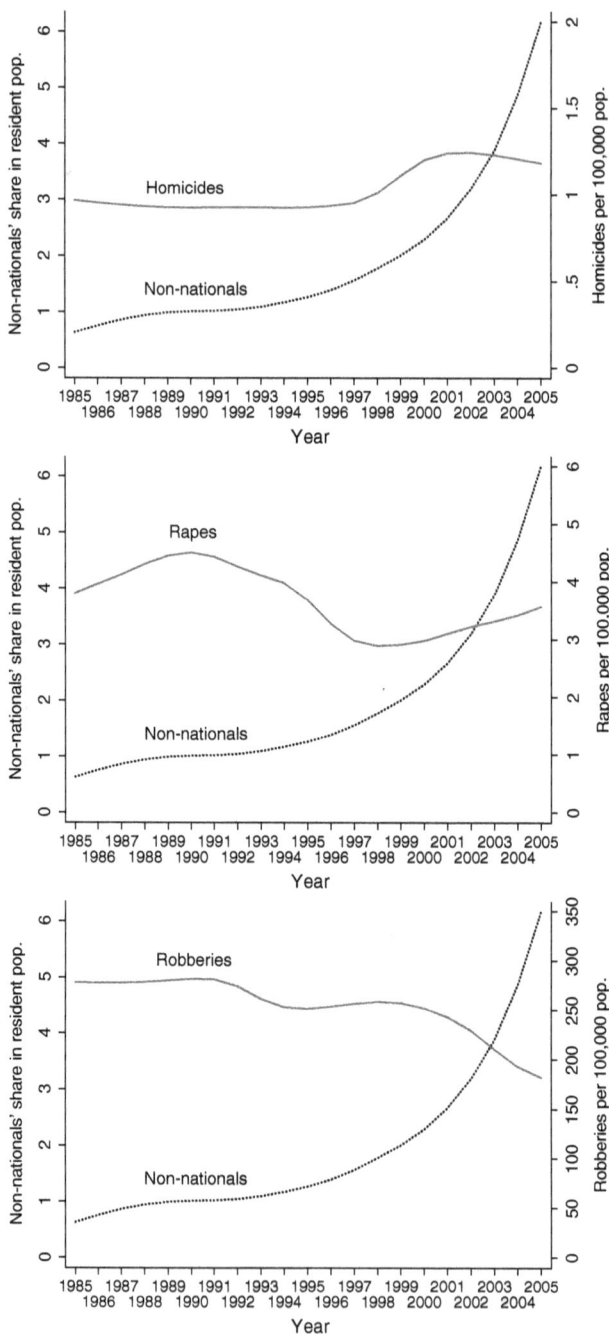

Figure 4.13 Spain: variation of the percentage of non-nationals among the resident population and of the rates of intentional homicides (including manslaughter), rapes and robberies (including bag-snatching).

Sources: Spain 1998 ff.; and data supplied by the Instituto Nacional de Estadística.

As regards robberies, the trend is clearly downwards, due especially to a decline in bag-snatching and bank robberies. However, in general the share of non-nationals among all those charged grew rapidly – as also grew the share of non-nationals in the resident population – and in more recent years has reached a share of roughly 30 per cent for major crimes: so a share far higher than the percentage of non-nationals among Spain's resident population. In substance, therefore, in the case of homicides and rapes, and even more clearly in the case of robberies, the trend has been for non-nationals to substitute citizens of the host country among those charged with these offences.

The situation in Austria shows similarities with Germany, Finland and especially with Greece in terms of the composition of its immigrant population, three-quarters of which are from non-EU countries in Europe. In contrast to Germany, however, most of the immigrants come from Eastern Europe. The trend of the non-nationals curve resembles that of Germany: a significant increase until the mid-1990s and then a stabilization.

The rate of intentional homicides in Austria has tended to drop since the early 1990s (Figure 4.14). The percentage of non-nationals among those charged for intentional homicide, on the other hand, has increased to the point of reaching, even surpassing, a third of the total. So we can assume that non-nationals have substituted nationals among the perpetrators of this crime, though within an overall trend of decreasing rates.

In contrast to the homicide rate, that for rape in Austria has more than doubled in the period being examined here. The percentage of non-nationals, which was already roughly a quarter of the total number of those charged for rape at the start of the 1990s, has gradually grown until it reached roughly a third of the total. It may be presumed therefore that the growth of the contribution of non-nationals has been accompanied by the growth also of the national (indigenous) component.

The rate of robberies in turn has grown in a very pronounced way, so much so that by the end of the period it was almost four times what it was at the start. The percentage of non-nationals, roughly a third at the start of the 1990s, has increased to over 40 per cent since the turn of the millennium. The sharp rise of robberies in Austria in recent years does not seem to find any explanation in the trend, a relatively stable one from the middle of the 1990s, in the share of non-nationals among the resident population, or in the growth of non-nationals among those charged with this offence.

Immigration to Denmark presents a trend characterized by a marked increase up to the middle of the 1990s and later by a stabilization (Figure 4.15). This situation therefore is similar to that registered in Germany and Austria. The non-national share of the resident population in Denmark, however, is lower than that in the other two countries. With regard to the provenance of its immigrants, Denmark is characterized by a balance between the three main components: that of non-nationals from the EU (and EFTA) is similar to those of non-EU Europeans and of non-Europeans.

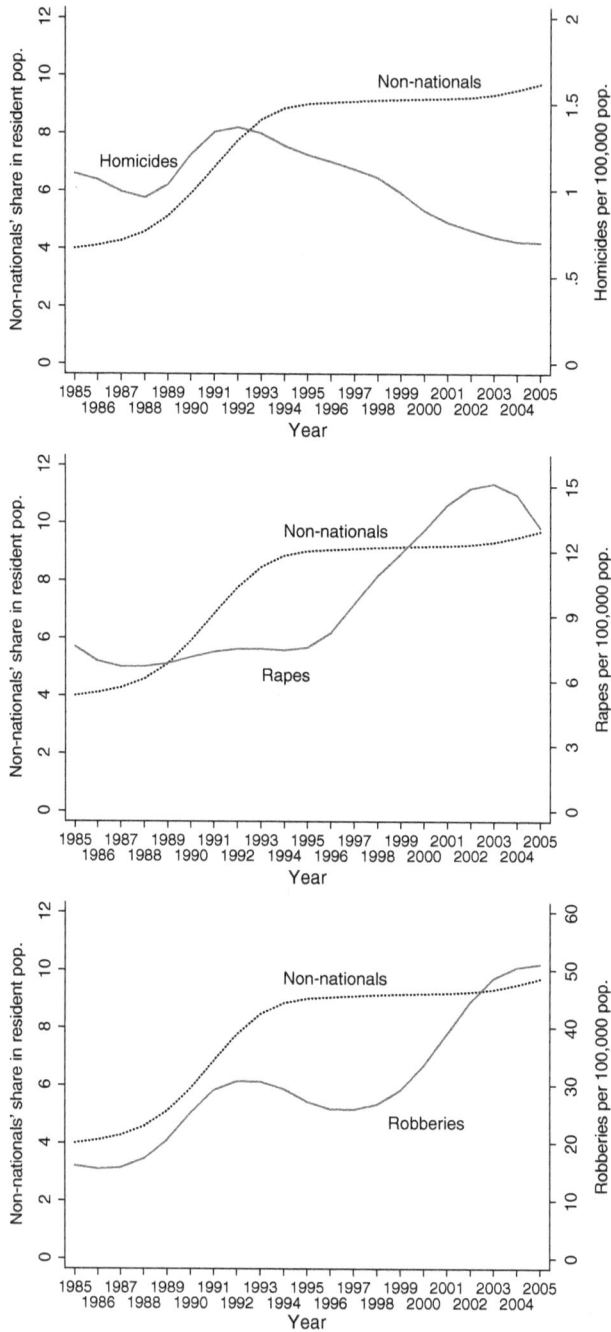

Figure 4.14 Austria: variation of the percentage of non-nationals among the resident population and of the rates of intentional homicides (excluding attempted homicides), rapes and robberies.

Sources: Austria 2008; and data supplied by the Bundesministerium für Justiz.

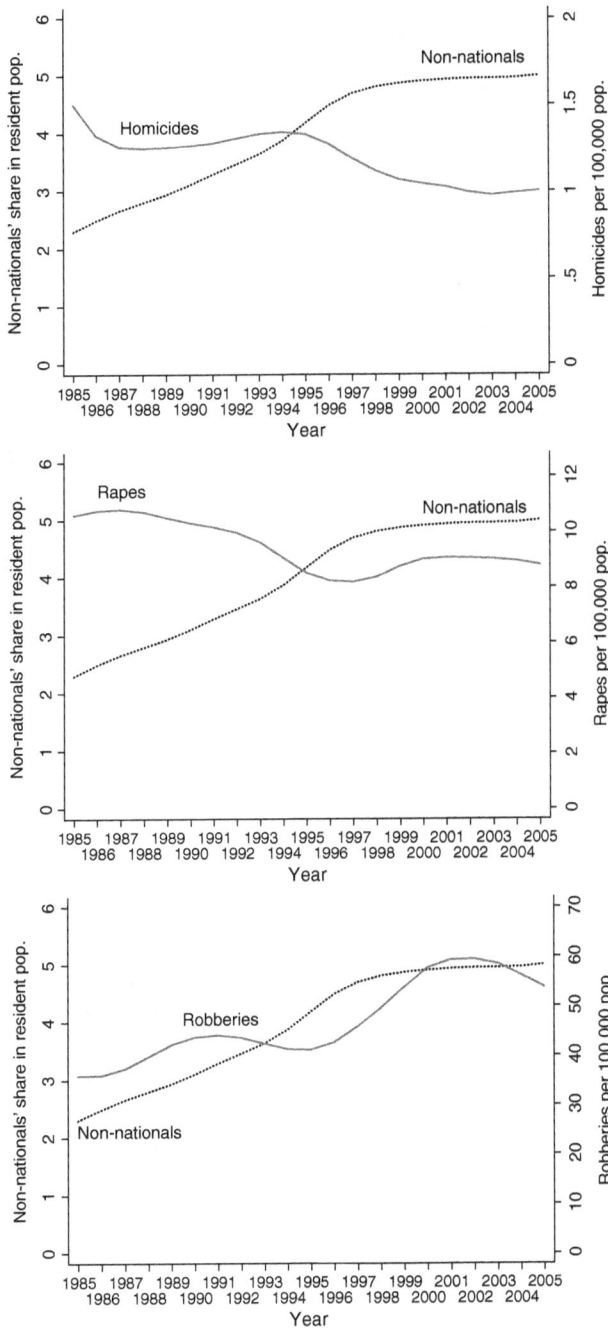

Figure 4.15 Denmark: variation of the percentage of non-nationals among the resident population and of the rates of intentional homicides (completed), rapes and robberies.

Sources: Denmark 2009 and previous years; and data supplied by Danmarks Statistik.

In the period 1985 to 2005, intentional homicide rate in Denmark presents a decrease (Figure 4.15). This is in contrast to the trend of the share of non-nationals in the resident population, which doubled during the same period. The share of non-nationals out of the total number of people charged with (and found guilty of) homicide presents a substantial growth over the last few years and has now reached a level of roughly a quarter of the total, compared with a non-national share in the resident population of c. 5 per cent.

The trend of rapes in Denmark is decreasing, and therefore it contrasts with the overall trend in Western Europe. For this offence, the share of non-nationals is almost a third of the total. There has been, therefore, a partial substitution of nationals by non-nationals, with regard to those charged with rape.

The trend of robberies in Denmark is quite different from that registered for intentional homicides and rapes. The robbery rate presents a definitely increasing trend, as has indeed occurred in most of the other European countries. The robbery rate has grown by c. 60 per cent and seems to graphically mirror (Figure 4.15) the increase in the non-national population that came about in Denmark in the period under review. Also the share of non-nationals charged with this offence did grow, though even now it doesn't go beyond a third of the total. All these facts, therefore, seem to suggest that the growth in the robbery rate is the result of the increase in the contributions of both non-nationals and natives.

* * *

The picture that emerges from the above analysis of the relation between non-nationals and violent crime in the various countries of Western Europe shows some interesting similarities with what has happened in the USA (Figure 4.16). First, the USA has registered a sharp growth in immigration since 1980. The percentage of foreign-borns almost doubled (from 6.2 to 12 per cent) in the period 1980–2004. The growth of non-nationals throughout Western Europe was close to 60 per cent in the period under review; but this figure does not include, as we have already pointed out, those who have in the meantime acquired citizenship in their host countries.

Yet, despite this sharp increase in immigrants, no corresponding growth in crime rates was registered in the USA. Crime rates had significantly grown in the period between 1960 and 1980; in particular, the homicide rate had almost doubled. Immigration to the USA had also increased during this period, and the association between the two phenomena had once again placed the relation between migration and crime, and the fears associated with it, in the spotlight. In the following years, however, the homicide rates did not grow (Martinez 2006). The rates indeed show a pronounced tendency to decline in the 1990s; and by the end of our period had almost been halved (from c. 10 to 5.5 per 100,000 population). The trend of the rate of rapes during this period is more uncertain, but it too altogether followed a downward curve.

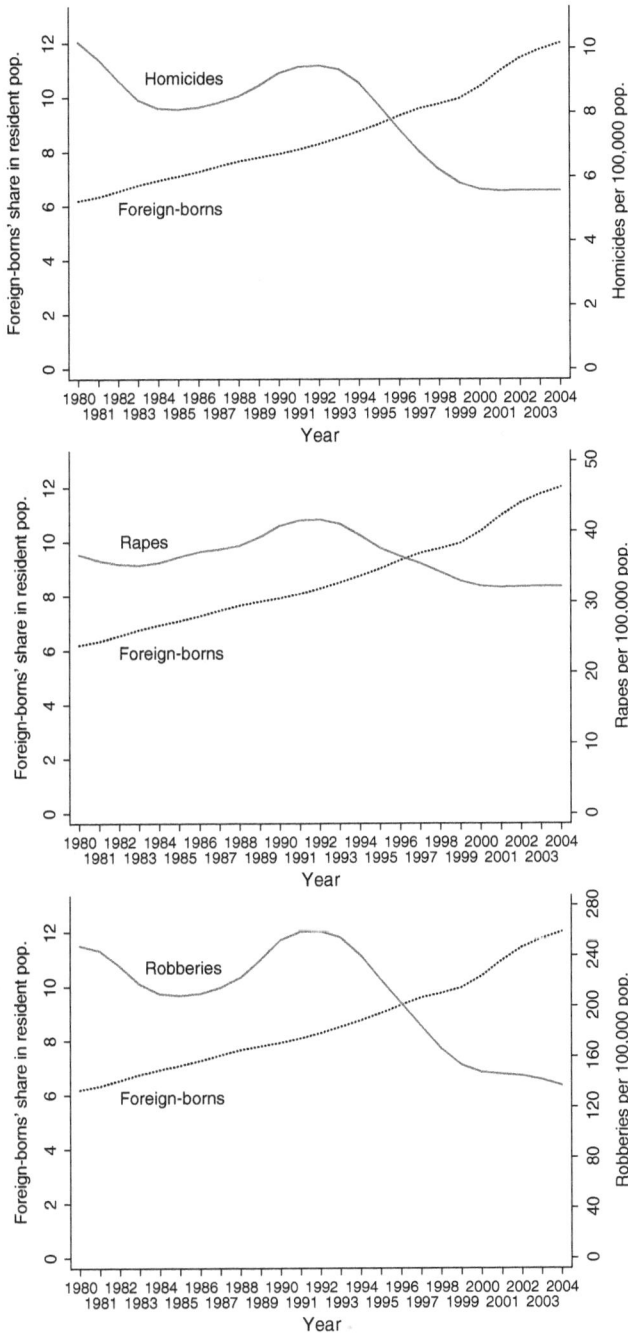

Figure 4.16 USA: variation of the percentage of foreign-borns among the resident population and of the rates of intentional homicides, including non-negligent manslaughter, rapes and robberies.

Sources: US 2007 and previous years.

The rate for robberies even more conspicuously followed a downward curve: by the end of the period it had almost been halved (from over 250 to 140). In this case, too, we may note that the downturn began around 1993.

To judge from the trend of the more violent criminality in the USA in recent decades – see also Figure 4.4 above – the relation between immigration and crime is the opposite of what might have been expected. The crime rates clearly declined precisely in a period characterized by a sharp growth in immigration and by the accentuation of its illegal component. This would agree with what had already been asserted by Sutherland back in the 1920s, namely, that immigrants in the USA don't bring criminality with them, but, if anything, gradually learn it from the host society. Adopting a similar perspective, Sampson (2006) has suggested that the diminution of criminality in the USA from the start of the 1990s onwards could have been determined precisely by the growing presence of immigrants. But this hypothesis would need to be further tested. The decline in crime rates in the USA is chronologically associated also with other phenomena. The start of the downturn in the rates for homicide, rape and robbery can be placed around 1993. It thus coincides with a policy of greater repression: the much-bruited policy of *zero tolerance* towards antisocial forms of behaviour and the provision of long and automatically inflicted custodial sentences on recidivist offenders responsible for graver crimes (so-called 'three strikes and you're out' law).

* * *

To sum up, there was on average a sharp growth in the presence of non-nationals in European countries in the years straddling the end of the twentieth and start of the twenty-first century. However, the data on the distribution of rates of criminality in the various countries – shown by the first Figures in this chapter – rebut the notion that, as far as major crimes are concerned, there is any relation between these rates and the share of non-nationals among the resident population. The rates for homicide, rape and robbery in the USA tend to confirm this lack of relation. So it would seem that the popular equation, that immigration = crime, needs to be reformulated. To explain the lack of relation between share of non-nationals and rates of criminality one could in the abstract advance two main hypotheses: (1) non-nationals make an essentially insignificant contribution to the criminality in the countries in which they reside; (2) the rates of criminality of non-nationals are very different in the various countries in which they reside. The first of these hypotheses is unrealistic, at least as far as Europe is concerned: in particular it flies in the face of the findings of a large number of empirical studies on immigration and crime in Europe in recent decades and also what has emerged in the course of this analysis (but see also Chapter 5 on non-nationals charged for various offences). The second hypothesis is realistic. The trends registered by the Figures published in this chapter in fact do not refute the proposition that immigrants contribute in a significant way to criminality in the various countries of Western Europe: they do, however, refute the proposition that immigrants present – at least for the major crimes of violence charted above – rates of criminality that are similar in the various countries. Otherwise the case of countries with a high share of non-nationals among their resident population and at the same time a comparatively low rate of criminality would not, in particular, be possible.

The second hypothesis brings with it some significant corollaries: first, that it is possible for a country to keep its crime rate low – at least for major crimes – even in the presence of a high percentage of immigrants; and second, that – given that non-nationals present a different rate of criminality in their various host countries – the characteristics of the host country and its immigration could play an important role in the determination of the criminality of immigrants. In short, the relevance of the *country factor* renders the equation immigration = crime at least inaccurate.

A second series of data – relating to the diachronic evolution of the rates for the more serious crimes – permits us a further elucidation of the picture described above. The on average sharp growth of the presence of non-nationals among the resident populations in the countries of Western Europe has not been accompanied – as many feared – by a growth of the rates of intentional homicides. Indeed these rates have on average remained more or less constant. The trend of the rates for robberies and rapes has shown, by contrast, an evolution characterized by overall *growth*. But the variations of the rates for these offences have not been associated with variations in the presence of non-nationals in the various countries. This implies that a growth in the share of non-nationals can be associated with a reduction in the rates of criminality, or their lesser growth in comparison with that registered in countries in which there has been less variation in the presence of non-nationals.

The analysis of the evolution of the rates of criminality and of the involvement of non-nationals in some specific countries permits us to refine these preliminary conclusions. The evidence seems to show, in particular, that – as regards the relation between non-nationals and crime – we find ourselves faced not by one evolutionary model but by several.

(A) In some cases, there has been a stabilization, or even a reduction, of the rates of criminality, even in the presence of a sometimes sharp increase in the non-national share of the total number charged. The case of the trend of intentional homicides in some European countries (e.g. Switzerland, Italy, Spain and Austria) is emblematic of this model. Another example is the trend of robberies in Switzerland and Finland, as well as the trend of rapes in Denmark. The model is that of the *substitution* of nationals by non-nationals in crime. The hypothesis that the criminality of nationals has been substituted by that of non-nationals is also supported by what has happened in the case of other offences, in particular, the exploitation of prostitution, which has become almost a monopoly of non-nationals in various European countries. The substitution model can be divided into two types: the first, *simple substitution*, is characterized by a largely constant trend in crime rates, combined with a decline in the contribution of nationals (e.g. homicides in Switzerland from 1985 to 2005); the second, *partial substitution*, consists of a growing contribution of non-nationals which compensates only in part the diminishing contribution of nationals, with the result that the rates of criminality are falling (e.g. robberies in Spain, homicides in Austria, and rapes in Denmark).

(B) In other cases, there has been a growth in the rates of criminality, associated with a growth of the involvement in criminal activities both by non-nationals and by citizens of the country in question (that's the case of intentional homicides in England and Wales, of rapes in Sweden, Italy and Austria and of robberies in Denmark). This trend corresponds to a model of *parallel evolution* in crime.

(C) Other trends have taken the form of a growth in the rates of criminality, in tandem with an increase only of the non-nationals component or that of nationals. An example of the first case is the trend of the rate of rape in Switzerland. An example of the second is the trend of the same crime in France. So in this case we are faced by a model of *divergent evolution* in crime.

It seems clear that this diversity of evolutionary models is connected not only with the different characteristics of the various offences, but also with more fundamental differences existing in the various European countries. In fact, if we combine what has emerged in the previous pages as regards both the synchronic and the diachronic dimension of the relation between immigration and crime, we cannot fail to observe that this relation assumes different characteristics within the various countries. It seems clear, therefore, that a *country factor* exists that needs to be considered with close attention. It might be assumed that this country factor is ethnically determined: that it consists of the different origin of the non-national population resident in the country in question. In effect, from the cases examined above, we do gain an impression that the countries with a strong component of non-nationals of EU origin also have a more stable, or at any rate less disturbing, situation in terms of their trends of criminality. However, the picture is far from homogeneous: it is enough to think, for example, of Germany and Finland, which have a high percentage of non-EU immigrants and at the same time a fairly contained involvement of non-nationals in crime. By contrast, Switzerland has a predominantly EU immigrant population, and yet has registered the growing contribution of this population to criminality. So the origin of the non-national population does not seem to be the decisive factor in explaining why the relation between immigration and crime should assume such different characteristics in the various European countries. Other aspects need to be identified.

4.3. Further remarks on variations of non-national populations and variations of criminality: what if the explanation is not immigration?

What has emerged from the above analysis is that, all things considered, there is no clear association between the share of non-nationals in the populations of the countries of Western Europe and their respective crime rates, nor even between the variations of non-nationals and the variations of the rates of criminality within these countries. In particular, variations of the rates for major crimes in these countries seem to be interwoven in a far from homogeneous or unambiguous way with variations in their non-national populations: in short, the curves of these separate variations do not coincide. All this leads us to infer that phenomena other than those we have considered so far have influenced the crime rates in these countries.

The variations we have registered in the crime rates may be studied in the light of historical tendencies and the hypotheses relating to them. We may begin by recalling that the authors of the Progressive Era had predicted that the more serious crimes would evaporate in tandem with the growth of material prosperity and of education: in short, the causes of crime, and with them crime itself, would be eliminated *pari passu* with the advance of civilization. The trend of intentional homicides lends itself very well to supporting this hypothesis. There has undeniably been a trend to a decline in the murder rate from the second half of the eighteenth century down to the Second World War; with a subsequent phase of increase followed by a process of stabilization in most European countries (Westfeld and Estrada 2005). Since the whole of this period coincided with a great growth in income and a no less considerable growth in education, the facts would seem to support the hypothesis. However, these optimistic predictions seem far less well-founded if we consider other crimes. For there has been, on the contrary, a demonstrable growth in the diffusion of many crimes, such as thefts, fraud, and white-collar crimes such as corruption in most of the countries of Western Europe in modern times. Even as regards robberies and rapes, there is sound empirical evidence to show their more or less generalized increase in recent decades (Entorf and Spengler 2002).

At this point some further corroboration and analysis are needed. Apart from the contribution of non-nationals, what other phenomena might have influenced the particular trends in Europe of the major crimes we have analysed and tabulated above? To answer this question, we have taken into consideration a series of indicators that are able to register the socio-economic and cultural differences that exist between the countries of Europe. What interests us in particular are the diachronic variations registered by these indicators, since our aim is to explain the *variations* of the rates of criminality, which, as we have emphasized, are a more reliable object of study than crime rates pure and simple. In selecting the indicators that could 'explain' these variations we took into account the main criminological theories presented above (see Chapter 1) and more specifically those that aspire to be *general theories*, given that the object of our investigation is not so much the contribution of immigrants to crime as the variations in criminality altogether.

We began by adopting some indicators that are usually defined as indicators of *context*: first, the classic indicator consisting of the country's *total economic activity value* (GDP per capita); and the more critical indicator of the country's *product at purchasing power parity* (GDP PPP per capita). Immediately after these indicators of material prosperity we considered the *percentage rate of inflation*: we did so on the basis of the hypothesis that a country with a high rate of inflation ought to present, *ceteris paribus*, a less reliable economic and social context. The relation between these indicators of material prosperity and crime presents some ambiguities. On the one hand, there is some evidence to support the hypothesis that the level of economic prosperity is inversely proportioned to overall criminality – greater prosperity, lesser crime – at least in the countries of Western Europe (Guajardo and O'Hara 1998). On the other hand, effects such as those already identified by Durkheim cannot be excluded: the proposition, namely, that sudden increases in material prosperity create a condition of *anomie*: they raise further expectations that society cannot satisfy, and the sense of frustration, or injustice, thus engendered, could in turn encourage recourse to crime. Moreover, material prosperity is associated with other collateral phenomena from which a growth in crime, or a criminal culture, might reasonably be expected: for instance, the generalized diffusion of passenger cars in Western society implies mobility on the territory and hence the ability to evade the social control exercised by the local community.

The effects of income distribution ought to be less ambiguous. A fairer distribution of income ought, in theory, to increase the material prosperity of the underprivileged classes and at the same time reduce their *relative deprivation*. In the presence of sharp inequalities between rich and poor, on the contrary, one might expect the latter to perceive themselves as comparatively deprived: denied the chance, that is, of realizing the 'universal' objectives of economic and social success. This is a situation that is considered particularly criminogenous by the proponents of *anomic strain* theory. To measure the distribution of income, and gauge the degree of income inequality in a society, we will use the classic *Gini Index*. We should point out, by the way, that the richer countries also have a fairer distribution of income (hence a lower value of the index), with some exceptions, notably the USA. The rapid growth of national income is initially associated, however, with a growth in income differentials.

The concept of income distribution, on the other hand, is interwoven with that of social protection. We can measure the propensity to a welfare approach in the various countries through e.g. *social benefits per capita*.

Not surprisingly, Eurostat (2003) considers these indicators as measures of *social cohesion*; the OECD prefers to call them indicators of *equity* (Martin and Pearson 2001): the phenomena they measure may also be placed in the wider sphere of solidarity. It should be borne in mind, however, that *social benefits per capita* are strongly conditioned by level of income. Consequently, they are also a measure of a country's average material prosperity.

The unemployment level represents another indicator that may impact on poverty and on *relative deprivation*. Among the unemployment indicators – that belong to the so-called category of *self-sufficiency* (Martin and Pearson 2001) – we have privileged those that regard the male population and the teenagers/young adults age groups, i.e. the population that makes the greatest contribution to crime. We have considered, for example, such indicators as the shares of *unemployed males* in the 15–24 age group and in the total labour force, as also the *long-term unemployment* that the UN Development Programme considers among the indicators of human poverty (UNDP 2003).

We have further used a series of indicators relating to level of education. Education ought to consist not only of knowledge, or skills, useful for material growth, but also of *civic values*, which could contain crime. We have already noted that historically the general growth of education was not accompanied by a reduction of particular crimes, in particular those against property. However, this could be the result of the counteracting influence of other concomitant phenomena, such as urbanization. We might adopt as a working hypothesis the proposition that – *ceteris paribus* – the countries with the highest levels of education are those best equipped to counter crime. In terms of education we considered some indicators such as the population's *average number of years of schooling* and the *percentage of population with at least a school leaving certificate*. These indicators, however, are not available for the whole period we intend to cover. Data are more readily available to measure the *percentage of GNP spent on public education* and the so-called *school life expectancy*. We further used, as a measure of education, what is in effect a composite indicator of development: this is the indicator of the UN Development Programme (UNDP), which in recent years has gained acceptance as a universal comparison gauge in this sector. The *Human Development Index* combines an educational variable (it is in turn the result of the combination of the literacy rate for adults and enrolments in primary and junior secondary schools and universities), with a purely economic variable, per capita income (though this is subjected in this Index to some major adjustments, in practice to a reduction of the weight of the richest economies) and a demographic variable, namely life expectancy at birth, strongly associated with education level.

We also considered the *number of dailies sold*. This indicator ought to measure the overall cultural level, and the level of interest in current affairs, knowledge and events. The indicator has met with wide approval and acceptance in social surveys, since it is held able to measure the level of *social capital* (Putnam 1993), and in particular citizens' interest in every-thing beyond their own personal world and that of their families: in short, their interest in and attention to an undifferentiated *alter*. These latter characteristics are unlikely to be accompanied by crime. We also considered that the number of *personal computers* (per 1,000 population) could be a valid cultural indicator comparable to the number of dailies sold. Admittedly for some the spread of PCs recalls in the first place online fraud, or even more criminogenous aspects of the world wide web; yet it's clear that it is also associated with a more specific and positive *cultural* aspect: that con-nected with the revolution of knowledge made possible by the Internet. Lastly, the spread of *mobile phones* may be considered a measure of com-munication; it is at the same time an indicator of wealth, since it is positively correlated with level of income.

A country's level of education, even more so than its level of income, is strongly correlated with its *infant mortality* rate. This latter indicator may be considered a measure of *social breakdown*. A deterioration of the social fabric is usually accompanied by an increase in infant mortality and a reduc-tion in life expectancy, as happened in the countries of the former Soviet bloc in the last decade of the twentieth century. In a situation of social breakdown of this kind one would also expect a concomitant breakdown in institutional measures for the containment of crime. A high infant mortality rate is also accompanied as a rule by a high *birth rate* and a high incidence of *tuberculosis*: a disease that remains typical of unfavourable socio-economic contexts.

The rate of *divorce* may be considered a further indicator of social break-down. While marriage itself may seem to some an even greater affliction, the divorce rate may well be considered an indicator of anomie in the sense described by Durkheim and by Thomas and Znaniecki: namely, the indica-tor of a situation in which traditional values are in decline, the individual feels himself less linked to the *alter*, and individualist pressures prevail. With an anomic situation of this kind it seems not unrealistic to associate a growth in crime.

A further indicator of social breakdown may be identified in urbaniza-tion. The urban context has been considered – at least since the onset of industrialization – as a less community-minded, more individualistic and socially less cohesive environment, as a result of widespread anonymity and also of the uprooting that urbanization implies. Even if contemporary urban environments have little in common with those social and demographic sinks that cities were in the first period of industrialization, it is not unreal-istic to imagine that a growth of urbanized population is accompanied by a growth in crime or at least a growth of certain crimes. For example, in France the overall rate of criminality in the Départements is strongly associ-ated with their population density (a proxy of urbanization). In Italy, the population density of the Provinces is closely correlated with the rate of crimes against property. In the USA, a close relation can be observed between urbanization and robberies in the various States. It is as well to recall, however, that urbanization is associated with high incomes: the negative influences of the urban context may thus be attenuated by the benefits accruing from economic prosperity. To measure urbanization – a characteristic that for the reasons set out above we may well call *structural* – we shall have recourse to the share of *urbanized population* and also to the share of *population living in cities larger than 1 million*. The persistence of a rural-agricultural context has been measured, instead, by means of both the share of *people employed in farming* and the share of *agriculture value added*.

Lastly, we considered the rate of *incarceration* in the various countries as an indicator of their level of punitiveness in tackling crime. The aim is to control whether variations in punitiveness are associated with variations in the rates of criminality.[1]

Basing ourselves on this series of indicators, we examined the changes that have occurred in time, subdividing the period already considered above (1990–2003) into several shorter periods. By this procedure we can ascertain whether the trend of criminality in the various European countries, as registered in the period 1990–2003, is reproduced in shorter segments of time: something that seems probable but not certain. Here too we have used – as regards rates of criminality – the data of the *European Sourcebook of Crime and Criminal Justice Statistics*; the variations are those registered in the period 1990–1994–1997–2000–2003. The tool used is that of the so-called *fixed effects models*, which analyse the repeated variations registered within the cases considered, here the various countries. An appreciable advantage of these models is that they permit a multiplication of observations, unlike those deduced from the variations registered in a single period of time, as in the case of the period 1990–2003 already examined above.

Let us begin with the results relating to robberies. The trend of robbery rates in the countries of Europe is either non-significantly or negatively correlated with variations in the percentage of non-nationals; and is also correlated negatively with the trend in the diffusion of dailies. Robbery rates, on the other hand, are correlated positively with variations in income (affecting social benefits per capita), as well as variations in the resident population, urbanization, spread of cars, and mobile phones and with persistence of rural-agricultural areas (Appendix II). In substance, increases in robbery rates are associated with increases in population, greater urbanization and mobility over the territory, greater material prosperity (social benefits, mobile phones, cars) but at the same time persistence of rural-agricultural regions, and diminishing interest in newspapers.

The results relating to the growth of rape are even easier to interpret. The trend in the rates of rape in the countries of Western Europe shows non-significant or negative correlations with variations in the percentages of non-nationals. It is positively correlated, instead, with growth of income, however calculated, growth of social benefits, cars, mobile phones, urbanization and divorces. It is correlated negatively with the trend of infant mortality and tuberculosis. In sum, the growth of the rate of rape registered in almost all the European countries in the years straddling the end of the twentieth and start of the twenty-first century is associated with a growth of material prosperity and mobility, urbanization and rising living standards (reduction of infant mortality and TB), and with increased marriage breakdown (Appendix II).

As regards the trend in homicides, the results of our longitudinal analysis show that this trend is negatively associated with the trend of the percentage of non-nationals. It is also negatively associated with variations of urbanization and of income and with variations in the income distribution index (negatively affected, in the short term, by the income increase). It is positively associated, on the other hand, with the rate of divorce and with infant mortality. In sum, homicide rates in Europe have tended to fall where material prosperity and urbanization have grown, social conditions (e.g. infant mortality) have improved, and the divorce rate has been contained.

Lastly, we found no significant association between the variation of punitiveness (incarceration rates) and the variation of rates for the three major crimes considered.

In conclusion, the study of criminality in the various countries of Western Europe between the late twentieth and early twenty-first century shows that the trends for the major penal offences examined here are far from homogeneous: for some the trend is downwards, for others upwards. The trends for homicides, on the one hand, and rapes, on the other, are emblematic: the one decreasing, the other increasing. The socio-economic context associated with these trends is understandably heterogeneous as well. A common denominator of great significance, however, consists of the fact that the trend of the share of non-nationals – almost always growing – shows no correlation with that of the major crimes. In substance, the finding that emerged in our previous pages has been confirmed: the increase in the non-nationals share of the resident population has not corresponded to any significant increase in the rates for the major crimes. So, to 'explain' the trend of criminality in Europe recourse must be had to phenomena other than the share of non-nationals among the resident population.

Chapter 5

Non-nationals in prison, non-nationals charged

5.1 Some data

So far we have dealt with the question of how criminality varies with the variation of the non-national population. It is now time to tackle directly the question of non-nationals involved in problems of criminal justice. Let us begin by analysing the data on the prison population in Western Europe. These data are the most complete of all those relating to the phenomenon of the criminality of nationals and non-nationals. Given the great differences in the resident population in the various countries taken into examination here, the absolute values of the prison population in the various countries are themselves of little significance: it is no surprise that countries with a large resident population (such as Germany or France) also present a large prison population.

What is a more interesting indicator is that of detainees per 100,000 population (Table 5.1). It shows a situation characterized by considerable differences between one country and another. In recent years, the highest rates of incarceration were registered in Luxembourg, Spain, Portugal, the UK and the Netherlands; the lowest in Iceland, Finland and Norway. It may be noted that the average value for all eighteen countries is always far lower than the total value, calculated on the whole population of Europe. This means that the countries with lesser population also have lower incarceration rates.

In terms of variations, it may be observed that from 1985 to 2005 a first period of essential stabilization was followed by a sharp increase of the overall rate, which rose from *c.* 73 to 108, with a variation of almost 50 per cent. Particularly noteworthy are the increases registered in Greece, Spain, Luxembourg, and Sweden. Even more momentous is the change in the Netherlands where, after a period characterized by a policy of lesser recourse to custodial sentences (Downes 1988), there was a clear reversal of the trend in penal policy (see also our remarks in Chapter 4), with the result that Holland's incarceration rate, which was the lowest in Europe in the 1980s, rose to become one of the highest twenty years later.

Table 5.1 Detainees per 100,000 population in the countries of Western Europe – Years: 1985–2005

States	1985	1987	1989	1991	1993	1995	1997	1999	2001	2003	2005
B	63.1	70.4	68.0	60.2	71.3	74.5	81.8	82.7	85.0	83.6	89.2
DK	63.6	68.5	65.8	62.8	71.2	65.5	62.3	62.8	58.7	66.3	76.1
D	72.3	68.1	65.4	61.9	80.9	80.8	90.6	95.6	95.5	96.4	95.8
EL	35.1	41.7	45.1	48.8	62.7	58.2	53.1	71.9	76.1	77.5	86.2
E	57.6	71.9	80.2	93.8	116.8	102.3	108.8	113.0	114.6	130.5	140.0
F	73.2	93.8	79.7	85.1	88.5	91.3	92.7	87.2	79.0	95.4	94.3
IRL	55.5	55.8	56.5	59.7	59.1	56.8	65.9	73.3	77.6	74.1	75.0
I	77.0	62.9	54.0	57.0	88.9	86.6	86.0	88.9	96.7	98.9	101.5
L	73.0	102.7	91.0	89.2	106.0	113.6	99.5	92.6	80.4	110.3	151.0
NL	33.6	36.0	43.4	44.0	51.1	64.9	87.0	85.7	94.7	112.2	133.6
A	109.8	96.0	75.0	84.6	88.6	76.7	86.0	85.5	85.7	96.0	106.1
P	91.4	82.4	85.3	82.1	110.2	122.0	147.0	141.0	130.7	135.9	122.0
FIN	81.0	77.4	62.4	62.2	61.7	59.0	54.4	51.0	58.5	65.8	72.7
S	48.4	61.2	56.2	54.7	66.3	65.3	59.0	61.9	68.3	75.3	78.0
UK	94.9	98.4	96.4	90.8	90.6	99.1	117.8	119.3	124.3	135.1	139.6
ISL	38.4	41.1	44.5	38.8	38.9	44.4	43.4	33.2	38.4	38.5	39.8
NOR	44.7	46.5	51.3	58.7	60.3	54.9	52.5	57.6	58.9	63.7	66.7
CH	63.2	75.7	70.6	83.1	80.7	80.1	88.2	86.8	71.1	71.5	81.9
Total	72.4	75.0	71.1	72.4	86.2	86.4	93.9	95.7	96.7	104.5	108.1
Aver. val.	65.3	69.5	66.2	67.6	77.4	77.5	82.0	82.8	83.0	90.4	97.2

Source: Conseil de l'Europe 1986 and following years.

NB: For 1999, the Conseil de l'Europe did not gather data on prison inmates for its periodical publication SPACE I; the data for the year in question were calculated by interpolation for the present study. Other annual data were also calculated by interpolation, more particularly: Germany 1992; Greece 1990 and 1995; Spain 1996; Ireland 1990; Netherlands 1995; Portugal 1995; UK 1995; Iceland 1996; Norway 1992; and Switzerland 1994.

The situation relating to non-nationals detained in prisons in the countries of Western Europe is shown in Table 5.2. The period taken into consideration is that from 1985 to 2005. No systematic survey of non-nationals in prison was conducted before the 1980s. So it has not been possible to go back any earlier in time, as has been possible, on the other hand, to monitor the non-national population resident in Western Europe. Indeed it should be premised that the data on non-nationals in prison gathered in the 1980s reveal various gaps and variations in the method of calculation that make them less reliable than subsequent data. The data presented are percentages: the percentage, namely, of non-national detainees out of the total prison population in the individual countries. The data are furnished in this form by our main source, the Council of Europe.

The data shown in our Table 5.2 are of undoubted interest for a number of reasons. First, there are countries, such as Switzerland, Luxembourg, Greece, and Austria, in which the number of non-nationals in prison has grown in recent years to represent a figure close to or even higher than 50 per cent of total detainees. In nine countries, i.e. half of the total, their share in the prison population is not less than c. 30 per cent. Second, the differences between the percentage values registered in the various countries are striking.

As regards the overall figures (see the total in Table 5.2), the latest data in the chronological sequence tell us that a quarter of the total prison population consists of non-nationals. The average value between the percentages of all countries is also higher than the total share, and in more recent years has grown to almost 30 per cent. The fact that the average is higher than the total share means that the countries that have a small number of detainees in absolute values – in practice the countries with lesser population – also have a higher percentage of non-national detainees. Belgium, Greece, Luxembourg, Austria and Switzerland are the best examples of this phenomenon. It is quite the reverse of what is ascertained with regard to the incarceration rate per 100,000 population, which is in general lower precisely in these countries.

If we look at the variations in the individual countries in the period in question (1985–2005), we cannot fail to notice the substantial percentage increases that have taken place in Finland, Ireland, Greece, Austria, Italy, Iceland, Spain (as well as in the UK, though there it is fair to say that down to 1990 we have to rely on estimates for non-nationals in prison and these are decidedly underrated, as comparison with the official data for the immediately successive period shows, so that we have had to have recourse to extrapolations for the period prior to 1990). Particularly relevant is the fact that during the period examined (1985–2005), the greatest increases in the percentage of non-nationals in prison were registered by countries in which this share had previously been lower (Figure 5.1). High shares of non-nationals in prison thus became a generalized phenomenon throughout Western Europe.

The total figures of non-national detainees (see in total in Table 5.2), if analysed diachronically, show a constant tendency to increase, with the result that the percentage of non-national detainees doubled between 1985 and 2000 and continued to grow further in the following years. The sharp increase in the rate of detainees per 100,000 population in the countries of Western Europe as a whole (Table 5.1) is in part explained by this increase in the percentage of non-national detainees as a share of the total prison population. The two indicators, however, do not have a parallel trend. The incarceration rate per 100,000 population followed a growing trend practically everywhere in Europe, at least since the start of the 1990s. The percentage of non-national detainees, by contrast, has declined in recent years in several countries – Germany, Greece, France, Sweden, Netherlands – and has remained constant in Belgium. The phenomenon finds no explanation in the trend of the non-national population resident in these countries.

Moreover, the entire aspect of the relationship between the presence of non-nationals and incarceration rates in Western Europe challenges some common beliefs. First, the belief that countries with high rates of non-nationals among their resident population would have – because of this – prisons bursting at the seams, is unsupported by evidence. In Europe, there is no relation at all between incarceration rates and non-national population. Besides, variations in the non-national share of population recorded from 1985 onward haven't been associated with variations in incarceration rates. For instance, the Netherlands, Luxembourg and the United Kingdom – which had the biggest increases in prison population – registered relatively contained variations in their non-national share of resident population. Second, the belief that high shares of non-nationals among the prison population are associated with high incarceration rates is also unfounded. Variations in the share of non-nationals in prison from 1985 onward show a negative correlation with variations in incarceration rates. Countries like Austria, Iceland and Finland, where huge increases in the share of non-nationals among the prison population were registered, had limited increases in incarceration rates. In countries like the Netherlands, Sweden and the United Kingdom, where on the contrary massive increases in incarceration rates were registered, the contribution given by the share of non-nationals in prison was limited. In other words, the growth of the share of non-nationals in prison has contributed to the general growth of prison population in Europe: however, in some countries non-national detainees have in part taken the place of national ones, as often the case with people charged with criminal offences (see Chapter 4); and the massive increases in prison population registered in some European countries aren't explained by variations of the share of non-nationals in prison.

Ultimately, the reasons for this overall increase of incarceration rates in Europe are not easy to identify. One can certainly speak of the emergence of a more punitive attitude at the popular level: a phenomenon that has

Table 5.2 Percentage of non-national detainees out of the total prison population in the countries of Western Europe – Years: 1985–2005

States	1985	1987	1989	1991	1993	1995	1997	1999	2001	2003	2005
B	27.6	27.4	31.1	33.7	40.6	41.0	38.2	38.4	40.7	41.0	41.2
DK	7.2	10.7	14.1	11.7	13.9	13.7	13.6	15.9	16.7	16.4	18.2
D	14.5	14.5	14.5	14.5	22.0	29.4	33.6	33.1	31.0	29.1	28.0
EL	16.3	18.7	26.6	21.8	25.6	32.3	38.6	46.8	47.2	42.3	41.6
E	10.6	13.0	15.2	16.3	16.0	15.5	17.8	18.3	22.1	26.5	30.1
F	26.4	26.6	27.8	29.8	29.8	28.5	26.0	23.7	21.6	21.7	20.5
IRL	1.8	1.1	1.1	1.3	4.9	6.4	8.3	7.5	7.8	8.8	9.5
I	8.9	8.7	8.6	15.2	14.9	17.4	22.1	26.4	29.3	30.8	33.0
L	43.3	38.5	41.2	39.7	49.2	53.9	54.6	57.6	61.5	69.3	71.4
NL	15.3	18.8	24.2	25.2	29.0	31.1	31.9	31.8	30.0	28.2	32.9
A	8.1	8.8	14.2	22.3	26.1	26.9	26.9	29.2	31.6	39.0	45.4
P	4.9	7.3	7.6	7.7	8.4	10.7	12.4	13.8	15.2	16.6	18.5
FIN	0.3	0.3	0.3	0.9	1.6	2.4	4.5	5.5	7.4	8.1	7.5
S	21.1	21.6	21.6	19.5	25.4	25.6	26.1	24.0	21.4	20.7	20.9
UK	2.9	3.8	4.7	7.1	6.0	7.8	7.8	8.2	9.8	11.7	12.7
ISL	1.1	1.3	1.8	2.2	2.0	1.6	2.9	4.0	6.2	8.3	11.8
NOR	8.1	10.7	11.9	11.0	13.1	14.1	14.6	12.7	14.0	17.1	17.8
CH	34.6	35.4	41.2	43.9	47.1	57.5	60.3	62.0	66.7	70.7	70.5
Total	12.5	14.0	15.1	17.3	19.3	21.5	23.2	23.7	24.3	24.9	26.2
Aver. val.	14.1	14.8	17.1	18.0	20.9	23.1	24.5	25.5	26.6	28.1	29.5

Source: Conseil de l'Europe 1986–1987–1988–1989–1990–1991–1992–1993–1994/95–1996, 2000, 2002; Council of Europe 2003.

NB: For 1999, 2001 and 2003, the Conseil de l'Europe did not gather data on non-national detainees in prison for its periodic publication SPACE I; we calculated the data for the years in question by interpolation. Denmark: the data for 1985, 1986, 1987 and 1988 have likewise been calculated by interpolation. Germany: 1985–91 data are estimates; the data for 1992, 1993, 1994, 1996 by interpolation. Greece: data for 1990, 1993, 1994 and 1995 by interpolation. Ireland: data for 1990 and 1993 by interpolation. Netherlands: data for 1995 by interpolation. Portugal: data for 1987 and 1995 by interpolation; data subjected to smoothing since the end of the 1990s, due to sharp annual variations. Sweden: the percentages refer to the population of sentenced detainees. UK: 1985–90 data by extrapolation. Iceland: data for 1990, 1991, 1992 and 1996 by interpolation; data subjected to smoothing, due to sharp annual variations resulting from low number of cases. Norway: data for 1989 and 1992 by interpolation. Switzerland: the percentages refer to the population of sentenced detainees; 1994 data by interpolation.

characterized the USA as also Europe in part (Garland 2001; Nelken 2009) and that is at variance with the downward trend of a part of criminality, as is the case of homicides in Western Europe, as we have seen (above, Chapter 4). The emergence of this 'popular punitiveness', in turn, is difficult to explain. Its causes might be sought in the contrast between the growing political autonomy of ordinary people and their decreasing ability to defend themselves against the threats of the competition of an ever more globalized world.

The overall percentages of non-nationals in prison are undoubtedly disturbing, since they are so disproportionate to the share of non-nationals out of the total population in Western Europe, as can also be shown by a rapid comparison with Table 3.6 in Chapter 3.

To sum up, three significant findings can be deduced from the data we have just presented: (1) the existence of considerable differences between the countries of Western Europe in terms of the share of non-nationals out of the total prison population; (2) an overall over-representation of non-nationals in the prison population; and (3) a sharp overall increase of non-nationals

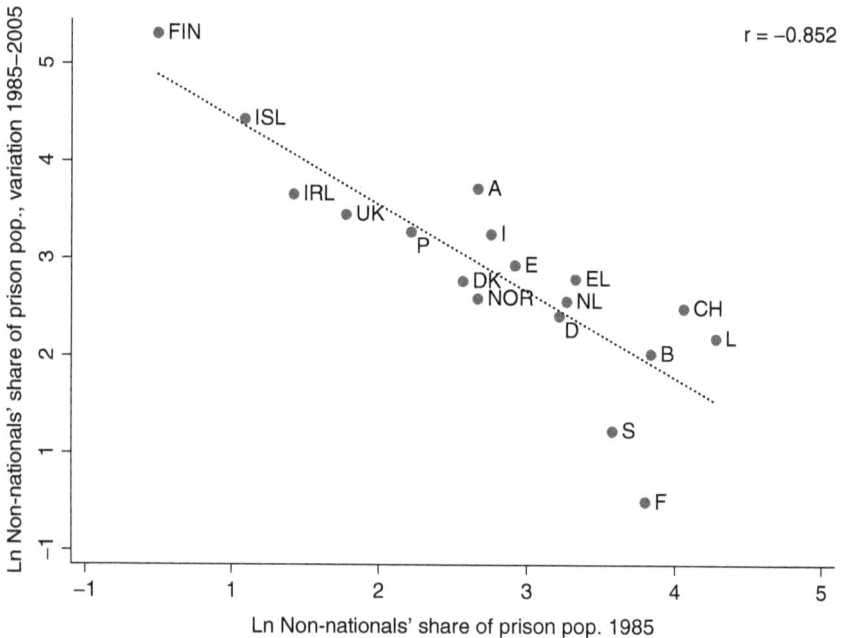

Figure 5.1 Distribution of European countries according to the share of non-nationals in prison in 1985 and the variation of the share in the following period (1985–2005): linear regression fit line and coefficient.

NB: Since Non-nationals' share 1985 => 0.3, then x = Ln (Non-nationals' share 1985 + 0.7); since Variation 1985–2005 => –1.12, then y = Ln (Variation 1985–2005 + 2.12).

in prison, with a generalization of the phenomenon of high shares of non-nationals among the prison population, though the trend is not uniform in the various countries.

Table 5.3 shows further relevant data: those relating to non-nationals charged for the various offences in each country. Unfortunately, the data in question are not available for all countries. The UK, as we have already pointed out, statistically surveys the *ethnic origin* of those charged, but not their citizenship; Ireland does not provide these data. In other countries, the data do not always cover all the categories of crime. Moreover, the data for charged offences in the various countries have characteristics that call for some degree of caution in using them in an investigation of comparative type. The problem consists in the main of the already underlined differences between one country and another. These differences especially derive from the inclusion or not of specific violations in the penal field, from procedural differences, and from the characteristics of national criminality. To overcome this problem as far as possible, here too we have preferred to concentrate our analysis on the *non-nationals share* in the criminal phenomenon of each country: in practice, that means we have privileged the data consisting of the percentage of non-nationals out of all those charged (both for the single types of offences and for their total), rather than the rates of charged non-nationals per non-national population. It is clear that not even this methodological procedure (as indeed any other) is watertight. If there are sharp differences in the level of involvement of non-nationals in the individual types of offence, the share of non-nationals out of the overall total of those charged could be at variance with the average share of non-nationals in the main types of crime. From Table 5.3 it may be deduced that cases of this kind were ascertained. This is the case of Italy, where this deviation is attributable in the main to the fact that while the most numerically widespread offence in the country has been the issuing of dud cheques, the involvement of non-nationals in this offence is far lower than that registered for homicide, theft, robbery, rape and drug trafficking. Moreover, if these differences in the level of involvement of non-nationals in the individual types of offence are compounded by differences in penal policy, further distortions could emerge. For example, if a particular country treats the exploitation of prostitution in a very tolerant way, and if at the same time non-nationals are significantly more involved in this crime than they are in others on average, then the share of non-nationals out of the total of those charged in that country will be influenced by that.

So the data on indictments need to be treated with caution; and to reduce the danger of comparisons between incompatible sets of data it is preferable to consider the figures relating to the individual categories of offence, as well as those relating to the total offences.

With these provisos in mind, we may note that Luxembourg is the country where charged non-nationals are most numerous in percentage terms.

Table 5.3 Percentage of non-nationals charged by types of offence (and total offences) out of all those charged for offences in the countries of Western Europe – Year: 2000 or the closest year for which data are available

States	Intent Homicides	Sexual Offences	Rape	Griev. Bodily Harm	Theft (All)	Aggrav. Theft	Robbery	Burglary	Car Thefts	Other Thefts	Fraud	Counter-feiting	Drug Offences	Total Offences
B	40.0		24.6	27.3	42.2		49.1				30.4	42.9	40.9	27.3
DK	12.5	22.5	41.2	23.4	17.2		30.5	11.2	11.6		12.3		17.7	16.6
D	34.0	20.9	33.2	27.3	22.3	25.9	31.5	23.5	22.0	21.5	22.8	48.4	23.5	27.1
EL	21.9	28.0	21.5	3.7	26.0	37.3	35.2	33.1	22.8	32.9	7.7	23.1	8.1	4.9
E	18.3	18.6		18.0	12.5	16.0	17.2	15.3		13.9	23.1		7.0	33.1
F	15.6	11.1	12.9	16.4	14.7	12.2	15.0	10.7	9.8	16.2	14.7	22.3	9.9	18.4
IRL														
I	22.1	30.4	25.5		31.9		29.5						35.3	19.0
L	100.0	34.0	39.5	46.2	52.1	45.5	42.7	42.6	34.1	58.1	77.4	75.0	53.5	52.0
NL	29.4	20.5	27.0		25.9	29.1	32.5	25.6			22.9	26.8	25.9	27.1
A	25.5		28.8	24.7	25.1	34.1	42.8	29.6	64.0	20.2	20.2	59.6	15.4	19.4
P	8.2		10.6		4.5	3.1	6.0						6.1	6.4
FIN	5	15	28	1	7		12			11	7	52	4	4
S	27		32	18	22	5	20	13	11				16	20
UK	20													
ISL	10.0	7.4	7.7	5.3	4.2	3.0	7.5	2.8			4.8	4.7	3.7	5.6
NOR	13	6	14	9	16	15	13		9	18	8	5	11	11
CH	59.7	37.0	65.9	54.6	59.8		53.4	63.2	54.4	34.0	39.5	29.5	29.5	43.7
Aver. val.	27.6	21.0	27.5	21.1	24.0	20.6	27.4	24.6	26.5	25.1	22.4	36.0	19.2	21.0

Source: Interpol 1996, 2000; Italy Istat 2002; Council of Europe 1999, 2003, 2006.

NB: For Belgium, Denmark, Portugal, the Netherlands and Iceland, data furnished by their Ministries of Justice, at our request. In the case of Belgium, the data comprise those recorded offenders who have already received a sentence. The data for Denmark comprise only those cases opened and closed in the course of the same year. For Portugal and Sweden, the total is represented by the average values for the various categories of offence.

Very high levels are also registered in Switzerland, Spain, Germany, Belgium, and the Netherlands. As regards the various types of offence, we may note the high percentage of non-nationals, on average, among those charged for homicide, theft, robbery, and counterfeiting. In the case of the UK, only a recent police estimate of the percentage of non-nationals among those charged for intentional homicide (20 per cent of the total) is available. On the other hand, the data on the percentage of non-whites among those charged are widely available. Clearly, there is no coincidence between non-whites and non-nationals: there are non-whites who are citizens of the UK (roughly half of them born in the UK) and non-nationals who are whites. The percentage of non-whites among those indicted for intentional homicide (20 per cent) coincides with the police estimates on the percentage of non-nationals out of the total charged for this offence. The percentages of non-nationals out of the total indicted for homicide in the UK are approximately four times higher than the percentages of non-nationals out of the total resident population; and also for the category of non-whites the over-representation is approximately four times (UK 2003: figures are based on England and Wales data, which represent *c.* 9/10 of UK homicides). The percentage of non-whites among those charged for robbery is approximately seven times higher than their share of the resident population; for sexual offences four times; for drug trafficking offences, more than four times.

Altogether, the percentages relating to the non-nationals' share of those charged for penal offences confirm what has already emerged from the figures for the non-nationals' share of the total prison population: namely, that (1) non-nationals impact in very different ways, from one country to another, on the official dimension of the criminal phenomenon, even taking into account their share of the population of the country in question; (2) non-nationals tend to contribute in a disproportionate way to the official dimension of criminality in the countries of Europe. As regards the second point, the figures show that the percentages of non-nationals among those charged are decidedly higher than the percentages of non-nationals among the resident population in their respective countries (Table 3.6). With the exception of Luxembourg and, to a lesser degree, of France and Iceland, the over-representation of the non-national population among those charged for the standard crimes is pronounced.

The convergence between the data relating to charged non-nationals and the data relating to non-nationals in prison is also striking. Let us consider in this regard the percentage share of charged non-nationals out of all those charged for the most significant offences (Table 5.3); and then calculate the mean value for all the countries for which we have available data. We thus obtain a mean value of 28 per cent for intentional homicide; 28 per cent for rape; 27 per cent for robbery; and 19 per cent for drug trafficking. For thefts, depending on type, the percentages of charged non-nationals out of the total charged vary from 21 per cent to 27 per cent. These are the offences that most impact on prison admissions. And the mean percentages for them are close to (and in general higher than) both the share of non-nationals out of the total number of detainees in Europe, which, as shown by Table 5.2, was of the order of 23–24 per cent in the final years of the twentieth century, and the mean share, for all countries, of detained non-nationals, which was of the order of 25–26 per cent (i.e. a quarter of the total prison population) during the same years.

This convergence provides further corroboration of the reliability of the measurements of the phenomenon studied, and indirectly of the soundness of the methodological procedures followed here. At the same time, in the light of the data relating to charged non-nationals, the problem of discrimination against non-nationals – a problem particularly posed by non-nationals in prison – is diminished. The data tabulated above do not invalidate the claim that custodial measures are used more frequently for non-nationals; a claim advanced, and backed up with considerable empirical evidence, by various studies (Chapter 1). The data show, nonetheless, that the very high rates of detention for non-nationals coincide with the high rates of indictment in which non-nationals are involved. And these high rates of indictment are, as we have explained, more difficult to impute to discriminatory attitudes.

The data on charged non-nationals also seem to invalidate another hypothesis: namely, that non-nationals are objectively discriminated against since the offences they commit tend to be among those characterized by greater visibility and hence less likely to vanish into the *dark figure* of crimes that remain unreported and hence ignored by criminal statistics. While some concentration of charged non-nationals may be ascertained in the perpetration of particular types of offence (e.g. counterfeiting), it may be noted, more generally, that charged non-nationals are distributed between a wide range of crimes, covering all the main forms of criminality: from those against the person (homicides, rapes) to those against property (thefts, robberies).

The fact that charged non-nationals are distributed between a wide range of crimes is also an obstacle to cultural conflict theory, given that this theory rests in part on the assumption that the criminality of non-nationals tends to be concentrated on some 'special' (culturally determined) offences. From Table 5.3 it emerges, on the contrary, that the percentage of non-nationals out of all those charged is high for all the standard forms of criminality, in short for all the 'banal' offences – from car theft to robbery – that do not usually imply any cultural peculiarity. Moreover, a particularly disproportionate involvement of non-nationals in some types of offence, such as counterfeiting, can be explained by the role played by non-nationals as intermediaries between different political and economic realities. It can therefore be explained by reference not to inherited cultural characteristics but to objective material conditions. The only crime for which the influence of cultural factors can more plausibly be alleged is rape. The share of non-nationals among those charged for rape is in general higher than that registered for total crimes in the various countries (with the exception of Belgium, France and Luxembourg).

5.2 Non-nationals' incarceration index

The substantial share of non-nationals in the official figures for criminality in Europe represents a macroscopic datum with which we need to come to terms. But this share does not seem particularly useful for explaining the relations between immigration and criminality. More useful, in this perspective, would seem to be an analysis of another significant aspect: that of the sharp differences that emerge in the various countries as regards the percentages of non-nationals among both those charged and those detained.

For purposes of this analysis, we first need to devise an indicator that may permit a better comparison of the involvement of non-nationals in the penal and penitentiary circuits in the various countries of Europe. Such an indicator ought, in the first place, to measure a relevant aspect in the framework of penal justice. At the same time, at a more technical level, it ought to be based on as complete, homogeneous and valid data as possible. More particularly as regards validity of data, it ought to satisfy two essential conditions. First, it ought to take into due account the size of the non-national population in the various countries. Second, it ought to reduce as far as possible the distorting influence of the differences between the various countries in terms of the actions of their law enforcement agencies in tackling criminality, for these differences, as we have already underlined, impact on the *dark figure* for crime in the various countries.

The indicator of the non-national population in detention presents some advantages in this perspective. Incarceration – depriving human subjects of some basic civil liberties as a result of the (grave) antisocial conduct attributed to them – is full of consequences not only for those who more directly suffer its effects, but also for the society responsible for its infliction. From a purely social point of view, incarceration assumes greater significance than, for example, penal indictments, or penal sentences, not to mention the mere fact of perpetrating deviant forms of behaviour in the first place. If it is true that a person may be sent to prison without having been sentenced, it is equally true that many sentenced offenders don't receive a custodial sentence. And if not everyone charged ends up in prison, all those detained in prison have at least been indicted for a criminal offence. The data on incarceration may not be the best indicator of criminality, but they are undoubtedly a sound measure of incrimination. By analysing the data on incarceration as an indicator of the problems of penal justice incurred by non-nationals in their host country, we will be dealing simultaneously with a central aspect both of the penal system and of social phenomena of adaptation, integration, and so on. We are persuaded, indeed, that even the most radical critics of the value of official criminal statistics would agree in attributing great importance to this indicator, at least as a reflection of the scale of the problems of interaction, reception, integration and adaptation between non-nationals and the host country.

In the second place, the data on the non-national population in detention represents, from a technical point of view, a valuable indicator since such data are readily available for all eighteen of the countries considered by the present research, and in general cover a fairly long time span. The data in question, moreover, have a high degree of reliability, for they share the advantage of all prison statistics, based as they are on counting a population that is almost by definition 'under control' and hence statistically verifiable. There can be few doubts about whether or not a person belongs to the category of prison inmates, or whether or not a person is in prison (Newman *et al.* 2007). But figures on the prison population, we should not forget, regard only a part of the officially registered criminality: that part of criminality whose perpetrators are being detained in prison either after sentencing by the courts or while awaiting sentence. All this could represent a limitation, since the remaining part of the officially registered criminality would be ignored; but on the other hand it represents a useful aspect, since figures on the prison population usually regard crimes of some gravity, the penal treatment and custodial sentences for which tend to be more homogeneous in the various countries. This fact differentiates the data for those imprisoned from the data for those charged: the latter, as we have already underlined, also regard violations of relatively minor importance, which in some countries are differently treated or even excluded from the list of those treated by the criminal justice agencies.

The data of the non-national population in detention also lend themselves to a calculation aimed at keeping under control the problem of the *dark figure*. The non-nationals' share of the total prison population in the countries of Western Europe is unlikely, we believe, to be unduly influenced by any differences between the size of the *dark figure* in the various countries. A country, for example, with a higher incidence of the *dark figure* would probably present lower official crime figures; in particular, proportionately fewer crimes reported to the police, fewer persons charged and fewer prison admissions. But the non-nationals' share of the total prison population ought not to be affected by all this.

The problem remains of how to take into account also the size of the non-national population in the various countries. As we have seen, the percentage of the non-national population is very different in the European countries to which this analysis is devoted: and an indicator that does not take this fact into account would not have much comparative value. This problem can be overcome by combining, in a single indicator, both information relating to the non-nationals' share of the prison population, and information relating to the non-nationals' share of the total population in the various countries. On the basis of these considerations, we have constructed an indicator for all countries, which we denominate the 'relative incarceration index'. It consists of the *percentage of non-nationals in prison out of the total prison population, divided by the percentage of non-nationals out of the total resident population.* In this way, a value for example equal to 2 means that the country to which the figure refers has a percentage of non-nationals in prison out of the total prison population that is twice that of non-nationals out of the total resident population.

This incarceration index has been calculated for all years from 1985 to 2005. From these data we have also derived the *average incarceration index,* for successive periods during this time span (Table 5.4). The periods are sufficiently long to keep under control short-term variations, variations that regard in particular the percentage of non-nationals out of the resident population, following new influxes of immigrants and the regularization of those already there.

Table 5.4 only adds further corroborating evidence to the general impression we already gained from Table 5.2, relating to the percentage of non-nationals in detention out of the total prison population in the countries of Western Europe. In fact, these two tables show in the first place that the non-nationals' share of the prison population is larger than their share of the resident population. If we observe the average incarceration index in the various periods considered in Table 5.4, we may note that on average the non-nationals' share of the total prison population is over four times higher than their share of the resident population.

This over-representation of non-nationals in prison is shown, moreover, in a way that remains fairly constant in time. This in itself suggests that the data are reliable. Yet, if we look at Table 5.4 more closely, we will see that diachronic changes *have* taken place. In the last decennial period examined we may note a diminution of the index for some of the countries that formerly registered the highest values. The countries in question, such as Portugal, Spain and Greece, are those in which the phenomenon of immigration was recent and at the same time underwent rapid growth. The decrease, in these countries, of the non-nationals' incarceration index suggests that a process of better integration might be underway and that the more recent immigrants might have benefited from the integration achieved by those who preceded them, in particular by those who belong to their same ethnic groups. The other countries, by contrast, don't show an improvement in the values of the index, so that the average value presents fractional variations.

At this point we should stress that the over-representation of non-nationals in the prison population, as shown by the incarceration index, cannot be explained by any structural dissimilarities existing between the national and non-national populations. The first of these dissimilarities consists of the respective size of the male and female populations. The contribution of

Table 5.4 Relative incarceration index of non-nationals in the countries of Western Europe – Average values for the periods 1985–1995; 1990–2000; 1995–2005; 1985–2005; the years 1990–2000 adjusted for gender, age groups and illegal immigration

States	Relative incarceration index				
	1985–1995	1990–2000	1995–2005	1985–2005	1990–2000 adjusted for gender, age & ill. immigr.
B	3.8	4.3	4.7	4.2	2.9
DK	3.9	3.5	3.2	3.6	2.4
D	2.5	3.1	3.5	3.0	2.1
EL	13.0	12.2	9.9	11.4	7.4
E	15.3	12.8	8.8	12.1	7.8
F	4.5	4.7	4.2	4.3	3.1
IRL	1.1	2.0	2.1	1.6	1.4
I	9.5	10.1	10.1	9.8	6.1
L	1.5	1.5	1.7	1.6	1.0
NL	5.5	6.5	7.1	6.3	4.3
A	2.7	3.1	3.5	3.1	2.1
P	8.4	7.0	5.6	7.0	4.5
FIN	1.1	2.1	3.2	2.2	1.5
S	4.3	4.2	4.2	4.2	2.9
UK	1.5	2.0	2.3	1.9	1.3
ISL	0.9	1.2	1.8	1.4	0.6
NOR	3.5	3.6	3.7	3.6	2.5
CH	2.5	2.8	3.3	2.9	1.9
Aver. val.	4.7	4.8	4.6	4.7	3.1

males to criminality is everywhere far higher than that of females, and so a large, or preponderant, share of males among the non-national population could, or more probably would, influence the rates of criminality. Now, in some non-national communities (e.g. those recently arrived and coming from Islamic countries) the percentage of males may be very high; but this is offset by other communities in which the female share in the non-national population is far higher. Throughout Western Europe the male share of all non-nationals is not in fact over-represented; it is around 48 per cent (see Chapter 6.3, Sopemi 2006), in other words, a percentage slightly lower than that registered in the resident population as a whole; and the differences registered between country and country are limited (Wanner 2002). There are exceptions, but these consist of countries in which it is women, and not men, who preponderate among the non-national population. That's the case of Iceland, of which we have taken account in our calculations. In short, we can conclude that the share of males and females among the non-national population is of little significance for the indices of criminality relating to *all* non-nationals; it could, on the other hand, be significant if we wanted to study the case of some specific non-national community.

The question of age groups is more significant for our purposes. Non-national populations tend on average to be more concentrated in particular age groups (those of adults and young adults). The problem is that it is just these age groups that make a greater contribution to the criminal phenomenon. Not surprisingly, only a small percentage of the prison population consists of the elderly. Half of the prison population in Western Europe is aged between 18 and 33 (Conseil de l'Europe 2001, 2003). And the share of the age groups above the age of 40 rapidly decreases. If we consider only the critical age group 18–39, we find that the percentage of non-nationals out of the prison population grows when compared with the percentage calculated without taking age groups into consideration (Table 5.2); but the increase shown by the share of non-nationals among the resident population – when we shift from all ages to only the 18–39 age group – is definitely bigger (Table 3.6). So when critical age groups are taken into account, the indices of the criminality of non-nationals are closer to those of nationals (Solivetti 1999; Holmberg and Kyvsgaard 2003). To obtain a non-nationals' incarceration index that takes into account the problem of age groups, reference could be made to the percentages of non-nationals belonging exclusively to a specific age group, both in prison and in the resident population. Precise calculations along these lines for all countries are difficult to carry out, because the data on the age groups of non-nationals present some gaps, and especially the data on the ages of non-national detainees are decidedly in short supply. So we are forced to have recourse to estimates to get round the problem. An increase of between 20 and 40 per cent – depending on case – of the percentage of non-nationals among the resident population ought sufficiently to compensate for the greater share of non-nationals in the critical age group between 18 and 39, both inside and outside prison (Eurostat 2006; see also Hagan and Palloni 1999). As a consequence, the values of the incarceration index decrease; but the overall over-representation of non-nationals in the prison population is far from disappearing.

This over-representation of non-nationals in the prison population, moreover, cannot be considered a mere effect of the number of non-nationals in a condition of irregularity or clandestinity, which in turn determines the underestimation of the resident non-national population. The clandestine or irregular component has reached a considerable level in some countries. European governments, however, consider its re-absorption an absolute priority in immigration policy (Sopemi 2000). This trend towards re-absorption has become almost universal in Western Europe; it is confirmed by the various regularizations implemented in the countries most affected by the phenomenon, to which we have already referred. Besides, it is also in the interest of almost all clandestine or irregular immigrants themselves that this component should be re-absorbed. So the clandestine condition can be assumed to have a transitory character (Garson and Loizillon 2003). In short, the share of clandestine immigration in a wide time span – such as that taken into consideration here for the average non-nationals' incarceration index – is likely to be substantially lower than that registered in particularly critical periods, not least as a result of the siphon-effect of successive regularizations.

The countries in which there is, in the view of a consensus of experts, a substantial share of clandestine immigrants are Spain, Italy and Greece. These countries are also those in which the highest values of the non-nationals' incarceration index are registered. If we were to re-calculate the incarceration index taking into account the most plausible estimates of the number of clandestine immigrants, the non-nationals' incarceration index would continue to show abnormal values for these countries, in comparison with those of other countries in Western Europe. The other countries, too, also have a share of clandestine non-nationals: and also for this reason the differences between the incarceration indices would not change much. However, to leave no stone unturned, we re-estimated the incarceration index also by calculating the clandestine component. To do so we availed ourselves of the most reliable international estimates (Wanner 2002; Jandl 2003; Sopemi 2004) and increased the figures of the non-national population in the various countries by 5 per cent, 10 per cent, and 20 per cent respectively, depending on their level of illegal immigration. The values of the incarceration index – recalculated for the intermediate period 1990–2000 – descend further (Table 5.4), but still remain very high for many countries, while in others they are substantially proportionate to the share of the immigrant population in the resident population.

The sharp differences between the various countries are shown by Chart 5.1, which shows – by means of value symbols – the figures for the relative incarceration index.

The fact that the non-nationals' incarceration index has higher values in countries in which there is also a high share of clandestine immigrants – as in Southern European countries – can hardly, in sum, be regarded as coincidental, or the consequence of a mere imprecision in the incarceration index estimate. It seems more likely to be a consequence of the social condition of such immigrants: a reflection, more especially, of the fact that a high share of clandestine immigrants is synonymous with a situation of social anomie, social hardship, and poor integration.

What is undoubtedly important to point out is that the countries that show a higher non-nationals' incarceration index also present a different profile in terms of their socio-economic and cultural characteristics and the type of immigration they attract. It is reasonable to assume that there may

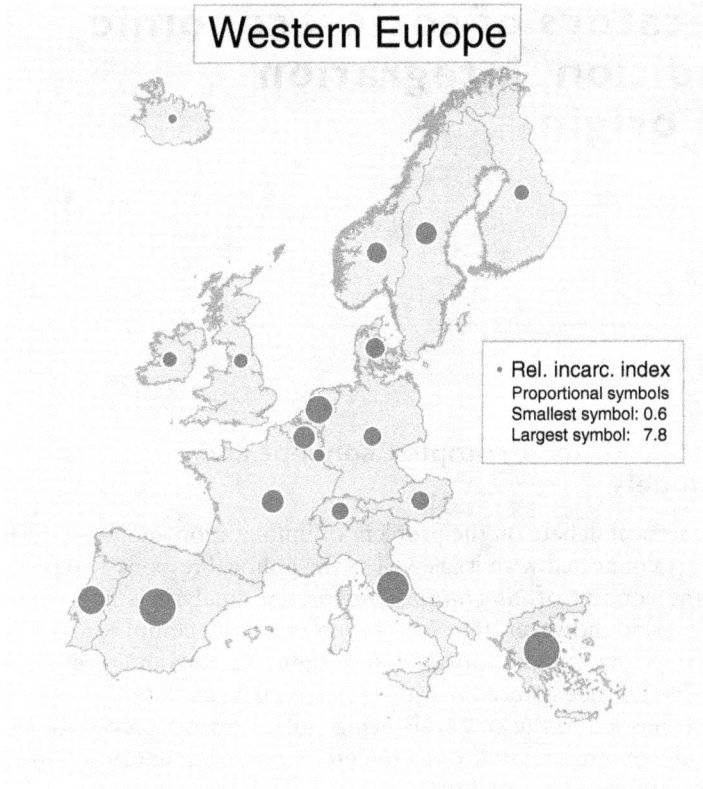

Chart 5.1 Non-nationals' incarceration index in the countries of Western Europe – Average values for the years 1990–2000 adjusted for gender, age groups and illegal immigration.

be a relation between these characteristics and the different share of non-nationals out of the prison population and out of the population of those indicted for criminal offences in the various countries.

In pursuing further our investigation we will use the values of Table 5.4 as a fundamental indicator of the different involvement of non-nationals in penal and penitentiary circuits.

Chapter 6

Indicators of socio-economic condition, integration and origin

6.1 Integration: a complex concept and five models

The theoretical debate on the problem of immigration and the hardships so frequently connected with it (as well as the political responses to it) revolves round the concept of *integration*. Our present analysis is no exception. It should be said, however, that *integration* is a more complex and less obvious concept than might appear at first sight. Various interpretations of it exist. Nor can it be ignored that there has been an *evolution* in conceptualization. It has led to the emphasis being shifted from a process of assimilation to one of integration, from a unilateral approach in terms of culture to a multicultural and intercultural approach.

We can identify at least three forms of integration in the broad sense: (1) *social integration*, represented by changes in immigrants' conditions, measured on the basis of the positions they occupy in the economy, in consumption, in habitat and in education; (2) *cultural assimilation*, which regards the cultural transformations connected with the process of immigration, including the immigrant's understanding of and adaptation to the fundamental rules of the host society; and (3) *political participation* (Dubet 1989). Socio-economic integration and cultural assimilation, and the interaction between them, are assumed to be the main processes for the immigrant's insertion in the host society. This scheme, however, seems somewhat reductive as regards both the aspect of integration and that of assimilation.

Assimilation, in our view, is a concept of many facets, many forms and many levels, some of which are particularly significant also in the light of the evolution of the migratory phenomenon itself. Assimilation may consist in an almost total rejection and abandonment of the immigrant's original culture. But it may also be a gradual learning process: a gradual adjustment to the basic values and norms of social life in the host country, but without the abandonment of the deepest core of the immigrant's original values. At the same time, these forms of assimilation may emerge in a more general context that imposes assimilation as the precondition for being accepted; or in a context so rich in opportunities for the immigrant, and so absorbing as to determine an assimilation by inner conviction; or in a context characterized by what used to be called *cultural pluralism*, and what is now more commonly called *multiculturalism*: in this case the adaptation will be partial; it will be a two-way process inspired by mutual cultural respect.

As for integration, some further qualifications need to be made. We could think of integration, understood in general terms, as a condition in which non-nationals achieve a stable and balanced relationship within the host society (Venchiarutti 2001). But that is undoubtedly a rigid and reductive conception. It implies that there is only *one* model of integration and this model is, so to say, the 'conformist' model of the host society. An example may help clarify the limitations of the model in question. It is by no means rare for immigrants to arrive in Western Europe from the Far East without any knowledge of the language, culture and organization of the host country, and yet who are immediately inserted into the commercial or other activities managed by their own compatriots and who in social terms mix only with their own ethnic community. It seems hard to deny that these immigrants have in some way been integrated: but it is an integration only within the microcosm of their own ethnic group within the host country. This is a scenario of integration that is limited to the immigrant's own ethnic community, and confined to legitimate activities. But far from unrealistic is another scenario: that of immigrants for whom integration is limited to their own ethnic community and accompanied by decidedly illegal activities: e.g. international drug trafficking. Nor should a form of integration of the immigrant directly in the criminal activities of the host society be ignored. This is a rarer event, because in general relations with criminal or delinquent groups in the host society are mediated by the immigrant's ethnic group. But it draws attention to the fact that the host society already contains processes of integration other than the 'conformist' one.

It would undoubtedly be misleading, however, to ignore or underestimate the model of conformist integration, not only because it is 'predominant' – in terms not just of power but also of consensus – but also because it makes no sense to speak of criminal activities unless in relation to parameters of legality connected to this model of integration. Yet if we wish to understand the mechanisms of criminality and their relation with immigration, it would be as well to bear in mind these alternative processes of integration. In short, there may be integration in work and integration in society, and these two forms of integration may not coincide; both may be achieved in the host society or in the ethnic group to which the immigrant belongs and which has been transplanted to the host society; both may be based on a conformist or on a deviant/criminal model.

In recent years there has been a lot of discussion about so-called *segmented integration* (Portes and Zhou 1993; Zhou 1997). The introduction of this concept has had the merit of rejecting the previous conception, prevalent in the social sciences in the USA, which regarded integration as a one-way process which – with the passage of time, through acculturation and parallel vocational integration – inevitably led the immigrant from outsider status to perfect integration in the middle class of the host society. The segmented integration approach suggests that it is now possible to combine vocational integration and economic success with the preservation of original values and ethnic community links.

However, if looked at more closely, there had long been abundant material in US social sciences to suggest a situation different from the unilinear model and more complex than that of segmented integration. Whyte, in his *Street Corner Society*, published in 1943, had shown that (1) both deviant and non-integrative choices and those of integration were well represented in the various immigrants belonging to the same generation; (2) it was possible for the same person to pass from the one to the other in time, but the processes of doing so were tortuous and not necessarily one-way; (3) not only the traditional values and those of the host society, but also deviant and integrative forms of behaviour could co-exist in the same person and criminality itself could pave the way for conformist integration.

In any case, as regards the problem of the immigrant's overall balance in the host society, we think it important to point out that the aspects of non-nationals' socio-economic integration and assimilation are inseparable from the socio-economic and cultural characteristics of the host society and from the characteristics deriving from non-nationals' origin. The problem posed by non-nationals' stability in the host country is not just a problem of their propensity or not to integration and assimilation; nor even a problem of the socio-economic and cultural 'opening' of the host society to them. It is an interactive relation. The factors that determine so-called 'integration' consist, in our view, of: (a) the sum of socio-economic conditions in the host country that directly influence social integration; (b) the cultural characteristics and behavioural models of the population of the host country that influence both the social integration of immigrants and their probability of cultural assimilation; (c) the professional skills and qualifications of immigrants that are reflected on their probabilities of social insertion and the attitude of the resident population to them; (d) the culture and ways of life of immigrants that influence their cultural assimilation and also the attitude of the population of the host country.

On the basis of these factors, we can hypothesize some basic models for the adaptation of non-nationals to the host society.

The first model, in analytical order, is the one we could call *integration* cum *assimilation*. Various factors may concur to determine this outcome: socio-economic conditions in the host country favourable to the social and professional integration of immigrants; a culture revolving around *universal* concepts of 'equal rules for everyone' and 'fair shares for everyone';

an attitude of the national population that is not on the whole hostile to immigrants, or at least not hostile to those who show some wish for integration and some effort to achieve it; not too great a disparity between the overall development of the country of origin and that of the host country, or at least a professional qualification of non-nationals that is compatible with the needs of the host country; culture and ways of life of non-nationals that are not too incompatible with those of the local population, or alternatively a willingness on the part of non-nationals to abandon their own culture and their own ways of life in favour of those of the host country; in this latter case, non-nationals will encapsulate their original values and models of conduct in a limited sphere of 'personal & private' type, in which scope will be found for little more than memories, religious beliefs tending to folklore, basic moral precepts especially relating to family life, typical linguistic expressions, and inherited 'ethnic' preferences in cooking and music. In this model, immigrants' links with their own national community *in loco* are not so strong as to prevent assimilation; they are a means to an end, in so far as they are especially aimed at promoting good social and professional integration. Within this model immigrants will seek to dissimulate or disguise their ethnic origin: they will take no pleasure in having others note their foreign accent, their foreign habits, in short their *diversity*. They will seek instead to disavow their roots and underline their dissociation from the society from whence they came. Only their descendents – in particular the third generation – having overcome their sense of ethnic inferiority, will once again be attracted by and seek to cultivate their roots. This model was historically represented, it seems to us, by European immigration to the USA. This was an immigration consisting in large part of those who had abandoned their own homelands for good, inspired by the hope of beginning a new life in a country rich in opportunities in which immigration was not a stigma but a 'normal' condition: a country at the same time in which, beyond the fascinating but somewhat rhetorical image of the *melting pot*, immigrants were obliged to meet precise stipulations for integration and the assimilation of at least some basic values (work, competition, meritocracy, rule of law). Within this model, the probabilities for non-nationals to engage in deviant or criminal activities were limited, or at any rate no higher than those of nationals. Indeed, immigrants were often transformed into diehard defenders of the social and legal system of the host society, critical of those who remained bound to the model of life of their country of origin, and openly censorious of the deviant conduct of fellow non-nationals: in short they became *more catholic than the pope*. In Western Europe, the national situation most similar to this model was probably France. In France, however, in contrast to the USA, the emphasis was placed on cultural assimilation and only secondarily on integration: and assimilation (watchword: 'becoming good Frenchmen'), under the aegis of a strong and homogenizing State (Melotti 1993) and of a culture inspired by *universalism*, was traditionally considered the key to integration. By contrast, the 'British variant' of the *integration* cum *assimilation* model has revolved far more round professional integration and political participation rather than assimilation, while at the same time remaining less open than the USA in terms of cultural differences.

A second and more complex model is characterized by a situation in which social and professional integration is accompanied not so much by *assimilation* as by *cultural adaptation in a multicultural context*. An important element of this version consists in the presence of a sharper differentiation in immigrants between primary and secondary values. Primary values are those that immigrants had learned in their formative years, within primary groups such as the nuclear family and the original community. These are values that concern basic principles of religion, morals, relations within the family and relations between friends, gender roles and the overall attitude in relations with others. Secondary values are those relating to different groups and associations with which immigrants later came into contact. The values in question are those that regard the regulation of social life in general, work, and relations with the institutions. In what we have called the version of *cultural adaptation in a multicultural context*, the immigrant will achieve a form of assimilation that essentially concerns the secondary values. But, in contrast to what happens within our first model, the immigrant will remain strongly attached to his own primary values and continue to cherish them. Indeed, he will feel he is the embodiment of a positive diversity precisely on the basis of these values. Instead of confining them to a sphere of 'personal & private' type, he will use them not only for his own greater security in more intimate relations, but also for the affirmation of his constructive diversity in the process of social and professional integration. It is clear that in this model immigrants' links with their own national community will be stronger and closer. As far as the host society is concerned, *cultural adaptation in a multicultural context* requires a more open, tolerant and flexible attitude on the part of the indigenous population. Without renouncing their own primary and secondary values, nationals can show themselves conscious of the fact that the cultural diversity of immigrants is not necessarily antagonistic to the objective of integration, indeed may help promote it, by exploiting to the best the cultural endowments that immigrants bring with them. *Cultural adaptation in a multicultural context* is also able to mediate between situations of sharp disparity between the socio-cultural heritage and values of immigrants and those of the national population. It has more probability of emerging where immigration has a medium and long-term prospect, not a short-term one. As in the more general *integration* cum *assimilation* model, the probabilities of deviant or criminal behaviour on the part of non-nationals are low. But critical areas remain: situations in which the primary values accidentally come into conflict with the legislative provisions of the host society ('clash of civilizations' scenario). The more probable offences are those relating to family and sexual mores. The model of *cultural adaptation in a multicultural context* has been the guiding principle of immigration policies in the EU in recent decades (watchword: 'unity in diversity'); and is well adapted to high-volume and long-term immigration, like that in Western Europe today. It is at the same time a model that requires of the host society a greater effort of adaptation; it places in question the cultural equilibria that society has acquired; and it always runs the risk of arousing reactions of nationalistic or xenophobic type, or at least of hostility, which are in general proportional also to the effort of adaptation required of nationals themselves.

A third model is characterized by *integration* sine *assimilation*. Here what non-nationals expect, and what they aspire to, is not overall adaptation, but professional integration in the labour market. Emigration in this sense is a less definitive once-and-for-all model. The predominant factors relate to the socio-economic conditions of the host country and the compatibility of immigrants' professional qualifications to them. The cultural disparity between non-nationals and nationals may be considerable. The attitude of nationals to non-nationals may be on the whole less open and *universal*, and less characterized by trust than had been the case not only in the second but also in the first model. Non-nationals may remain strongly attached to their own culture and their own existential values, also on the basis of strong links of community type. Their interest in the host country is usually reduced to the realization of specific material objectives (Albrecht 1997). Their condition may be summed up by the concept of *separation* (Berry 1992), especially as regards social integration (Ambrosini 2005). Situations characterized by a radical version of the *integration* sine *assimilation* model arise in particular: (1) when immigrants work for their compatriots in an ethnic social context within the host country (as mentioned at the beginning of this chapter); (2) when immigrants work in large factories or building sites that employ a sizeable number of their compatriots and keep the immigrant workers separated from the native population. In this model, the probabilities of deviant and criminal forms of behaviour are greater than in the previous case, but not necessarily great. They are linked to the opportunities to engage in occasional criminal acts (e.g. thefts on the workplace) or to commit offences linked to cultural conflicts (physical assault/grievous bodily harm, sexual offences). These criminal activities are incited by the strong links that immigrants retain with their own culture of origin, the cultural gulf that exists between the two populations and the limited trust that may exist between them; but these criminal activities are at the same time limited by non-nationals' positive socio-economic integration. An historic example of this model may readily be found in the emigration of temporary character (that of guest workers) from some European countries with a surplus of labour to other European countries with a deficit of it (e.g. Germany) in the period 1950–1970; an emigration characterized by a prevalence of *pull factors*.

The fourth model is characterized by the combination *assimilation* sine *integration*. In this model, the decisive factors consist, on the one hand, of the socio-economic conditions of the host country and the professional qualifications of non-nationals, both in tendency unfavourable to integration or at odds with each other; on the other hand, by the gradual detachment of non-nationals from their own culture and their own ways of life, and by their at least partial acceptance of the model of life of the host country. This combination has been present in some measure in all historic migratory phenomena (e.g. it was clearly present also in European migration to the USA). It emerges, however, more strongly wherever economic crises intervene and the chances of social and professional integration are diminished; or wherever more simply integration is unsatisfactory, or difficult to achieve, due to the prevalence of a *non-universal* culture in the host society. This combination may also be fostered by the great diffusion, typical of more recent years, of the mass media (film, television, Internet).

Immigrants to Western Europe in recent decades are on average different from those, for instance, of the period 1940–50, due to the fact that they know a good deal more about their country of election. Nonetheless, it is a knowledge that is often distorted. It prospects the existence of a *Schlaraffenland*, a land of milk and honey. And to obtain it, emigrants are willing to renounce even their own way of life, which they perceive as inferior. But the model of life to which they aspire turns out to be in large part unrealizable. The upbeat tales of other emigrants – since it is human to underline success rather than failure – that filter back to the homeland may also have an effect similar to the mass media in their effects on future migrants. There is reason to believe that this combination, *assimilation* sine *integration*, has found a more fertile terrain in Europe in recent times, in combination with the *diffusionism* of the migratory phenomenon and the ever more powerful influence of *push factors*. Push factors in the country of origin (deterioration of social, economic and environmental conditions, political and ethnic conflicts, etc.) understandably encourage a certain disenchantment with the emigrant's original culture and models of life, and a greater propensity to assimilate the models of the host country. But they don't guarantee integration in it. On the contrary, they may even hamper it, favouring as they do a more improvised and 'desperate' emigration. This fourth model is undoubtedly criminogenous. Non-nationals, in this perspective, may stoop to crime (theft, robbery, drug trafficking) to obtain what their poor socio-economic integration denies to them. Crime may also be a way of expressing a negative reaction against the frustration bred of the mismatch between expectation and reality, and against the apparently futile sacrifice of their original values (by committing such crimes as grievous bodily harm, homicide, or rape). Since *assimilation* sine *integration* represents the most criminogenous model – together with that of *non-assimilation* cum *non-integration* (see below) – it will be as well to devote some further remarks to it.

The picture so far presented shows an individual immigrant having to come to terms with the culture of the host country – a culture he has nominally adopted as his own – and with the chances of finding personal satisfaction in it, by the process of social and professional integration in the host country. The image of the social actor as an isolated individual faced by these problems of social and cultural adjustment, however, fails to take into consideration the ethnic community to which the immigrant belongs and to which he continues to refer. This may be of greater or lesser importance, but in any case will not be irrelevant. It may have a crucial importance in the case of *delinquent gangs of immigrants*: in other words, groups of delinquents that emigrate for no other purpose than greater criminal opportunities. In this case, the assimilation of the culture of the host country is likely to be decidedly reductive and linked to such images as 'here you can get rich quick', 'live like kings' etc., while detachment from their culture of origin can be inferred from their contempt for those 'who remained at home' and for the 'closed' society and lack of opportunities they left behind them. Integration in the host country, still less in the labour market, is not even attempted. The ethnic group to which such delinquent immigrants belong – and in particular the criminal sub-group within it – forms the context of social and economic integration, through crime. This mode of adaptation, exemplified by the 'plundering migrant', has long been the nightmare of many natives as also of many immigrants themselves who have achieved conformist integration in their host countries. To ignore this mode would be foolish; to exaggerate its importance an error. Far more common and far more relevant is another mode of adaptation in which migration is not predicated on a criminal project. The links with the ethnic group of origin are less exclusive. Assimilation is less reductive, but the ethnic group of origin diffuses a version of the culture of the host country in which more superficial aspects and secondary values (material success, power with a high visibility over persons and things) prevail. The socio-economic ambitions of the immigrant, in this case, derive at least in part from the general environment, but also take into account the parameters of the society of origin and the local ethnic community ('making good', from the viewpoint of the family of origin, 'sending money home').

Sub-groups of the local ethnic community provide information and opportunities for insertion in illegal income-generating activities that seem more viable, immediate and rewarding than those possible within conformist integration. In this situation, immigrants' investment in social relations within the ethnic community and in power over persons can unsurprisingly prevail against investment in learning, practice and hard work. Conformist integration remains, however, an objective. But it's an objective deferred to a better day: meanwhile the age group within the same ethnic community offers to adolescent non-nationals the social participation and integration that otherwise seems difficult, or impossible, to achieve in the world outside. But tendencies to forms of deviance from the conformist model also emerge in the ethnic group of those of the same generation, and these forms of deviance may all too easily degenerate into criminal activities proper.

The fifth model consists of the combination *non-assimilation* cum *non-integration*. Here the decisive factors may be those linked to a socio-economic situation in the host country and the professional characteristics of non-nationals, both negative, or at least not converging; as also the factors linked to the huge gap between the cultures of the two populations and the strong and enduring bond of non-nationals with their culture of origin and way of life. A crucially important element in this scenario is the strong community links between non-nationals. It's an emigration more easily determined by *push factors* of political or ideological type. Migrants abandon their country of origin, spurred by contingent push factors, but in general they have every intention of returning home one day and retain a strong interest in the culture and situation in their homeland. They frequent subgroups of their compatriots with values similar to their own and show little interest in adapting to the host society. Their social and professional integration oscillates between zero and little. It is in any case temporary and strictly a means to an end, with low personal involvement. The probabilities of deviant forms of behaviour in this situation are high; but those of specifically criminal activities are low. This is because the marginalization of these non-nationals, which is ideologically rather than economically conditioned, and frequently assumes the character of self-exclusion, concurrently reduces their chances of getting involved in crime. Activities of a criminal character may occur on an occasional basis or as a consequence of cultural conflicts (physical assault, homicide), also favoured by their indifference, if not contempt, for the laws and mores of the host country and the hostility with which the local population treats them. The character of marginalization and self-exclusion of these groups makes it likely that any criminal acts they commit are more readily directed at other members of the same ethnic group (political adversaries, compatriots perceived as deviants). The recent emergence in Europe of non-national groups with strong ideological and religious character, such as Islamic fundamentalists, exemplifies this model. In this case, cultural conflicts are exacerbated and have also given rise to forms of criminality of terrorist type. The case of immigrants who form terrorist groups, or are associated with jihadist circles, has assumed particular political and criminal significance in Europe in recent years. It does not exhaust however, the *non-assimilation* cum *non-integration* model.

Other cases, far less topical, have long existed in Europe: for instance, there are Rom communities that are strongly self-referential from a cultural and very little integrated from a social and professional point of view. In contrast to the groups we mentioned above, these do not have ideological motives as the cause of their emigration and do not aspire to return to their country of origin. They exclusively cultivate ties with their own community, and share with those other groups cohesion based on language and culture, as well as the consciousness – untinged by regret – of their own diversity. From a social and professional point of view, they too are characterized by a marginal and temporary integration, to which they add the pursuit of criminal activities on a professional basis (especially car theft, burglary, bag-snatching and petty theft). The perpetration of other crimes is minimized, or precluded, by their lack of interaction with the indigenous population, also due to the suspicion that the latter openly manifests towards them. Other cases of ethnic communities could be cited as exemplifying the model in question: but the cases described here probably represent the extreme examples of a phenomenon with a wide range of intermediate situations.

In conclusion, it should be pointed out that none of the five models identified here is exclusive to any particular migration of the past. They are all present, in varying degrees, in all historical situations. In the current historical phase they are also to be found in all the European countries here being examined. Moreover, they are not stable, in the sense that an immigrant, in the course of his life abroad, may pass from one model to another: in particular, both the *integration* sine *assimilation* model, and that of *assimilation* sine *integration* may be transformed in time into *integration* cum *assimilation*. The value of these models is therefore more analytical than empirical. Yet the factors that contribute to determining them can be empirically ascertained, and measured, in the various national situations. And we believe these factors can be present in significantly different ways in these various situations. In the following pages we will therefore try to identify the differences that exist in the various countries in terms of the relevance of these factors. With a view to greater clarity of exposition, we have subdivided these factors into three groups, also on the basis of what we have said so far. The first group concerns in general the socio-economic and cultural differences between the host countries; the second, aspects of the integration of non-nationals in the host countries; the third, aspects of the origin of non-nationals.

As we have seen above, the involvement of non-nationals in penal offences – in the light of the official figures for criminality – is far from homogeneous in the various European countries. In some countries, the over-representation of non-nationals among those charged and detained is modest and even irrelevant; in others it is very pronounced. Our working hypothesis in what follows is that the marked diversity of this over-representation may be associated with a different overall socio-economic and cultural scenario in the various countries.

The data we have used, throughout this chapter, refer to repeated measurements relating to the first and second half of the 1990s.

6.2 Socio-economic and cultural differences between the host countries

Interest in the socio-economic and cultural differences between the host countries flows from the findings that emerged from our discussion of the models of integration. In practice, the countries in which disadvantageous conditions for a 'conformist' integration of non-nationals are ascertained are those in which the probabilities of experiencing grave forms of maladjustment, and the criminal proclivities that flow from them, are likely to increase.

To measure the differences between host countries we will use indicators already used to explain the variations registered in the rates for major crimes. So we will not repeat what we have already said in our previous chapter on crime statistics. It should be borne in mind, however, that here it is a case of analysing not overall rates of criminality, but of the involvement of non-nationals in penal offences. Some further preliminary remarks in this regard will be necessary.

Let us begin, here too, with indicators of *context*. The countries with greater socio-economic development and prosperity ought to possess, *ceteris paribus*, greater potential for the support and integration of immigrants. The contribution made by the socio-economic prosperity of the host country may take two directions. The first regards the greater availability of resources for immigrants; where there's *more*, and especially where there's more for everyone, comprising those at the foot of the social ladder, there's usually more also for non-nationals in need. The second direction regards the contribution that greater prosperity can make to the attitude of the national population towards non-nationals. Where there's *more*, and especially where prosperity trickles down even to the less privileged classes, it is less probable that there will be hostility towards immigrants. For in such situations insecurity and the fear of seeing one's own livelihood threatened are reduced. The perception of immigrants as *economic threat* seems an important factor of hostility towards them (Palmer 1996; Espenshade and Hempstead 1996; Kühne 2002). On the other hand, as we have already emphasized, the integration of non-nationals is connected with the problem of observance of rights, in particular human rights; and comparative empirical research has long shown that socio-economic development has a decisive influence on the observance of such rights (Lipset 1959; Hughes 2001). Observance of human rights, in other words, tends to be affirmed and to grow in a situation of high development; and vice versa.

To measure the economic and social prosperity of individual countries in Western Europe, we used as our indicators *per capita gross national product* and *per capita gross national product at parity of purchasing power*. To these two indicators we added the *gross domestic product (per cent) spent on food*: this indicator represents an excellent measure of effective economic prosperity. In fact, as GDP grows there will be a corresponding reduction of its percentage allocated to food consumption – which is a form of primary consumption. So, where expenditure on food is higher, prosperity will be lower. Immediately after these indicators of material prosperity we considered the *percentage rate of inflation*.

We then considered some indicators of social equity. The first is *per capita gross national product for the poorest 10 per cent of the population*, i.e. the income band to which a large number of immigrants belong, especially more recent immigrants. The second is the relation between the percentage of income at the disposal of the richest 20 per cent of the population and the percentage at the disposal of the poorest 20 per cent. A value equivalent to 5, for example, means that those who belong to the richest 20 per cent of the population enjoy an income that is on average five times higher than that belonging to the poorest 20 per cent. The two indicators are significantly correlated with each other and with the Gini index: all three measure the material prosperity of the less well-to-do and the distribution of income. But they also measure the social policy of the country.

The social policy of governments and their propensity to a welfare approach was measured through their expenditure on *social protection*. This variable seemed to us important, given its impact on the conditions of socio-economic precariousness to which many immigrants are reduced, especially in the years immediately following their arrival, but also in a longer time-frame (Martens 1997). In a rare empirical study on the relation between social protection and criminal conduct on the part of non-nationals (Denmark 2002), it emerged in particular that the latter registered a sentencing index for penal offences decidedly higher than that registered by nationals: but the disparity between the two indices was reduced to practically zero if one took into consideration non-nationals and nationals on parity of social benefits received (see also Holmberg and Kyvsgaard 2003).

All the indicators of *social equity*, and in particular the Gini index and the relation between the income of the richest 20 per cent of the population and that of the poorest 20 per cent, may also be considered empirical measures of the *relative deprivation* of the underprivileged classes and hence of a large part of immigrants.

The overall levels of employment/unemployment were regarded as significant for their consequences in terms of the opportunities for the economic and social insertion of immigrants. We took into consideration the *unemployment rate* for males in the 15–24 age group. We have already stressed that the growth of unemployment in Europe has not arrested or decelerated the influx of immigrants, also because the disaffection of European nationals for the more demeaning and poorly paid jobs has simultaneously grown. So immigrants can still find work, even if in conditions of marginality or irregularity ('off-the-books' work); in short they can find what with a degree of cynicism is called *immigrants' work*, even in the presence of high rates of unemployment. It seems logical to assume, however, that the higher the unemployment rate for the labour force as a whole, the lower will be the scope on the labour market also for non-nationals. Moreover, high unemployment in the general population may contribute to a greater sense of insecurity, and thus to greater hostility towards non-nationals (see Palmer 1996; Eurobarometer 2001; Kühne 2002).

We then took into consideration indicators relating to education. Educational levels are closely correlated with the growth of material prosperity. At the same time, they are correlated with observance of human rights (McMahon 2002). More specifically, the higher the educational level, the greater ought to be knowledge of *others'*, understanding of *diversity*, and the lesser tendency to perceive foreigners as 'different'. Empirical research (Eurobarometer 2001) shows that citizens' educational level is inversely proportioned to their racist attitudes. Low levels of education seem to be a characteristic of the perpetrators of *hate crime* (Kühne 2002). Better educated citizens seem more favourable to immigration (Simon and Alexander 1993; Chandler and Tsai 2001) and are presumably more sympathetic to the problems of immigrants' rights. On the basis of these considerations, we examined the *percentage of GDP spent on public education*, the *percentage of the population with at least a school-leaving certificate*, the *Human Development Index* and the *number of newspapers sold*. We next took into consideration a corruption index: namely, the *index of the perception of corruption*, calculated by Transparency International (1995). The coupling between this corruption index and that of the number of newspapers sold is not without reason. A widely disseminated press increases the transparency of political, economic and social events and at the same time reduces the scope for corruption. Comparative empirical research, using data from all over the world, shows that this corruption index is strongly correlated with the diffusion of dailies (Adserà *et al.* 2001). The level of corruption, in our view, may also furnish us indirectly with an indication on the level of solidarity and trust. Lesser solidarity and trust ought to correspond to greater corruption, and in short to a climate less favourable *also* to immigrants. Corruption also implies the prevalence of *particularism* (clientele-based relations, favouritism, individualistic and anti-social relations) over *universalism* (impartial application of the same rules no matter to whom) (Parsons 1951). And *particularism* tends to favour the socially stronger and to trample over the hopes and rights of the weakest, among whom non-nationals are undoubtedly over-represented. Particularism, corruption, and violation of rights abound wherever good governance and the rule of law are weak. So the indicator of the *certainty of the law*, formulated by the World Bank (2004), which combines measurements relating *inter alia* to the predictability of judicial sentences and the ability to appeal to a higher authority to enforce the terms laid down in a contract, may be a significant tool here. It is clear that the condition of non-nationals, who, in view of their vulnerability, have greater need for the protection of the law, may be decisively influenced by the level of the certainty of the law.

If the certainty of the law is a support for the socially weak, the excess of regulation tends to create difficulties for them. Moreover, the relation between certainty of the law and over-regulation is generally negative rather than positive. Of course, Montesquieu was right when he pointed out that the number of laws grows in proportion to the growth in complexity of economic systems and in particular to the transition from a pastoral to an agricultural and thence to an industrial economy. But the societies we are dealing with here belong to the same level of development, approximately. *Ceteris paribus*, the hypertrophy of rules and regulations makes us think of a State that is afflicted by a delirium of omnipotence; that is enforcing rather than enabling; that is obsessed more by bureaucratic regulation than by being a prompt, efficient and moderate machine for government. A system that is too coercive, too bent on the application of rules in the field of commercial and business activities – a system characterized by the complexity of the required documentation, long waiting times for the issuing of permits, inevitable uncertainty about the results, etc. – will restrict access to the market and stifle development. The excess of red tape is likely to penalize in particular all those who are seeking entry into the labour market, i.e. the majority of immigrants. Moreover, the hypertrophy of rules and regulations in the commercial and business sectors is inevitably associated with powerful bureaucracies, which favour corruption and particularism. The social marginality of immigrants represents a handicap when they are forced to deal with these bureaucracies. To measure the hypertrophy of rules and regulations in the commercial and business sector we used the *Freedom from Business Regulations* index devised by The Fraser Institute (Gwartney and Lawson 2002; Gwartney *et al.* 2006).

Corruption control, rule of law and freedom from excessive business regulations could be regarded as institutionalized social capital: a form of social capital that – as in Machiavelli's vision – could represent the translation of the virtues of individuals into a virtuous State, more particularly into State agencies inspired by civic values. This form of social capital could act as a vertical linkage between State and immigrants, favouring their integration and respect for the rules.

Together with these indicators, we also took into consideration the share of the *hidden or informal economy*. Though this is an economic indicator, its connections with the cultural, institutional and legal aspects are significant. The hidden economy can only flourish in the presence of a high level of corruption, a low level of certainty of the law, and a cultural attitude tending on the whole to *particularism*. The hidden economy is also encouraged by an excess of red tape in the commercial and business sectors and by a hyperdevelopment of the bureaucracy that operates in these sectors. The relation between hypertrophy of regulations and development of the hidden economy is only an application of the well-known model that regulates relations between customs duties and contraband or between jealousy and adultery. The effects of the hidden economy on the conduct of the individuals who come into contact with it are also understandable. It seems logical to assume that, in general, illegality will breed illegality and, more specifically, will facilitate the slide into common criminality. At the same time, the hidden economy especially involves marginal, borderline individuals and *outsiders* such as immigrants. The share of the hidden economy has been calculated as a percentage of GDP, according to the estimates of the main studies in the sector (Friedman *et al.* 2000; World Bank 2004).

To assess the level of development of telecommunications and digitalization we used as our indicators the number of *telephone lines per 1,000 population* and the number of personal *computers per 1,000 population*. This latter indicator seems to us of particular interest, given that it includes a specific cultural aspect: that connected with the 'opening' to the world made possible by the Internet.

A further hypothesis regarding the social and cultural characteristics of the host country is that there is a relation between the propensity to punitiveness in general and the propensity to punitiveness towards non-nationals in particular. If a high propensity to punitiveness is fuelled by *exclusionary cultural attitudes* (Cavadino and Dignan 2006) and by intolerance of those who don't seem *mainstream*, the non-nationals' incarceration index might be expected to grow in proportion to the growth in the propensity to punitiveness. This is a hypothesis that conforms with labelling theory, since it assumes that the involvement of non-nationals in penal and penitentiary circuits is the result of *biases* against them. To put the hypothesis to the test we need a measure of *punitiveness*. The most obvious measure is the incarceration rate (Cavadino and Dignan 2006). We have calculated this rate for all the European countries over a period sufficiently long to offset the distorting effects of any amnesties and pardons. As can be deduced from Table 6.1, the countries that emerge as most punitive on the basis of their incarceration rate are Portugal, Spain, the UK, Luxembourg and France. The Nordic countries (Sweden, Finland, Norway, Denmark and Iceland) are the least punitive.

However, it might be objected that a society is *punitive* not when its incarceration rate is high, but more precisely when its incarceration rate is higher than its level of criminality. We have taken this argument on board and therefore calculated, first, for all countries, the average rate for the most serious crimes, intentional homicides, rapes and robberies. The values of this rate (Table 6.1) obviously echo what was already said apropos of the distribution in Europe of non-nationals and crime rates (Chapter 4, in particular Figure 4.3). The highest average rates are registered in France and Belgium – where the rates for all the three major crimes are high – in Sweden – high rate of rapes – and in Finland – mainly due to its homicide rate – the lowest ones in Norway, Switzerland and Iceland. We then calculated an indicator of relative punitiveness, based on the ratio between the incarceration rate and this average rate for the three most serious crimes. These three crimes, however, do not concur in the same measure to determining the prison population. In Western Europe, on average, those charged with homicide in prison are double the number of those accused of rape; and those charged with robbery thrice as numerous. So we calculated a second indicator of relative punitiveness: unlike the first, it is based on rates of crimes weighted according to the contribution each of them makes to the prison population.

Table 6.1 Western Europe, indicators of punitiveness: incarceration rate per 100,000 population; idem (maximum = 100); average rate per 100,000 pop. for intentional homicide, rape and robbery (maximum = 100); ratio between incarceration rate and average rate for the above-mentioned crimes (maximum = 100); idem, with weighted crimes rate – Period: 1991–2000

States	Incarceration rate	Incarceration rate (max.=100)	Crimes rate (max.=100)	Incarc. rate/ crimes rate (max.=100)	Incarc. rate/wgtd crimes rate (max.=100)
B	75.3	61.5	99.7	37.0	36.0
DK	65.0	53.1	53.5	59.5	65.1
D	83.8	68.5	59.1	69.5	70.0
EL	61.5	50.3	30.2	100.0	100.0
E	106.2	86.8	76.7	67.8	51.3
F	88.9	72.7	100.0	43.6	41.9
IRL	63.8	52.2	54.2	57.8	50.5
I	84.0	68.7	70.7	58.3	47.3
L	98.6	80.6	55.9	86.5	84.1
NL	68.2	55.8	72.3	46.2	45.5
A	84.8	69.3	53.0	78.4	92.1
P	122.3	100.0	66.7	89.9	75.5
FIN	57.1	46.7	84.3	33.2	34.5
S	62.4	51.0	87.0	35.2	42.0
UK	105.3	86.1	80.4	64.3	62.8
ISL	38.6	31.5	51.9	36.4	51.5
NOR	57.3	46.8	44.7	62.8	75.6
CH	83.6	68.4	45.7	89.7	87.5
Aver. val.	78.2	63.9	65.9	62.0	61.8

NB: Since the rates for the three major crimes are not numerically homogeneous, we have standardized them.

If we move from absolute punitiveness (incarceration rate) to relative punitiveness (fifth column figures *vis-à-vis* third column ones), we will see that France becomes far less punitive (for the above-mentioned reasons); the same is ascertained for Belgium, and to a lesser degree for the UK (high rates for robberies and rapes), Spain and Sweden; instead, punitiveness sharply grows for Greece, Austria, Norway and Switzerland, i.e. for the countries with lower rates for the three major crimes. If finally we move to the second index of relative punitiveness (last column on the right), based on weighted crime rates, a decrease emerges in the figures for Portugal, Spain and Italy (where robbery rates are relatively high) and an increase in the figures for Austria and the Nordic countries (where robbery rates are relatively lower).

Our above remarks on the general propensity to punitiveness, and its possible effects, suggests further tests. In particular, it seems logical to control whether the attitude of the national population *specifically* to immigrants is related in any way with the involvement of non-nationals in activities considered criminal. Various indices are available to this end, relating for instance to the diffusion of xenophobia, anti-Islamic and more generally racist attitudes in the various European countries. It has to be said, however, that the use of these indices presents logical problems. Hostile attitudes to immigrants are not necessarily xenophobic or racist; they may be generated by other causes (Palmer 1996; Chandler and Tsai 2001), for example economic anxieties. But it is difficult to contest the hypothesis that non-hostile attitudes to non-nationals contribute to the formation of the *social capital* of the nation; in particular, to the social capital of the host society towards its immigrants; therefore, to a form of inter-ethnic social capital, a 'bridging' social capital between heterogeneous groups.

Xenophobic and racist attitudes, by contrast, would prejudice the adaptation and integration of non-nationals, and increase their probabilities of committing criminal acts. In this regard, there is good evidence in the field of social psychology to support the hypothesis that prejudices (positive or negative) towards pupils at school heavily influence their results (Rosenthal and Jacobson 1992). This is the so-called *Pygmalion effect*: it seems to be triggered also where prejudices are essentially racist. Pupils treated as racially inferior will end up producing inferior results, as shown by the well-known blue eyes / brown eyes experiment of Jane Elliott, in which pupils were classified for a given period as *diverse*, and treated accordingly, on the basis of the colour of their eyes (Peters 1971). The results of these studies of social psychology could be repeated in the far more macroscopic context of the problems of immigration and integration. We will therefore try to measure the association between xenophobia and the involvement of immigrants in activities considered criminal.

What we have said risks, however, ignoring the fact that xenophobic attitudes may be in turn a reflex of a real and threatening level of criminality among immigrants. Now, as we already remarked, hostility is not necessarily equivalent to xenophobia and racism, which are prejudicial and generalized attitudes, closer in kind to emotions and sentiments, to *residues* as Vilfredo Pareto calls them. However, the circularity of the relation between hostility (of nationals) and deviance (of non-nationals) seems difficult to overcome. To remove these uncertainties, at least in part, we considered the fact that the recent wave of migration towards Europe does not involve, or does so only marginally, populations of Jewish faith: it involves, instead, populations of Islamic faith. So a high level of criminality in immigrants in Europe ought in theory to increase the level not of anti-semitism, but of Islamophobia. A high level of anti-semitism could indicate, on the other hand, an unfavourable attitude more generally to those who present features of *otherness*; and this would probably be extended to current immigrants, with the predictable negative consequences we have already pointed out.

On the basis of this argument, we thought it useful to analyse the level of *anti-semitism*, measured by the percentage of persons who 'would not like to have Jews as their neighbours' (European Values Study Group and World Values Survey Association 2006).

On the basis of these same arguments, we also adopted an indicator of the level of *multiculturalism* in the population. In general, multiculturalism seems to be positively associated with education and income levels (van de Vijver *et al.* 2008); in turn multiculturalism seems to favour immigrants' presence (Lappi-Seppälä 2008). The indicator adopted is based on the percentage of persons who agree with the proposition that 'diversity in terms of race, religion and culture increases a country's strength' (Eurobarometer 2001).

6.3 Differences in the integration of non-nationals in the various countries

The socio-economic and cultural situation of the host countries, which we have just been examining, represents only the premise of more specific aspects of the integration of non-nationals. Let us now concentrate our attention on these specific aspects. The chosen indicators concern the aspects linked to the acquisition of citizenship, world of work, demographic structure of immigration and its characteristics.

The *percentage of non-nationals who have acquired citizenship* of the host country may be considered an indicator of social integration in the broad sense. Incorporated in *citizenship* are a series of civil, political and social rights: *civil* rights, such as individual civil liberties; *political* rights including the right to vote in elections and participate in political life; and *social* rights relating to social and economic participation in the community. If there is consensus about the importance of granting citizenship for the integration of immigrants, that does not mean there is consensus about the need to extend this prerogative to the mass of non-nationals. The policies of the various States may vary on this point: non-nationals may be accepted for their contribution to the national economy, but not as permanent members of the national population (Cornelius *et al.* 1994: 5).

The data on the granting of citizenship in any case need to be treated with caution, because they are based on different definitions and policies. In more recent years, the countries of the EU have gradually converged on a policy of granting citizenship to non-nationals on the basis of the requisite of a sufficiently long residence in the host country (5–10 years) and a condition of legality and regular employment. As far as the children of non-nationals are concerned, the principle of *jus soli*, i.e. the granting of citizenship of the host country to those born there, has in general been upheld. But exceptions to this rule are not lacking. For example, up to 2000 Germany applied the *jus sanguinis*, which restricted the granting of citizenship only to those born to at least one parent of German nationality (Sopemi 2001). The policy of

Switzerland has always been inspired by the concept of the *jus sanguinis* and not that of the *jus soli*. Some countries – notably Switzerland – require citizens to be sufficiently fluent in the language of the host country as a condition for the granting of citizenship. Others, such as Sweden, are particularly generous in granting citizenship. These differences could have repercussions, *ceteris paribus*, on the chances for the integration of non-nationals. The countries in which it is easier to obtain naturalization ought, in theory, to present fewer problems in terms of the integration of non-nationals, and a lower share of non-nationals in criminality.

Another factor that needs to be taken into consideration, however, is that an interest in obtaining the citizenship of their host country is not the same for all non-nationals. In the EU, the problem of citizenship only secondarily concerns non-nationals who are already citizens of another EU member state: they are already protected by a series of provisions in force in all EU countries. The problem primarily concerns those who are *not* citizens of the EU. Those belonging to communities in conditions of relative *weakness vis-à-vis* the host country are particularly interested in acquiring citizenship: just those communities with greater problems of integration. Since the various national communities of immigrants (and in particular these disadvantaged communities) are not present in a homogeneous fashion in the various European countries, the interest of immigrants in acquiring citizenship of their host country is not homogeneous. And hence also the indicator of the acquisition of citizenship will be negatively affected by this diversity.

Other indicators are specific to immigrants' integration in the workforce. They include the *non-national workforce rate* and the *relative non-national workforce index*, the latter based on both the national and non-national workforce rates. These indicators present margins of uncertainty, since it is well known that the analysis of the basic data on immigrants in employment is handicapped both by differences in national procedures for gathering this information and by the size of the *dark figure* of workers in a condition of irregularity. Moreover, even if the majority of immigrants are keen to be integrated in the workforce, there are immigrants with quite different interests, for instance those who come to Europe to study or for purely residential purposes. So the data for the non-national workforce are not entirely indicative of the level of integration.

Other indicators relating to integration in the workforce are the *non-nationals' unemployment rate*, and the *relative non-nationals' unemployment index*. What these indicators are meant for is fairly clear: where the non-nationals' unemployment rate is higher, the difficulties of integration and the pressure towards deviant forms of behaviour are also likely to be higher. We devised a relative unemployment index to measure the difference between the unemployment rate of non-nationals on the one hand and that of nationals on the other. On average, the non-nationals' unemployment rate in Europe is roughly double that of nationals, but sharp differences are registered between one country and another. However, in this case too, and for the same reasons mentioned above apropos of the non-national work-force, the data in question are of dubious validity.

We then examined the percentage of non-nationals with *schooling no higher than lower secondary school*: hence with low levels of education. Now, education – with its contents of cultural and technical knowledge – ought to represent a powerful factor of integration. So, the lower the educational level of the non-national population, the greater the risk of lack of integration and of a slide into illegality and crime will be. It should further be recalled that *control* theory considers a person's dedication to his/her own education a sound defence against the temptations of illegality: education involves self-discipline and the pursuit of conformist goals. It is therefore likely to be synonymous with a low propensity to deviance.

Another dimension that ought, we believe, to be taken into account con-sists of the *variation of the non-national population* in the individual host countries. Now, a massive increase of this population within a limited period of time implies a mass of new immigrants, all simultaneously having to grap-ple with the problems of adjustment to the host society. As we have already recalled, the theory of *social disorganization*, propounded by the Chicago School, had emphasized the dangers of poor integration connected with high mobility and lack of roots in the territory. It is presumed that a rapid increase of the immigrant population would exacerbate these negative aspects. In addition, it is precisely in the first years that immigrants experience the great-est difficulties of adaptation and integration; this is all the truer for a migra-tion propelled by *push factors*. In other words, for immigrants the passage of time ought to be synonymous with mitigation, if not solution, of the prob-lems of integration. But more negative consequences are likely to derive from a situation characterized by a non-national population within which the per-centage of recently arrived immigrants is very high: in other words, the higher the percentage of immigrants with difficulties of integration, the greater the probabilities of criminal activities. On the other hand, where the variation is contained, and the percentage of new immigrants is low in comparison with the mass of 'old' immigrants, the more limited is likely to be the percentage of those with greater problems of adaptation. Very high variations in the size of the non-national population have been registered in recent decades in such countries as Greece, Finland, Spain, Italy and Portugal.

It may further be assumed that the heterogeneity of the immigrant popu-lation, the multiplicity of its ethnic origins, will have negative consequences on integration. An immigrant population subdivided into many ethnic groups is likely to reduce the probabilities of finding support from other immigrants to seek integration in the host society: *ethnic heterogeneity*, in other words, would reduce the availability of intra-ethnic social capital. At the same time, it may be presumed – also in agreement with the Chicago School – that the heterogeneity of immigrants will increase prejudice and suspicion towards other immigrants and weaken the sense of belonging to a community. To test this hypothesis, we calculated for each country the percentage of immigrants *not belonging* to the two national groups with the largest share of the total non-national population. The higher this percentage, the greater the heterogeneity will be. The ratio between the values presented by the less heterogeneous and by the more heterogeneous countries is approximately one to two.

We then took into consideration various characteristics of immigrants such as *gender* and *age*, based on the presupposition that the demographic structure of the immigrant population will condition the type of problems and needs to which the host society must respond.

As regards the *gender composition* of the non-national population, we assume that greater problems of adaptation and integration, and greater probabilities of deviant and criminal conduct, will be posed when the male immigrant population is substantially larger than the female one (cf. Baldacci and Natale 1995). We have seen that a situation of this type sometimes occurs within an ethnic group; but if we consider the immigrant population as a whole in the various countries of Europe, we will find – as already pointed out – that disparities in the male and female shares of the non-national population are limited. We therefore don't expect much from this indicator.

The *distribution by age groups* of non-nationals in Europe, in turn, differs from the distribution of the general population, as we have already noted. In simplified terms, the demographic situation of non-nationals, in contrast to nationals, is characterized, comparatively, by a greater percentage of the young adults and adults age groups and, simultaneously, by a lesser percentage of the older age groups. In general, these *irregularities of the demographic structure* of the non-national population imply social disadvantage/ deprivation (cf. Casacchia and Strozza 1995). In seeking indicators of the disadvantage of the non-national population, we were interested in particular in the percentage of young children as share of the non-national population. A low share of the children's age groups implies a non-national population in which there is little room for families and in particular for young families. This in turn would presuppose greater social problems and deprivation, and concomitantly greater exposure to deviant forms of behaviour.

Lastly, the indicators of the integration of non-nationals should also include a measure of the presence of *clandestine or irregular immigrants*. As already pointed out, the number of clandestine or irregular immigrants has soared in Western Europe in recent decades. This is no surprise, given the current situation, characterized by migrants propelled by *push factors* and often by dramatic conditions of poverty, famine, war, displacement and oppression in their countries of origin, which make clandestine emigration, however dangerous, an attractive proposition. These clandestine immigrants could also represent the category in which the recourse to deviant forms of behaviour is more frequent (Barbagli 1998; Albrecht 2002; FAIR 2007).

The relation between clandestine immigration and crime has various roots. First, clandestine immigrants evade the normal filters applied to legal immigration. These filters are aimed at preventing the admission into the country of subjects with a criminal record. Thus, in the USA, those who apply for a 'green card' or for citizenship are subjected to a vetting procedure to ascertain whether they have any criminal past. In Western Europe, the controls vary depending on country of origin. While the citizens of other States of the European Union are exempted from them, such vetting procedures are in place for those coming from other countries for which an entry visa is required. There are reasons to believe that individuals with criminal records are in percentage terms more numerous among clandestine immigrants and that their average propensity to criminality is higher.

The propensity to criminality of clandestine immigrants is also favoured by their condition in the host country: in other words, they are forced to live in a situation of illegality. Illegality is structured in their very condition, in rather the same way as it is in the condition of the drug addict who depends on the illegal market for the drugs he uses. The condition of illegality of clandestine immigrants, moreover, does not just regard their arrival in the host country and their continued presence in it. It regards their daily working activities, given that these activities can only be offered by the *hidden economy*, a euphemism for the economy outside the rules. Their belonging to, and dependence on, the area of the economy outside the rules multiplies their experiences of contact with illegality and leads them to believe that illegality is normal, thus inevitably reducing their cultural resistance to crime. At the same time, their condition of illegality, especially in employment, exposes them to particular precariousness and vulnerability, to a high probability of being exploited, maltreated, defrauded, robbed, and physically assaulted (Valenzuela 2006). In sum, the diffusion of the condition of clandestine immigrant – with its inevitable corollary of the hidden economy – significantly contributes to the creation of an underworld of illegality and violence, exploitation and abuse that forms the very antithesis of the ideals of justice and equity.

In the second place, in large part as a result of the aspects we have just described, the condition of clandestinity is synonymous with particular economic and social exclusion. It may reasonably be assumed that clandestine immigrants are on average characterized by conditions of greater disadvantage, of greater *strain*: and that they are therefore more prone to deviant and criminal acts. Besides, their condition as outsiders itself has a deviant effect: it makes them feel they have less to lose from the host society: the anxiety of losing their job or simply 'losing face', as a consequence of a penal indictment, is unlikely to disturb them, given that they already find themselves in a condition of illegality and marginality.

So an indicator of the level of clandestinity of non-nationals in the various countries would be useful. Of course it is impossible to have precise values for a phenomenon that is by its very nature shrouded in obscurity. We can, however draw on the estimates contained in various international publications (Sopemi 2000, 2002, 2003, 2004; Wanner 2002; Jandl 2003), which we had already used to evaluate the scale of the non-national population. On the basis of these estimates, we then constructed a *dummy* variable, in other words a variable that transforms into numerical values (1, 2, 3) the data for categories of clandestine immigrants classified as *low, medium and high level* of clandestinity.

6.4 Differences in the origin of non-nationals present in the various countries

Foreign immigration in Western Europe, as we have already seen, is characterized by the presence of populations coming not only from various countries but from various areas/regions; and the share of national and regional groups is very different from one country to the next. It is natural to ask ourselves whether the data on origin can help to explain the share of non-nationals among the crime figures in Europe. It should be noted, however, that the already underlined phenomenon of the *diffusionism* of immigration to Europe has had the result that at the present time there are, in practically all Western countries, significant representations of all the main national groups of migrants, even if the share of these groups out of the total non-nationals is not the same in the various countries. In any case, the hypothesis of a direct relation between origin of migrant influxes and rates of criminality encounters various obstacles. For example, France and Italy presented, between 1980 and 1990, similar percentages of EU and non-EU immigrants, and also of immigrants coming from Africa among their non-national populations; but the relative contribution of non-nationals to the crime figures was very different in the two countries. Moreover, as we have already underlined (in our Introduction), the national groups that are distinguished for the highest rates of criminality are not the same in the various countries. A confirmation of this fact comes from the USA, where ethnic groups of immigrants present rates of involvement in criminal activities that vary greatly from state to state (Martinez and Lee 2000). This implies that origin probably represents a parameter that should be considered not in isolation but together with other parameters relating to the socio-economic conditions of the host country and the characteristics of migratory flows.

At the same time, it is obvious that each national group of immigrants and each group from a specific geographic area of origin presents peculiar characteristics and an often different history of migration. These basic differences may also imply cultural disparities with the host country, whether of religion, level of socio-economic development, and so on; and these aspects may in turn represent further significant factors for the integration and assimilation of non-nationals. Differences of origin may coincide with differences in the process of adjustment to the host society. The integration of non-nationals will presumably present fewer difficulties if they come from areas less culturally dissimilar from the host country.

A first parameter that should be taken into account in this perspective is that of the percentage of *non-nationals respectively from EU member states, non-EU European states and non-European countries*: a parameter we already presented earlier. As noted in Chapter 3.3, the distribution of immigrants from the EU, other European countries and non-European countries is extremely heterogeneous in the various European countries. For the reasons set forth above, we assume that higher percentages of EU non-nationals would be associated with lower levels of criminality, and vice versa (cf. Albrecht 2002).

But since the distinction between *EU, non-EU* and *non-European* continues to lump together countries that are clearly very dissimilar to each other, especially so in the case of the non-EU and non-European categories, more precise indicators can be used, based on the percentages of non-nationals that come from particular geographic areas. We have thus made reference to a distinction already made in Chapter 3, where we showed the percentages of non-nationals coming from the countries of *Central and Eastern Europe*, the *Rest of Europe, Africa, North America, Latin America, Asia* and *Oceania*.

Lastly, we took into account the *percentages of non-nationals coming from specific countries*, such as Poland, Romania, the former Soviet Union, Turkey, Morocco, Algeria, Tunisia, the USA, Canada, Brazil, India, Iran, Pakistan, China, Australia and New Zealand.

We then devised other indicators of origin that are able to measure even more specific aspects. We thus formulated an indicator consisting of the percentage of non-European non-nationals coming from the less developed countries alone: in practice, we thus excluded from the calculation of non-Europeans those coming from North America, Japan, Australia and New Zealand. There are empirical data supporting the hypothesis that non-nationals in Europe coming from *less developed* countries present higher rates of criminality (Denmark 2002, Netherlands 2008b).

All the indicators so far considered in this chapter refer to measurements of the presence of the various populations of non-nationals in the countries of Western Europe *in a particular phase or period*. So the data in question are so-called *stock*. However, if looked at more closely, the aspect of the diachronic variation of this presence is no less important. While we expect, for example, that a high proportion among non-nationals of non-Europeans coming from the less developed countries is associated with a high rate of criminality, we would also expect an increase over time of the share of these populations to be accompanied by an aggravation of this situation. This is especially so if the variations in question occur in the short term, because, as we stressed above, the integration and adaptation of immigrants require time. We thus thought of combining in a single indicator data of *stock and flow*.

In practice, we will use, for example, an indicator that measures the share of non-Europeans in a given year and the percentage variation of this share in the following decade. For the construction of indicators of this type we used the technique of *principal components analysis*.[1]

6.5 Association between the incarceration index and the socio-economic parameters in the various European countries

Let us now see whether, and to what degree, the sharp differences in the incarceration index of non-nationals, as registered in the European countries, are associated with differences in terms of the socio-economic situation, characteristics of integration and characteristics of the influx of migrants. The values of the incarceration index consist of the average values for two five-year periods, 1991–1995 and 1996–2000. This permits us to smooth out the short-term variations and increase the number of occurrences. The values of the indicators relating to the socio-economic situation of the countries also refer to these two periods. It proved impossible to have more time-series sections because some of the indicators (e.g. that of the hidden economy) are not available on a continuous basis. In any case, it should be noted that here the dependent variable – i.e. the incarceration index – is based on hard data and hence particularly reliable; it does not present those weaknesses (already adverted to) that undermine the value of data relating to rates of criminality. So we can study the association between this index and the variables relating to the socio-economic situation of the countries, without having recourse to the analysis of their variation in time.

The results obtained by this analysis – for further information see Appendix III – show that the non-nationals' incarceration index is higher in countries with lower and unstable (or inflation-prone) economic development, particularly low income for the poor, unfair income distribution, ungenerous social protection, high corruption level, ineffective rule of law, widespread hidden economy, limited education and culture, limited diffusion of knowledge and communication media (dailies, personal computers). The incarceration index is higher also where non-nationals rapidly grew over the last few years; where their children's percentage of the non-national population is lower – i.e. where families are less numerous and rooting in the community is limited; where illegal immigration is common; and where non-nationals from non-European and less developed countries are more numerous.

Indicators of economic well-being, social equity and relative deprivation show, *vis-à-vis* the incarceration index, coefficients lower than those shown by PC diffusion and indicators of legality, such as corruption, rule of law, hidden economy and illegal immigration. Legality indicators present coefficients also higher than those shown by origin indicators.

To this we can add that the incarceration index is associated with the diffusion of anti-semitism, and negatively associated with the percentage of the population with multicultural attitudes; but the associations in question are modest in scale.

Decidedly non-significant, moreover, is the association between the punitiveness of the host society – however measured – and the non-nationals' incarceration index. For example, the four countries with the highest incarceration index in the period 1991–2000, i.e. Portugal, UK, Spain and Luxembourg, present – for the non-nationals' incarceration index – values that vary from the lowest to the highest registered in Europe as a whole. These results, therefore, offer no support to labelling theory.

The incarceration index is also associated – predictably – with the percentage of non-nationals with low levels of education – no higher than lower secondary school – but the degree of association is decidedly less than that between the same incarceration index and the education of the resident population, i.e. substantially the natives. So the indicator of *context* seems to prevail over that of the characteristics of the immigrants themselves. We may note that non-nationals' educational level is significantly correlated with that of nationals; immigrants with lower average levels of education are mainly found in the countries with less-educated populations. Immigrants with lower education, moreover, are more numerous in the countries with higher levels of corruption, lesser diffusion of newspapers, and lower prosperity.

The data also show that the association between the incarceration index and the percentage of non-European non-nationals is less strong than that with non-Europeans from the *less developed countries alone*. So the greater the disparity from Europe is – economic disparity primarily, but not only that – the higher is the level of imprisonment.

Lastly, the index of the heterogeneity of the non-national population is not significantly associated with the incarceration index.

There are strong correlations between the majority of the indicators relating to the overall socio-economic situation in the various countries. In particular, the variables that measure material prosperity and its distribution – GDP for food, social protection, etc. – are all strongly correlated. But the variables that measure the cultural level and more generally the *social capital* also show strong correlations. For instance, dailies and PC diffusion are strongly correlated ($r > 0.77$) with control of corruption and rule of law; control of corruption and rule of law are even more correlated ($r = 0.92$) with each other. Revealingly, illegal immigration is strongly correlated with corruption, rule of law and hidden economy. Last, the three origin indicators are all inter-correlated.

To sum up these relations, we had recourse to factor analysis.[2] This enabled us to identify – below the network of the correlations between the explanatory variables – at least three main factors or latent variables (see further, Appendix III). Figure 6.1 (first chart) shows that the first factor, on the

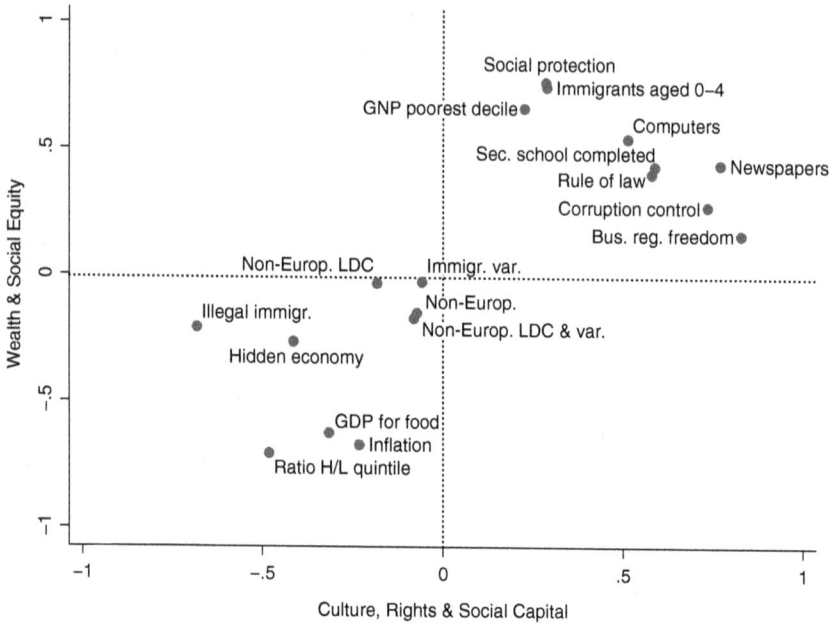

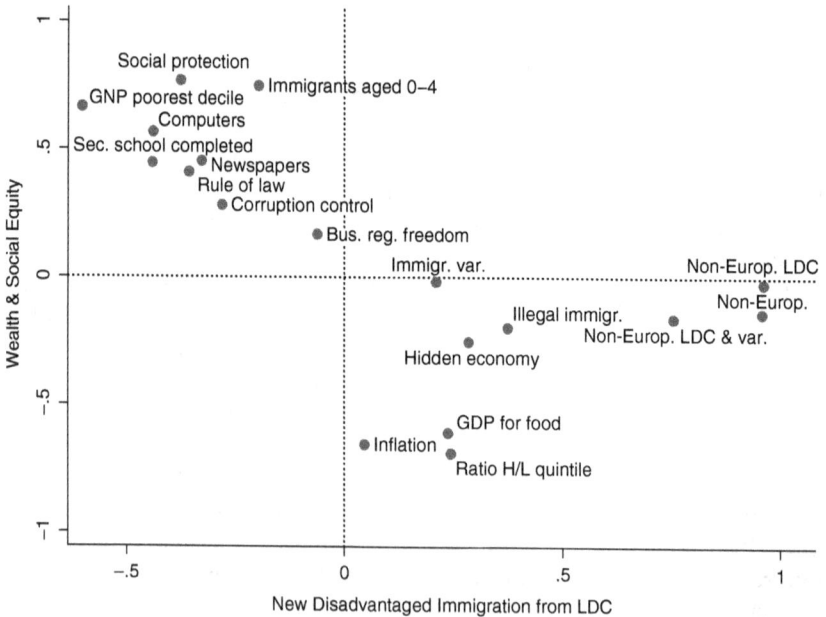

Figure 6.1 Distribution of the main variables regarding the socio-economic situation, integration and migratory flow in the countries of Western Europe: first and second factor; second and third factor.

horizontal axis, is characterized by high loadings for the variables of population with school-leaving certificate, newspaper diffusion, corruption control, rule of law, business regulation freedom, PC diffusion (on the right) and by equally high loadings, on the negative side, for illegal immigration and hidden economy (on the left). In other words, the countries that present good rule of law, strong corruption control, better educated population, and so on, also have low levels of illegal immigration and hidden economy, and vice versa. We can define this factor as 'Culture, Rights and Social Capital'.

The second factor, on the vertical axis, is especially characterized by variables relating to income, economic stability, and social protection: the countries that present high social protection and high income for the poorest decile are also characterized – not surprisingly – by a high percentage of infant children of immigrants (in the upper part on the vertical axis) and by low values in terms of the gap between rich and poor and the percentage of income spent on basic needs (ratio H/L quintile and GDP for food: in the lower part on the vertical axis). High average levels of income are therefore associated not only with higher absolute levels of income for the poorest but also with fairer distribution of wealth. We could therefore call this factor 'Wealth and Social Equity'.

The third factor (second chart) is characterized by high loadings (on the right) for all three origin indicators: we could call it 'New Disadvantaged Immigration from the Less Developed Countries'. We may note from the second chart that the variables of this third factor are graphically differentiated from other variables (on the left) that measure GNP for the poorest decile, secondary school completed, social protection, rule of law, etc. So, the new disadvantaged immigration from the less developed countries is in percentage terms stronger in those countries that are characterized by less material prosperity, less culture, less social equity and more illegality.

Subsumed in the first factor, the rule of law, corruption control, and illegal immigration variables may be considered as a latent sub-factor corresponding to the concept of 'prevalent legality/illegality'.

From Figure 6.2 we may deduce that lower values of the non-nationals' incarceration index correspond to growing levels of 'prevalent legality'. We may also notice the large disparities that exist between the various countries both in terms of the values of the non-nationals' incarceration index and in terms of the values of the sub-factor 'prevalent legality/illegality'.

At the same time Figure 6.2 suggests the existence of groups of countries with very similar values, in contrast to the values of other groups, as diagrammatically shown by the distances between the countries in the chart. This encourages us to pursue our analysis in this direction, and try to identify the degree of similarity/dissimilarity between the countries studied, on the basis of the characteristics measured by the variables taken into consideration.

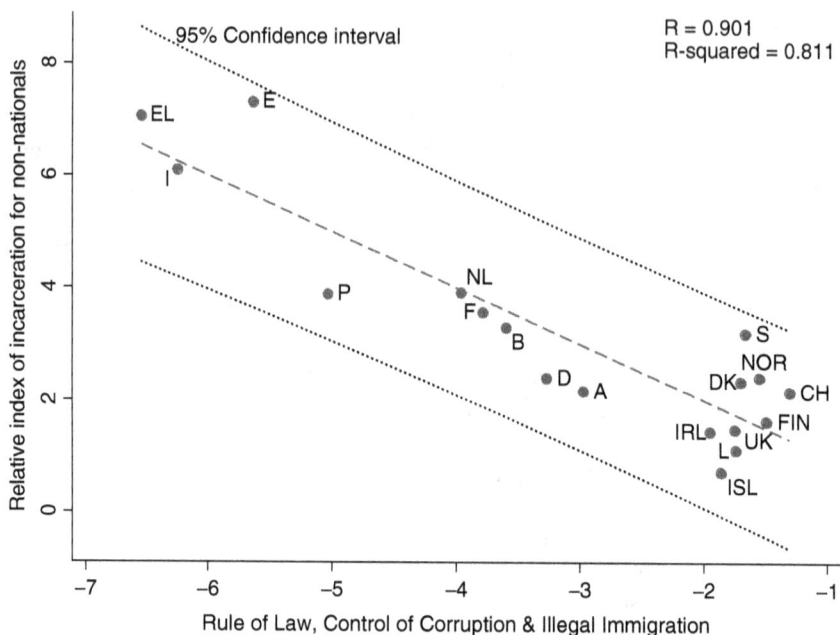

Figure 6.2 The countries of Western Europe in relation to some variables of the first factor (rule of law, corruption control and illegal immigration) and to the non-nationals' incarceration index: linear regression fit line, confidence interval and coefficients.

An easily understandable diagrammatic representation of the differences between the countries of Western Europe in terms of the non-nationals' incarceration index and of all the chosen variables regarding the situation in the various countries may be obtained by the *Multidimensional Scaling* technique.[3]

It may be noted (Figure 6.3) that Greece, Italy, Spain and Portugal are placed in fairly close conjunction in this chart (and thus have similar characteristics), and at the same time are far removed from most of the other countries. These are the four countries with a high non-nationals' incarceration index and with a less favourable overall situation of integration. The Nordic/Scandinavian countries form a separate cluster, sharply demarcated from the Mediterranean countries and hence characterized by a sharp dissimilarity from them. All the countries on the right – and hence including Luxembourg and Switzerland as well as the Nordic/Scandinavian countries – are grouped together, also thanks to the common denominator of a relatively low non-nationals' incarceration index. Luxembourg and Switzerland seem to resemble each other and to be very dissimilar not only from the Mediterranean countries but also from those in the lower part of the Figure (France, UK). Germany and Austria present similar characteristics. UK and

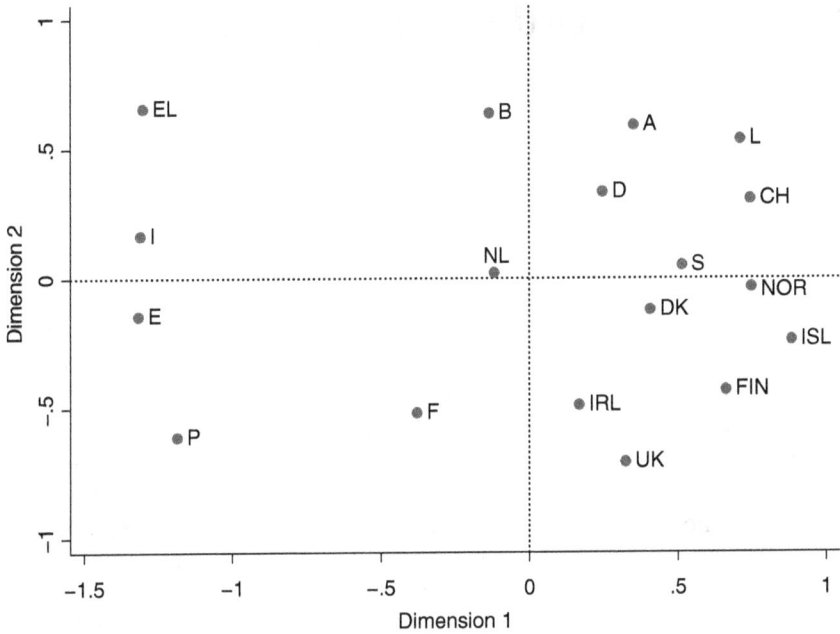

Figure 6.3 Chart plotting the differences between the countries of Western Europe on the basis of the values of the non-nationals' incarceration index and of all the variables regarding socio-economic situation, integration and migratory flow (Appendix III).

Ireland are also placed in close conjunction. Holland is situated close to the intersection of the two axes, which coincides with the mean of the values of all the variables for all the countries, and which may thus be considered the point of intersection that represents Western Europe as a whole.

Summary and conclusions

After the years of reconstruction, following the end of the Second World War, Western Europe assumed a profile that made it ever more dissimilar from the countries of the Third and the former Second World. Three factors, in particular, have contributed to the creation of this peculiar profile: first, the demographic decline in Europe; second, the very high level of economic prosperity achieved, with trade and demographic mobility hugely facilitated by the creation of a new political and economic entity, the European Community (later Union); and third, a level of respect for human rights far higher, and far more diffused, than that existing in most of the developing countries. The emergence of this *differential* of conditions has, not surprisingly, coincided with a growth of migration towards the countries of Western Europe. This migration has in large part come precisely from those countries more disparate from Europe in demographic, economic and political terms.

During the same period, a significant growth of non-nationals (i.e. non-naturalized immigrants) charged and imprisoned has seemed to emerge in Western Europe – in spite of doubts about the scale and structural characteristics of the phenomenon. Non-nationals, in particular, would seem to be over-represented among the prison population: their share of it being higher than their share of the total resident population. Current research on this problem – introduced and discussed in Chapter 1 – has tried to analyse, and find plausible answers to, some basic questions in this regard: in particular, whether the criminality of immigrants is quantitatively and qualitatively *different* from that of nationals, and whether it can be traced back to causes that are essentially different from those of nationals. The problem of the links between immigration and criminality has bulked large in the socio-criminological literature. Experts in this field have contextualized and interpreted the phenomenon from many widely different points of view. Yet, while the existence of a strong link between the deviance of immigrants and their level of socio-economic and cultural integration has emerged as a plausible hypothesis, scientific research in this field encounters some serious obstacles: notably the lack of homogeneity of the available data for a comparative study at the international level and the difficulty of tracking down some basic data.

In the attempt to contribute to a solution of this still unresolved problem, we mapped out a process of exploratory research, assuming as our units of analysis 18 countries of Western Europe: in practice, all the countries for which sufficient data exist for a comparative analysis. First, we traced the main lines of the situation of immigration in Western Europe and its evolution in recent decades, starting from the 1950s but focusing in particular on the period from 1985 onward. Second, we tried to evaluate the scale of the criminal phenomenon, and the share of it attributable to the non-national population, or at any rate its degree of involvement in cases that fall within the field of penal and penitentiary justice.

As regards more generally the presence of non-nationals in the countries of Western Europe, our data show, unsurprisingly, that they have grown in recent years, both numerically and as a percentage of the resident population. All this is in conformity with the general trend of the non-national population in Western Europe: a trend that has always been one of growth, at least since the 1950s, i.e. at least since the period for which the available data are sufficient to trace a profile of the situation for all the countries taken into consideration. This growth in the presence of non-nationals has been accompanied by a transformation of the characteristics of non-nationals, their countries of origin and their modes of 'adjustment' to the host societies. There has been, especially since the early 1980s, a sharp decline in the share of non-nationals coming from other countries in Western Europe itself. Migration to Western Europe, more generally, has been characterized by a process we have described as *diffusionism*: in other words, the migratory phenomenon has been extended through a multiplication of the goals in Europe to which migrants are directed and a diversification of their nationalities of origin. There has been, in particular, a growth of non-nationals coming from non-European countries and an even more pronounced growth of immigrants from the countries of Central and Eastern Europe (former Soviet bloc, Balkan countries). In other words, there has been a growth of non-nationals from countries with a relatively greater differential from those of Western Europe in terms of their economic, social and cultural condition. In addition, the non-national model in Europe typical of the 1950s and 1960s has become obsolete: namely, the model of the foreign worker (or guest worker) – usually coming from Western Europe itself – who emigrated especially on the basis of *pull factors*, in other words, the high probability – if not the guaranteed certainty – of finding an advantageous and remunerative job in the host country. This foreign worker was characterized by a high level of vocational integration, even if his assimilation of the model of life of the host society often remained marginal or perfunctory.

The predominant model of non-nationals today is very different: it seems to consist of immigrants who come from relatively more distant – cultural as well as geographical – countries and whose emigration is driven especially by *push factors*, often dramatic in kind: civil wars, various conflicts, deterioration of living conditions and systematic violations of human rights. Their emigration understandably has a character at once more casual – in terms of what country of Western Europe is their chosen destination – and compulsive – in terms of what motivations they have for emigrating in the first place. Their position in the country of immigration is often conditioned right from the start by the fact that their arrival in the country was neither planned nor authorized by the authorities: it was *clandestine*. Their chances of integration in the host society and in its labour market, now that the link between immigration and the official request for manpower had been broken, are reduced, and often limited to the *hidden economy*. Their assimilation of the model of life of the host society is on the whole superior to that of their predecessors, but often distorted by the mass media, by unrealistic (or rather unrealizable) expectations and by an ambiguous and frustrating rapport with the culture of their own country of origin.

The situation in the various European countries is, however, differentiated. This differentiation consists first of all of the size of the immigrant population as a share of the local population and the pace of growth of the migratory phenomenon in the various countries. Other differences consist of the origin of immigrants. Some countries are characterized by, and have to come to terms with, foreigners coming in large part from areas of the world very different in cultural, economic, social and religious terms. A basic change has been registered in some European countries, which were themselves formerly the origin of a sharp migratory outflow towards foreign countries: with the virtual extinction of this *emigration*, these countries have rapidly been transformed into countries of *immigration*. This phenomenon has contributed in large part to the strong growth of their non-national population, in the period from the 1980s on.

The rapid and often dramatic transformations of the scenario of the presence of non-nationals in Western Europe not surprisingly seem to be reflected on the phenomenon of criminality.

The data gathered in the course of the present research show that, as regards subjects charged, the share of non-nationals out of the total number of those charged for penal offences is on the whole higher than their share of the resident population. This share seems particularly high in the case of such offences as counterfeiting, robbery, homicide, and rape. Thus the data on the prison population (data that are more exhaustive than those of persons charged) show that non-nationals form over a quarter of the total detainees in Western Europe. The phenomenon of high percentages of non-nationals among the prison population tends, moreover, to be generalized throughout Western Europe, also involving those countries that until just a few years ago had only a small percentage of non-nationals among their detainees.

The incarceration index for non-nationals used in the present research, specially devised to have a comparative measure of the phenomenon, has shown that the share of non-nationals out of the prison population is over four times higher than their share of the resident population. It is interesting that this finding coincides with the data calculated for immigrants in France almost a century and a half ago. The current situation thus seems to have precedents. The current over-representation of non-nationals in the prison population decreases if we take into consideration the greater share of young adults among the non-national population and the presence of clandestine or irregular immigrants. Nonetheless it still remains disproportionately high.

All this dispels some basic doubts about the share of non-nationals in the official crime figures. The conclusions reached by a series of studies in Western Europe, especially in the 1950s and 1960s – according to which non-nationals made no significantly different contribution to crime than nationals – are thus to be rejected, as far as the present situation is concerned. A mistaken acquiescence in the vogue for the 'politically correct' has probably hampered a full and unbiased understanding of this situation; and by denying some basic, disturbing facts it has indirectly favoured a popular xenophobic reaction.

However, if one were to deduce from all this – as many have done and continue to do – that immigration is synonymous with criminality, one would be committing a grave error. The popular opinion according to which immigrants in general, and some national groups in particular, are crime-prone, is challenged by some facts: in some countries the non-national contribution to crime figures is limited and the same national groups show – in the various countries – a dissimilar contribution to crime. If we add that the immigrant crime rate was much lower in the 1950s and 1960s in Europe and is still low in the USA and Canada, we can conclude – against stereotypical beliefs – that the migration-crime relationship is (1) historically contingent, and therefore changing over time, and (2) significantly dependent on the context in which immigration occurs. Immigration therefore is not tantamount to high crime rates, and the experience of some countries shows that it is possible to keep immigrant crime under control.

Our data further show how unfounded is the idea that a growth of criminality is a necessary consequence of a growth of immigration. In Western European countries, as far as the 'classic' crimes of major gravity are concerned, namely, intentional homicide, rape and robbery, there is no relation between the percentage of immigrants in the resident population and the rates of criminality registered in our 18 countries. Even more important, and statistically reliable, is the fact that – again in terms of the 'classic' crimes of major gravity – there is no relation between the variations of the percentage of immigrants in the resident population and the variations of the rates of criminality in the host country. There may be significant variations in the share of non-nationals in the resident population without there being a parallel growth in crime rates. Our longitudinal comparative study of all the countries of Western Europe shows that in the crucial years straddling the end of the twentieth and start of the twenty-first century, the variations in the rates of criminality were associated with such phenomena as urbanization, material prosperity, territorial mobility, divorces, living conditions, spread of infant mortality and tuberculosis, but not with variations in the presence of immigrants. In fact, depending on country, different models of interaction between immigration and criminality emerge. In some cases we have a model of parallel evolution, in which the contribution of immigrants to criminality grows but in a similar way to the contribution of nationals. In other cases, the contribution of nationals to crime is substituted by the new contribution of immigrants, giving rise on the whole to stable or even decreasing rates of criminality. Only in a few cases do we ascertain a growth of the rates of criminality associated with a growth of the sole contribution of non-nationals. In other words, the variations of the rates of criminality seem to follow logics internal to the individual societies rather than any general equation between criminality and immigration. These conclusions are also corroborated by the results of a further analysis of the situation in the USA, which ascertained that diachronic variations of the rates of criminality registered in the various States of the Union are not associated with variations of the immigrant population.

Our research has helped, we believe, to elucidate an aspect that seemed of great significance: namely, the fact that the contribution of non-nationals to criminality is decidedly different from one country to another. Our data corroborate the conclusion that, in some national contexts, non-nationals do not contribute to the official crime figures disproportionately to their share of the resident population. In other national contexts, by contrast, their involvement in criminal cases seems abnormally high. These great differences between one country and another seemed to us a central factor on which to base our attempt to gain a better understanding of the phenomenon, and more generally to suggest more appropriate policies in terms of immigration, integration and social control.

On this basis, we tested several hypotheses belonging to the theoretical and empirical 'state of the art'. First, the concepts of so-called *culture conflict* theory (which sees crime as a *direct* consequence of the cultural gap between the national and non-national populations living together in the same land), seemed ill-suited, or insufficient, to provide an overall explanation of the current phenomenon. The situation of immigrants at the present time seems to be characterized not by problems of cultural assimilation but by a kind of assimilation that is not accompanied by integration (in accordance with what we have called the *assimilation* sine *integration* model). In fact, the crimes commonly attributed to non-nationals in Europe are mainly common offences: they are not the kind of crimes which could by any stretch of the imagination be described as 'culturally determined'. Scope for cultural conflict theory remains, at best, only for a few particular offences such as rape. But the theory seems unable to explain the enormous differentials in terms of the contributions of non-nationals to criminality in the various countries.

The concepts of so-called *control* theory also seemed rather unconvincing, especially when applied to non-national populations mainly composed of first-generation immigrants. It is almost axiomatic that such recently arrived immigrants, and in particular the more marginal groups such as clandestine immigrants, find themselves in a situation with little, or perhaps without any, *external controls* by the host society, precisely due to their lack of integration in it. It may be presumed, however, that they are subject at least to *internal controls*, derived from the influence on them of the culture, education and moral constraints of their society of origin. Moreover, emigration ought to be synonymous with commitment to conventional lines of action, e.g. making sacrifices to improve one's own condition. And this, too, ought to act as a curb on any slide into crime.

So other explanations were sought. We tried to ascertain whether the differences in the involvement of non-nationals in penal and penitentiary circuits between the various countries of Europe might correspond to other differences upstream: different situations, and in particular different socio-economic conditions in the host countries, different characteristics of migrant influxes, and differences in the degree of immigrants' integration.

What emerged from a more detailed analysis was an association between the incarceration index of non-nationals and some key indicators of the socio-economic and cultural development of the host countries. Greater overall development, in particular greater economic development, greater social protection, greater education and culture, greater opening to *diversity*, and especially greater transparency (high levels of diffusion of newspapers and personal computers and hence access to new means of information and communication, less corruption, less bureaucracy-controlled economy), greater respect for civil rights (certainty of the law), and less diffusion of the hidden economy, are all associated with a lower share of non-nationals among the prison population.

The incarceration index also seems associated with the characteristics of the migratory flow: in particular, our findings show that a sharp increase, in the space of a few years, of the presence of non-nationals, and a low presence of children among immigrants (implying a lack of nuclear families and hence of *rooting*), are associated with a high incarceration index. We also ascertained a strong correlation between the share of clandestine immigrants among the non-national population and the incarceration index: clandestine immigrants, it goes without saying, are in a particularly difficult situation in terms of integration.

The positive association between the incarceration index and the growth of the immigrant influx seems to be a point in favour of the 'old' theory of *social disorganization*. But the negative effects of a rapid growth in immigration are also compatible with other major explanations. Moreover, the heterogeneity level of the non-national population – a point emphasized by proponents of *social disorganization* theory – seems to be scarcely influential.

The data on the nationality of immigrants did not add any decisive explanatory factors. A high share of immigrants from societies more dissimilar from, and less developed than, those of the countries of destination is associated with a high incarceration index. All the indicators of *origin* are, however, less associated with the incarceration index than are the indicators of *legality*, and are non-significant when used together with these latter. This suggests that the characteristics of *context* (host society) and the modes or processes of integration/poor integration (e.g. hidden economy) could be more relevant as explanatory factors than the characteristics of immigrants themselves, their origin included. The modest association between incarceration index and *education of non-nationals* seems to lend further credence to this hypothesis. Other factors, moreover, concur to invalidate the hypothesis of any direct influence of the *origin* factor on the values of the incarceration index. Many national groups of immigrants in Europe coming from less developed countries (e.g. groups coming from the Philippines and Sri Lanka) present decidedly low rates of incrimination and incarceration. The rates of criminality of national groups moreover are not constant in time. The same groups – as already pointed out – present different rates of criminality in different countries.

Analysis of the *origin* factor has, however, led to the emergence of other aspects to which attention needs to be paid. Our findings show that the percentage of immigrants from the less developed countries is associated with many variables regarding the characteristics of the host country, such as material prosperity, education/culture, rights and social capital. Something very similar happens with the indicator of the average education of immigrants, it too associated with the same variables of the host country. In practice, immigrants from the less developed countries with an average level of lower education are especially concentrated in European countries with a relatively lower level of material development and a less advanced level of culture, rights and social capital. So immigrants are not distributed in a casual way in the various countries of Europe, but according to opportunities/preferences that are correlated with the average characteristics of the immigrants themselves and those of the society of destination. This is in part predictable. Agricultural labourers will have better chances in a country with a developed agricultural sector; nuclear engineers, in a country with an advanced technological sector, and so on. However, the fact that immigrants in Western Europe are not casually distributed raises a question. Is it not possible that the high incarceration rates registered for immigrants in some countries are due to the fact that those who are (whether by character, inclination or duress) prone to crime choose to emigrate precisely to those countries in which illegality is widespread and the control of the law weak? To this disturbing question no conclusive answer can be given. Reliable data are lacking – as we have noted – on the criminal curriculum of immigrants. Besides, it will never be possible to know what their attitude to legality is. But some more general remarks on this score can be made. First, the propensity to criminality does not remain constant throughout a person's life. Still less is it an inherited trait. Even those who have committed crimes generally stop doing so as they grow older and as their living conditions change. The abandonment of crime is not something that is found only in the pages of novels like *Les Misérables*. Moreover, the original propensity to criminality of immigrants, assuming there is one, does not tell us much about their conduct in their new country of election. It should not be forgotten that immigration to North America did not consist merely of devout Pilgrim Fathers. As for immigration to some other countries, perhaps it's better to pass that over in silence. Even if we admit that the hypothesis of a higher proportion of those with criminal records among immigrants bound for certain countries has some basis in fact, it seems difficult to attribute to this alone the high rates of incarceration of non-nationals registered in those countries.

It is more realistic to assume that the interaction between the characteristics of the host society and the migrant influx has an effect on these rates. The analysis of the differentials that exist between the various European countries, in terms of all the indicators used in this study, has furnished further data in this regard. We have been able to identify a limited group of countries materially more disadvantaged, economically more unstable, with a more modest cultural level and a propensity to *particularism*, characterized by a surge in the growth of their non-national population in recent years, and by an immigration less linked to the presence of nuclear families and culturally more 'alien' to Europe. It is just this group of countries that presents an abnormally high level of imprisonment of non-nationals. Contrasting with this group are those countries characterized by material prosperity even for the poorer classes, high social protection, high level of culture, information and communication, prevalence of a universalist conception, contained growth of immigration, and a non-national population more culturally 'attuned' to Europe. These latter countries are characterized by an incarceration index that – once differences in age groups and the presence of clandestine immigrants are taken into account – is not too different from the share of non-nationals out of the resident population.

On the whole, the findings of our analysis suggest that the incarceration index tends to rise wherever socio-economic and cultural conditions unfavourable to integration are registered. These conditions relate both to the characteristics of the host country, and to the characteristics of the immigrant influx and the population that gives rise to it. Our data analysis seems to indicate, therefore, that the difficulties of integration and the

conditions of economic and social marginality of the non-national population are factors not unrelated to the emergence of higher levels of criminal
charges and imprisonment for non-nationals.

The having identified conditions unfavourable to the integration of non-
nationals as the background associated with their high levels of criminal
charges and imprisonment does not, however, imply a confirmation of the
anomic strain thesis, i.e. of the model most commonly used. Indicators of
inequality and of *relative deprivation* – such as the income of the poorest
10 per cent of the population, and the ratio between the income of the richest
and that of the poorest – are closely correlated with the incarceration index.
This is in conformity with the hypothesis that recourse to criminal forms of
conduct can be linked to the gulf existing between the 'universal' goal of full
social and economic success and the limited means that these non-nationals
generally have at their disposal – as indeed the proponents of anomic strain
theory argue. New immigrants are drawn by the great hopes that an ever
richer Europe engenders in them: but too often their hopes are dashed and
they find themselves to be *poor amidst wealth*.

Nonetheless, our analysis has pointed to various factors that are difficult
to reconcile with anomic strain. In the first place, one would expect that the
immigrants on which our attention has been especially focused – those without citizenship of the host country, usually immigrants of the first generation, often coming from countries with decidedly lower wage levels and
living conditions – would have more limited and more easily realizable
expectations. They ought by the same token to be less disturbed by situations of *relative deprivation*, of the kind from which, on the contrary, immigrants of the second generation, *caught between two worlds*, probably suffer.
Immigrants of the second generation, in turn, are usually citizens of the host
country, and therefore no longer registered as non-nationals. In the second
place, given that anomic strain is dependent on the level of expected success
in the host country, we would expect the strain to which non-nationals are
subjected to be stronger where the emphasis on economic success and on the
effort everyone ought to make to achieve this objective is greater. This is
more likely to happen in those countries in which, under the influence of
Protestant-Calvinist culture, economic success assumes the character of a
personal duty and a means of gauging one's own moral standard (when one
is successful) and that of others (when they are not). However, the data on
the involvement of non-nationals in criminal activities show us that such
involvement is particularly high in countries impervious to the Protestant
ethic, such as Greece, Italy and Spain. Nor does comparison between Europe
and the USA help to corroborate anomic strain theory. The data we have
gathered and those of other similar studies in a European framework show
an overall over-representation of non-nationals in the figures for subjects
charged and subjects detained. The US data, by contrast, show no over-
representation, in spite of the fact that the USA is a society that not only

idealizes personal achievement, through a winner/loser culture, but also has an inequality of income greater than any country in Europe. The different contribution of immigrants to criminality in the USA, besides, is difficult to attribute to a more rigid selection of immigrants, given that the USA has to cope with a sizeable proportion of illegal immigrants on whom no selection is conducted.

Lastly, the fact that variables concerning legality, such as corruption, certainty of the law, hidden economy and clandestinity, are more strongly associated with the incarceration index than the variables concerning inequality and relative deprivation, ought not to be ignored.

In other words, the current expansion of the presence of non-nationals in penal and penitentiary circuits seems to be associated with a scenario characterized not only and not so much by inequality and relative deprivation as it is with one of widespread illegality and violation of the right to justice, with its corollaries of corruption and abuse/exploitation of the condition of deprivation and vulnerability of immigrants, especially those most marginalized such as clandestine immigrants (through the hidden economy). It seems realistic, moreover, to conclude that a society inspired by the rule of law and a culture of fairness (equity), in which arbitrary powers are curbed – in other words, a society characterized by a high level of legality and, more indirectly, by a substantial amount of institutionalized social capital – is able to keep under control even a high level of socio-economic inequality and relative deprivation. Contrariwise, a society in which legality is weak, corruption rife and arbitrary powers rampant, will have difficulty in preventing, in the same situation, the diffusion of antisocial activities. These activities indifferently assume – among non-nationals in Europe – the form of crimes of *acquisition* (theft, robbery, drug trafficking) and crimes of *violence* (homicide, rape).

In any case, the involvement of non-nationals in penal and penitentiary circuits seems to be 'explained' not by a particular phenomenon but by a combination of phenomena. This combination seems to merge basic characteristics of the host country and characteristics of immigrant influxes. This should be no cause for surprise. A variety of different but interacting aspects influences integration. Thus, if the presence of clandestine or irregular immigrants is synonymous with poor integration, the share of clandestine immigrants among the non-national population is associated with the level of corruption and that of the certainty of the law in the host society, which are in turn dependent on its social and cultural characteristics. The diffusion of the hidden economy, which is strongly associated with the share of non-nationals among the prison population, is dependent on corruption, promotes clandestine immigration, exploits it, and is in turn perpetuated by it; and so on. Three factors associated with the incarceration index of non-nationals have emerged from our analysis. Each of them combines different specific variables. The first of these factors is the one we have called 'Culture, Rights and Social Capital'; the second, 'Wealth and Social Equity'; and the third, 'New Disadvantaged Immigration from the Less Developed Countries'. In the first factor we can identify a more specific latent variable: 'widespread legality/illegality'. Widespread illegality, as a characteristic of context, seems to be extended, almost automatically, to new residents of it, i.e. immigrants, and to encourage their involvement in criminal activities.

In sum, if the alienation – social, cultural, religious – of at least a part of current immigrants seems to contribute to the involvement of non-nationals in penal and penitentiary circuits, economic generosity to the poorest and, more generally, respect for civil rights, the rule of law, and the tolerance and openness shown by the host society, seem to represent effective anti-dotes to counteract this involvement. For the host society, openness, transparency, probity, fairness and generosity may constitute forms of enlightened egoism or, to put it in the words of Alexander Pope (1733–4: *Essay on Man*, III, 6, 311–312):

> *Man, like the gen'rous vine, supported lives;*
> *The strength he gains is from th' embrace he gives.*

Notes

4 Criminality in the countries of Western Europe

1 The incarceration rate is expected to be affected by the preceding crime rate: therefore, we tested the model: Crime rate variation$_t$ = α + β Incarceration rate variation$_{t-1}$ + γ Crime rate variation$_{t-1}$ + ε.

6 Indicators of socio-economic condition, integration and origin

1 By using Principal Components Analysis we can summarize a series of interrelated variables in a small number of *principal components*. The new indicators used here are the product of the *linear combination* of the two basic variables; in practice, they represent the *optimal association* of the original variables.
2 Factor Analysis is a technique aimed at identifying a restricted number of underlying factors capable of representing the relations between many manifest variables that are inter-correlated. The factors are identified on the basis of the contribution of the variables to the factors themselves; in practice, through the value of the coefficients of the variables, shown here by the matrix of the factors (Appendix III). Our group of explanatory variables is ideal for factor analysis because it is characterized by a high level of correlation. The specific method used is that of the *principal components*. The matrix was rotated, for easier interpretation, by the *equamax* method. The first three factors explain 84 per cent of the overall variance.
3 Multidimensional Scaling is aimed at analysing the distances that exist within variables that refer to two or more cases (here countries), and at producing a geometric figure that represents these distances. The distances are based on correlations with the Sammon loss criterion.

Bibliography

Aalberts, M.M.J. 1990. *Politie tussen Discretie en Discriminatie: Operationeel vreemdelingentoezicht in Nederland*. Antwerpen: Kluwer.

Adserà, A., Boix, C. and Payne, M. 2001. 'Are You Being Served? Political Accountability and Quality of Government'. Pp. 293–295 in *Global Corruption Report 2001: Data and Research*, ed. Transparency International. Berlin: Transparency International.

Aebi, M.F., Killias, M. and Tavares, C. 2002. 'Comparing Crime Rates: The International Crime (Victim) Survey, The European Sourcebook of Crime and Criminal Justice Statistics, and Interpol Statistics'. *International Journal of Comparative Criminology*, 2: 22–37.

Agnew, R. 1985. 'Social Control Theory and Delinquency: A Longitudinal Test'. *Criminology*, 23: 47–63.

Agnew, R. 2001. 'Building on the Foundation of General Strain Theory: Specifying the Types of Strain Most Likely to Lead to Crime and Delinquency'. *Journal of Research in Crime and Delinquency*, 38: 319–361.

Albrecht, H.-J. 1987. 'Foreign Minorities and the Criminal Justice System in the Federal Republic of Germany'. *The Howard Journal of Criminal Justice*, 26 (4): 272–286.

Albrecht, H.-J. 1988. 'Ausländerkriminalität'. Pp. 183–204 in *Fälle zum Wahlfach Kriminologie, Jugendstrafrecht, Strafvollzug*, ed. H. Jung. Munich: Beck.

Albrecht, H.-J. 1993. 'Ethnic Minorities: Crime and Criminal Justice in Europe'. Pp. 84–100 in *Crime in Europe*, eds F. Heidensohn and M. Farrell. London: Routledge.

Albrecht, H.-J. 1995. 'Ethnic Minorities, Culture Conflict and Crime'. *Crime, Law and Social Change*, 24 (1): 19–36.

Albrecht, H.-J. 1997. 'Ethnic Minorities, Crime and Criminal Justice in Germany'. Pp. 31–99 in *Ethnicity, Crime and Immigration: Comparative and Cross-National Perspectives*, ed. M. Tonry. Chicago and London: The University of Chicago Press.

Albrecht, H.-J. 2002. 'Fortress Europe? Controlling Illegal Immigration'. *European Journal of Crime, Criminal Law and Criminal Justice*, 10 (1): 1–22.

Ambrosini, M. 2005. *Sociologia delle migrazioni*. Bologna: il Mulino.

American Academy of Political and Social Sciences. 1966. *The New Immigration*. New York: Annals of the American Academy of Political and Social Sciences.

Andersson, J. 1984. 'Policing in Multi-Ethnic Areas in Stockholm'. Pp. 57–60 in *Policing and Social Policy*, ed. J. Brown. London: Review Publishing.

Austria. 2008. *Gerichtliche Kriminalstatistik*. Wien: Statistik Austria.

Baldacci, E. and Natale, L. 1995. 'Devianza e integrazione degli immigrati stranieri: una verifica empirica'. Pp. 545–552 in *Continuità e discontinuità nei processi demografici – L'Italia nella transizione demografica*, ed. Società Italiana di Statistica. Soveria Mannelli: Rubettino.

Barbagli, M. 1994. *L'occasione e l'uomo ladro: Furti e rapine in Italia*. Bologna: il Mulino.

Barbagli, M. 1998. *Immigrazione e criminalità in Italia*. Bologna: il Mulino.

Barbaret, R. and García-España, E. 1997. 'Minorities, Crime and Criminal Justice in Spain'. Pp. 175–197 in *Minorities, Migrants and Crime*, ed. I.H. Marshall. Thousand Oaks, CA: Sage.

Basdevant, C. 1983. 'Les carrières scolaires. Étude comparative de la trajectoire scolaire d'adolescents français et immigrés'. *Annales de Vaucresson*, 20: 89–101.

Becker, H.S. 1963. *Outsiders: Studies in the Sociology of Deviance*. New York: The Free Press.

Berry, J.W. 1992. 'Acculturation and Adaptation in a New Society'. *International Migration*, XXX (3/4): 69–85.

Blau, P.M. and Blau, J.R. 1982. 'The Cost of Inequality: Metropolitan Structure and Violent Crime'. *American Sociological Review*, 47: 114–129.

Bonifazi, C. 1998. *L'immigrazione straniera in Italia*. Bologna: il Mulino.

Bottoms, A.E. 1967. 'Delinquency among Immigrants'. *Race*, 4: 357–383.

Bursik, R.J., Jr. 2006. 'Rethinking the Chicago School of Criminology: A New Era of Immigration'. Pp. 20–35 in *Immigration and Crime: Race, Ethnicity, and Violence*, eds R. Martinez Jr. and A. Valenzuela Jr. New York and London: New York University Press.

Burton, V.S., Jr., Cullen, F.T., Evans, T.D. and Dunaway, R.G. 1994. 'Reconsidering Strain Theory: Operationalization, Rival Theories, and Adult Criminality'. *Journal of Quantitative Criminology*, 10: 213–239.

Butcher, K.F. and Piehl, A.M. 1997. *Recent Immigrants: Unexpected Implications for Crime and Incarceration*. Cambridge, MA: National Bureau of Economic Research.

Canada, Department of the Solicitor General. 1974. *An Estimate of the Present and Future Costs and Involvement of Immigrants in Crime in Canada*. Ottawa: Department of the Solicitor General.

Caritas Roma. 1995, 1996. *Immigrazione – Dossier statistico*. Roma: Anterem.

Carr-Hill, R.A. 1987. 'O Bring Me Your Poor: Immigrants in the French System of Criminal Justice'. *The Howard Journal of Criminal Justice*, 26 (4): 287–302.

Casacchia, O. and Strozza, S. 1995. 'Il livello di integrazione socioeconomica degli immigrati stranieri: un quadro di riferimento'. Pp. 553–560 in *Continuità e discontinuità nei processi demografici – L'Italia della transizione demografica*, ed. Società Italiana di Statistica. Soveria Mannelli: Rubettino.

Caselli, G. 2001. 'Le migrazioni internazionali'. Pp. 622–640 in *Enciclopedia Italiana: Eredità del Novecento*. Roma: Istituto della Enciclopedia Italiana.

Casman, M.-T., Gailly, P., Gavray, C. and Pasleau, J.P. 1992. *Police et immigrés: Images mutuelles, problèmes et solutions*. Brugge: Vanden Broele.

Cavadino, M. and Dignan, J. 2006. 'Penal Policy and Political Economy'. *Criminology & Criminal Justice*, 6 (4): 435–456.

Chandler, C.R. and Tsai, Y. 2001. 'Social Factors Influencing Immigration Attitudes: An Analysis of Data from the General Social Survey'. *The Social Science Journal*, 38: 177–188.

Cheong, P.H., Edwards, R., Goulbourne, H. and Solomos, J. 2007. 'Immigration, Social Cohesion and Social Capital: A Critical Review'. *Critical Social Policy*, 27 (1): 24–49.

Cheung, Y.W. 1980. 'Explaining Ethnic and Racial Variations in Criminality Rates: A Review and Critique'. *Canadian Criminology Forum*, 3: 1–14.

Clancy, A., Aust, R., Hough, M. and Kershaw, C. 2001. *Crime, Policing and Justice: The Experience of Ethnic Minorities, Findings from the 2000 British Crime Survey*. London: Home Office.

Cloward, R.A. and Ohlin, L.E. 1960. *Delinquency and Opportunities. A Theory of Delinquent Gangs*. Glencoe, IL: The Free Press.

Cohen, A.K. 1955. *Delinquent Boys. The Culture of the Gang*. Glencoe, IL: The Free Press.

Coleman, J.S. 1988. 'Social Capital in the Creation of Human Capital'. *American Journal of Sociology*, 94: S95–S120.

Conseil de l'Europe. 1984. *Évolution démographique récente dans les états membres du Conseil de l'Europe*. Strasbourg: Conseil de l'Europe.

Conseil de l'Europe. 1985, 1986, 1987, 1988, 1989, 1990, 1992, 1993, 1994–95. *Bulletin d'information pénologique*. Bruxelles: Conseil de l'Europe.

Conseil de l'Europe. 2000, 2001, 2002, 2003, 2004, 2007. *SPACE I*. Strasbourg: Conseil de l'Europe.

Cornelius, W.A., Martin, P.L. and Hollifield, J.F. 1994. 'Introduction: The Ambivalent Quest for Immigration Control'. Pp. 3–41 in *Controlling Immigration: A Global Perspective*, eds W.A. Cornelius, P.L. Martin and J.F. Hollifield. Stanford, CA: Stanford University Press.

Council of Europe. 1996. *Penological Information Bulletin 1994–1995*. Brussels: Council of Europe.

Council of Europe. 1999, 2003, 2006. *European Sourcebook of Crime and Criminal Justice Statistics*. Strasbourg: Council of Europe.

Council of Europe. 1999a. *Recent Demographic Developments in Europe*. Strasbourg: Council of Europe.

Crook, E.B. 1934. 'Cultural Marginality in Sexual Delinquency'. *American Journal of Sociology*, 39: 493–500.

Crow, I. 1987. 'Black People and Criminal Justice in the UK'. *Howard Journal of Criminal Justice*, 26: 303–314.

Debuyst, C. 1970. 'Notes sur la délinquance des étrangers'. *Annales de Droit*, 4: 557–568.

Denmark. 2002. 'Immigrants Are Convicted of More Criminal Offences'. Danmarks Statistik *NYT*, 191.

Denmark. 2009. *Statistical Yearbook 2009*. Copenhagen: Statistics Denmark.

Dentler, R.A. and Erikson, K.T. 1959. 'The Functions of Deviance in Group'. *Social Problems*, 2: 98–107.

Desdevides, M.-C. 1976. *La délinquance étrangère*. Université de Rennes: Thèse pour le doctorat.

De Valkeneer, C. 1987. *Missions de policiers patrouilleurs et des agents de quartier. Volume I et II.* Louvain-la-Neuve: Université Catholique de Louvain.

Downes, D. 1988. *Contrasts in Tolerance: Postwar Penal Policy in the Netherlands and England and Wales.* Oxford: Clarendon Press.

Downes, D. and Rock, P. 2003. *Understanding Deviance.* Oxford: Oxford University Press.

Dubet, F. 1989. 'Trois processus migratoires'. *Revue française des affaire sociales,* 3: 7–28.

Du Camp, M. 1870. 'La mendicité dans Paris'. *Revue des deux mondes,* Mai: 175–212.

Durkheim, É. 1893. *De la division du travail social.* Paris: Alcan.

Durkheim, É. 1897. *Le suicide. Étude de sociologie.* Paris: Alcan.

Ehrlich, I. 1974. 'Participation in Illegitimate Activities: An Economic Analysis'. Pp. 68–134 in *Essays in the Economics of Crime and Punishment,* eds G.S. Becker and W.M. Landes. New York: NBER.

Entorf, H. and Spengler, H. 2000. 'Socioeconomic and Demographic Factors of Crime in Germany: Evidence from Panel Data of the German States'. *International Review of Law and Economics,* 20: 75–106.

Entorf, H. and Spengler, H. 2002. *Crime in Europe: Causes and Consequences.* Berlin – Heidelberg: Springer.

Erikson, K. 1962. 'Notes on the Sociology of Deviance'. *Social Problems,* 9: 307–314.

Espenshade, T.J. and Hempstead, K. 1996. 'Contemporary American Attitudes towards U.S. Immigration'. *International Migration Review,* 30: 535–570.

EUICS. 2007. *The Burden of Crime in the EU: A Comparative Analysis of the European Survey of Crime and Safety (EUICS) 2005.* Bruxelles: EUICS.

Eurobarometer. 2001. *Attitudes towards Minority Groups in the European Union.* Vienna: Eurobarometer.

European Values Study Group and World Values Survey Association. 2006. *European and World Values Surveys Four-Wave Integrated Data File, 1981–2004.* Madrid and Tilburg: ASEP and JDS.

Eurostat. 1988. *Censuses of Population 1981–1982.* Luxembourg: Office for Official Publications of European Communities.

Eurostat. 1994a, 1995, 1996. *Migration Statistics.* Bruxelles-Luxembourg: ECSC-EC-EAEC.

Eurostat. 1996a, 1997, 2000, 2002. *Yearbook.* Bruxelles-Luxembourg: Office for Official Publications of European Communities.

Eurostat. 2000a, 2002a. *European Social Statistics: Migration.* Bruxelles-Luxembourg: Office for Official Publications of European Communities.

Eurostat. 2003. *Structural Indicators: Social Cohesion.* Luxembourg: Eurostat Metadata.

Eurostat. 2004. *European Social Statistics: Social Protection.* Luxembourg: Office for Official Publications of European Communities.

Eurostat. 2004a. *Living Conditions in Europe.* Luxembourg: Office for Official Publications of European Communities.

Eurostat. 2004b. *Education.* Luxembourg: Eurostat Website.

Eurostat. 2006, 2008. *Non-National Population in the EU Member States.* Eurostat Website.

Eurostat. 2007. *Population and Social Conditions.* Eurostat Website.

Eysenck, H.J. 1972. *Psychology Is about People*. Harmondsworth: Penguin Books.

FAIR. 2007. *Illegal Aliens and Crime Incidence*. Washington, D.C.: FAIR.

Fante, J. 1985. *The Road to Los Angeles*. Santa Barbara, Cal.: Black Sparrow Press.

Fassmann, H. and Münz, R. 1994. 'Patterns and Trends of International Migration in Western Europe'. Pp. 3–33 in *European Migration in the Late Twentieth Century*, eds H. Fassmann and R. Münz. Aldershot: Elgar.

Ferracuti, F. 1968. 'European Migration and Crime'. Pp. 189–219 in *Essays in Honor of Thorsten Sellin*, ed. M. Wolfgang. New York: Wiley.

Ferrari, R. 1913. 'Report of Robert Ferrari'. Pp. 530–548 in 'Crime and Immigration (Report of Committee G, of the Institute)', Chairman G.C. Speranza. *Journal of the American Institute of Criminal Law and Criminology*, 4 (Nov.): 523–548.

Finland. 2004. *Statistical Yearbook of Finland*. Helsinki: Statistics Finland.

Flowers, R.B. 1990. *Minorities and Criminality*. New York: Praeger.

Friedman, E. *et al.* 2000. 'Dodging the Grabbing Hand: The Determinants of Unofficial Activity in 69 Countries'. *Journal of Public Economics*, 76: 459–493.

Garland, D. 2001. *The Culture of Control*. Oxford: Oxford University Press.

Garson, J.-P. and Loizillon, A. 2003. *L'Europe et les migrations de 1950 à nos jours*. OECD: Paris.

Gellner, E. 1983. *Nations and Nationalism*. Oxford: Blackwell.

Germany (Federal Republic) Bundeskriminalamt. 2007a. *Polizeiliche Kriminalstatistik 2006*. Wiesbaden: Bundeskriminalamt.

Germany (Federal Republic) Bundeskriminalamt. 2007b. *Police Crime Statistics 2006*. Wiesbaden: Bundeskriminalamt.

Giddens, A. 1998. *The Third Way: The Renewal of Social Democracy*. Cambridge: Polity Press.

Giffen, P.J. 1976. 'Official Rates of Crime and Delinquency'. Pp. 66–110 in *Crime and its Treatment in Canada*, ed. W.T. McGrath. Toronto: Macmillan.

Gillioz, E. 1967. 'La criminalité des étrangers en Suisse'. *Revue pénale Suisse*, 83: 178–191.

Gilroy, P. 1982. 'Police and Thieves'. Pp. 143–182 in *The Empire Strikes Back: Race and Racism in 70s Britain*, ed. Centre for Contemporary Cultural Studies. London: Hutchinson.

Glazer, N. 1997. *We Are All Multiculturalists Now*. Cambridge, MA: Harvard University Press.

Golini, A. 2000. 'I movimenti di popolazione nel mondo contemporaneo'. Pp. 89–160 in *Migrazioni: Scenari per il XXI secolo*, a cura di Agenzia romana per la preparazione del Giubileo, vol. I. Roma: Agenzia romana per la preparazione del Giubileo.

Greenberg, D.F. 1999. 'The Weak Strength of Social Control Theory'. *Crime & Delinquency*, 45: 66–81.

Guajardo, S.A. and O'Hara, P. 1998. 'Diversity, Economics and Crime in Europe'. *Security Journal*, 11: 273–278.

Gusfield, J. 1963. *Symbolic Crusade*. Urbana, IL: University of Illinois Press.

Gwartney, J. and Lawson, R. 2002. *Economic Freedom of the World 2002*. Vancouver, BC: The Fraser Institute.

Gwartney, J., Lawson, R. and Easterly, W. 2006. *Economic Freedom of the World 2006*. Vancouver, BC: The Fraser Institute.

Hagan, J. and Palloni, A. 1999. 'Sociological Criminology and the Mythology of Hispanic Immigration and Crime'. *Social Problems*, 46: 617–632.

Hagan, J., Levi, R. and Dinovitzer, R. 2008. 'The Symbolic Violence of the Crime–Immigration Nexus: Migrant Mythologies in the Americas'. *Criminology & Public Policy*, 7: 95–112.

Hanak, G., Pilgram, A. and Stangel, W. 1984. 'Die Strafverfolgung an Ausländern – Eine Sekundärauswertung zweier soziologischer Studien zur Rechtsanwendung'. *Kriminalsoziologische Bibliographie*, 11: 41–53.

Hart, T.C. and Rennison, C. 2003. *Reporting Crime to the Police, 1992–2000*. Washington, D.C.: US Department of Justice.

Haskey, J. 1992. 'The Immigrant Populations of the Different Countries of Europe: Their Size and Origins'. *Populations Trends*, 69 (Autumn): 37–47.

Hebberecht, P. 1997. 'Minorities, Crime and Criminal Justice in Belgium'. Pp. 151–174 in *Minorities, Migrants and Crime*, ed. I.H. Marshall. Thousand Oaks, CA: Sage.

Hindelang, M.J. 1978. 'Race and Involvement in Common Law Personal Crimes'. *American Sociological Review*, 43: 93–109.

Hirschi, T. 1969. *Causes of Delinquency*. Berkeley, CA: University of California Press.

Hofer, H., von. 2000. 'Crime Statistics as Constructs: The Case of Swedish Rape Statistics'. *European Journal on Criminal Policy and Research*, 8: 77–89.

Hofer, H., von, Sarnecki, J. and Tham, H. 1997. 'Minorities, Crime, and Criminal Justice in Sweden'. Pp. 62–85 in *Minorities, Migrants and Crime*, ed. I.H. Marshall. Thousand Oaks, CA: Sage.

Hollifield, J.F. 1994. 'Immigration and Republicanism in France: The Hidden Consensus'. Pp. 143–175 in *Controlling Immigration: A Global Perspective*, eds W.A. Cornelius, P.L. Martin and J.F. Hollifield. Stanford, CA: Stanford University Press.

Hollinger, R.C. 1984. 'Race, Occupational Status and Pro-Active Police Arrest for Drinking and Driving'. *Journal of Criminal Justice*, 75: 234–249.

Holmberg, L. and Kyvsgaard, B. 2003. 'Are Immigrants and Their Descendants Discriminated Against in the Danish Criminal Justice System?'. *Journal of Scandinavian Studies in Criminology and Crime Prevention*, 2: 125–142.

Hood, R. 1992. *Race and Sentencing*. Oxford: Oxford University Press.

Horowitz, C.F. 2001. *An Examination of U.S. Immigration Policy and Serious Crime*. Washington, D.C.: Center for Immigration Studies.

Hughes, B.B. 2001. 'Global Social Transformation: The Sweet Spot, the Steady Slog, and the System Shift'. *Economic Development and Cultural Change*, 49 (2): 423–458.

Ianni, F.A.J. 1974. *Black Mafia: Ethnic Succession in Organized Crime*. New York: Simon and Schuster.

INSEE. 2006. *Annuaire statistique de la France*. Paris: INSEE.

Institute for Social Research. 1994. *World Values Study*. Ann Arbor, MI: Institute for Social Research.

Interpol. 1985–86, 1987–88, 1989–90, 1991–92, 1993, 1996, 2000. *Statistiques Criminelles Internationales*. Lyon: Interpol.

Italy, Istat. 1985 ff. *Statistiche giudiziarie penali*. Roma: Istat.

Jandl, M. 2003. *Estimates on the Numbers of Illegal and Smuggled Immigrants in Europe*. Vienna: International Centre for Migration Policy Development.

Junger, M. 1989. 'Ethnic Minorities, Crime and Public Policy'. Pp. 142–173 in *Crime and Criminal Policy in Europe*, ed. R. Hood. Oxford: Centre for Criminological Research, University of Oxford.

Junger, M. 1990. 'Studying Ethnic Minorities in Relation to Crime and Police Discrimination'. *British Journal of Criminology*, 4: 493–503.

Junger, M. and Polder, W. 1992. 'Some Explanations of Crime Among Four Ethnic Groups in the Netherlands'. *Journal of Quantitative Criminology*, 8: 51–78.

Junger-Tas, J. 1985. *Young Immigrants in the Netherlands and their Contacts with the Police*. The Hague: Ministry of Justice.

Junger-Tas, J. 1992. 'An Empirical Test of Social Control Theory'. *Journal of Quantitative Criminology*, 8: 9–28.

Junger-Tas, J. 1997. 'Ethnic Minorities and Criminal Justice in the Netherlands'. Pp. 257–310 in *Ethnicity, Crime and Immigration: Comparative and Cross-National Perspectives*, ed. M. Tonry. Chicago and London: The University of Chicago Press.

Kaiser, G. 1988. *Kriminologie: Eine Lehrbuch*. Heidelberg: Müller.

Kammhuber, S. 1997. 'Ausländerkriminalität. Eine bittere Realität und ihre Bewältigung'. *Kriminalistik*, 8–9: 551–556.

Kanellopoulos, C.N. and Gregou, M. 2006. *Policy Report on Migration, Asylum and Return in Greece*. Athens: Centre of Planning and Economic Research.

Kennet, L. and Martin, W.A. 1989. 'On the Structure of Ethnic Crime in America: The Modern Form of Buccaneer Capitalism'. Pp. 91–102 in *Crime and the New Immigrants*, eds H.M. Launer and J.E. Palenski. Springfield, IL: C.C. Thomas Publisher.

Kidd, R.F. and Chayet, E. 1984. 'Why Do Victims Fail to Report? The Psychology of Criminal Victimization'. *Journal of Social Issues*, 40: 39–50.

Killias, M. 1988. 'Diskriminierendes Anzeigeverhalten von Opfern gegenüber Ausländern?'. *Monatsschrift für Kriminologie und Strafrechtsreform*, 71: 156–165.

Killias, M. 1989. 'Criminality among Second-Generation Immigrants in Western Europe: A Review of the Evidence'. *Criminal Justice Review*, 14 (1): 13–42.

Killias, M. 1997. 'Immigrants, Crime and Criminal Justice in Switzerland'. Pp. 375–405 in *Ethnicity, Crime and Immigration: Comparative and Cross-National Perspectives*, ed. M. Tonry. Chicago and London: The University of Chicago Press.

Killias, M., Haymoz, S. and Lamon, P. 2007. *Swiss Crime Survey: Die Kriminalität in der Schweiz im Lichte der Opferbefragungen von 1984 bis 2005*. Bern: Stämpfli.

Kühne, H.-H. 2002. 'Culture Conflict and Crime in Europe'. Pp. 89–99 in *Migration, Culture Conflict and Crime*, ed. J.D. Freilich *et al.* Aldershot: Ashgate.

LaFree, G. and Russell, K.K. 1993. 'The Argument for Studying Race and Crime'. *Journal of Criminal Justice Education*, 4 (2): 273–289.

Landau, S.F. and Nathan, G. 1983. 'Selecting Delinquents for Cautioning in the London Metropolitan Area'. *British Journal of Criminology*, 23: 128–149.

Lappi-Seppälä, T. 2008. 'Trust, Welfare, and Political Culture: Explaining Differences in National Penal Policies'. Pp. 313–387 in *Crime and Justice: A Review of Research*, vol. 37, ed. M. Tonry. Chicago: University of Chicago Press.

Laughlin, H.H. 1922. 'Analysis of America's Melting Pot'. *Hearings before the Committee on Immigration and Naturalization, House of Representatives*. Washington, D.C.: US Government Printing Office, Serial 7-C: 725–829.

Layton-Henry, Z. 1994. 'Britain: The Would-Be Zero-Immigration Country'. Pp. 273–295 in *Controlling Immigration: A Global Perspective*, eds W.A. Cornelius, P.L. Martin and J.F. Hollifield. Stanford, CA: Stanford University Press.

Lee, M.T., Martinez, R., Jr. and Rosenfeld, R. 2001. 'Does Immigration Increase Homicide?: Negative Evidence from Three Border Cities'. *The Sociological Quarterly*, 42: 559–580.

Lemert, E.M. 1972. *Human Deviance, Social Problems and Social Control*. Englewood Cliffs, N.J.: Prentice-Hall.

Liben, G. 1963. 'Un reflet de la criminalité italienne dans la région de Liège'. *Revue de Droit Pénal et de Criminologie*, 44: 205–246.

Lipset, S.M. 1959. 'Some Social Requisites of Democracy'. *American Political Science Review*, 53 (1): 69–106.

Macura, M. 1994. 'Overview'. Pp. 1–20 in *International Migration: Regional Processes and Responses*, eds M. Macura and D.A. Coleman. New York: UN.

Malewska-Peyre, H. 1982. *Crise d'identité et déviance chez les jeunes immigrants*. Vaucresson: La Documentation Française.

Marshall, I.H. (ed.) 1997. *Minorities, Migrants and Crime*. Thousand Oaks, CA: Sage.

Martens, P.L. 1997. 'Immigrants, Crime and Criminal Justice in Sweden'. Pp. 183–255 in *Ethnicity, Crime and Immigration: Comparative and Cross-National Perspectives*, ed. M. Tonry. Chicago and London: The University of Chicago Press.

Martens, P. and Holmberg, S. 2005. *Crime among Persons Born in Sweden and Other Countries*. Stockholm: National Council for Crime Prevention.

Martin, J.P. and Pearson, M. 2001. 'OECD Social Indicators: A Broad Approach towards Social Reporting'. Pp. 1–10 in *Journées de la statistique publique*, sous la direction de l'Office Fédérale de la statistique. Neuchâtel: Office Fédérale de la statistique.

Martinez, R., Jr. 2006. 'Coming to America: The Impact of the New Immigration on Crime'. Pp. 1–19 in *Immigration and Crime: Race, Ethnicity, and Violence*, eds R. Martinez Jr. and A. Valenzuela Jr. New York and London: New York University Press.

Martinez, R., Jr. and Lee, M.T. 2000. 'On Immigration and Crime'. Pp. 485–524 in *Criminal Justice 2000. The Nature of Crime: Continuity and Change*, ed. G. LaFree, Washington, D.C.: US Department of Justice.

McClintock, F.H. and Gibson, E. 1961. *Robbery in London*. London: Macmillan.

McMahon, W.W. 2002. *Education and Development: Measuring the Social Benefits*. Oxford: Oxford University Press.

Melossi, D. 2000. 'The Other in the New Europe: Migrations, Deviance, Social Control'. Pp. 151–166 in *Criminal Policy in Transition*, eds A. Rutherford and P. Green. Oxford: Hart.

Melotti, U. 1993. 'Migrazioni internazionali e integrazione sociale: Il caso italiano e le esperienze europee'. Pp. 29–65 in *Immigrazione in Europa – Solidarietà e conflitto*, a cura di M. Delle Donne, U. Melotti and S. Petilli. Roma: CEDISS.

Merton, R.K. 1949. *Social Theory and Social Structure*. Glencoe, IL: The Free Press.

Microcase. 1996. *International Data Files*. Bellevue, Wash.: Microcase Corporation.

Morenoff, J.D. and Astor, A. 2006. 'Immigrant Assimilation and Crime: Generational Differences in Youth Violence in Chicago'. Pp. 36–63 in *Immigration and Crime: Race, Ethnicity, and Violence,* eds R. Martinez Jr. and A. Valenzuela Jr. New York and London: New York University Press.

Morris, T. 1958. *The Criminal Area: A Study in Social Ecology.* London: Routledge & Kegan Paul.

Natale, L. 1988. 'Stranieri e criminalità: alcune considerazioni basate su un'analisi strutturale'. *Rivista Italiana di Economia, Demografia e Statistica,* XLII (3–4): 133–150.

Natale, M. and Strozza, S. 1997. *Gli immigrati stranieri in Italia: Quanti sono, chi sono, come vivono?.* Bari: Cacucci.

Nelken, D. 2009. 'Comparative Criminal Justice: Beyond Ethnocentrism and Relativism'. *European Journal of Criminology,* 6 (4): 291–311.

Netherlands (The). 2008a. *Statistical Yearbook.* The Hague: Statistics Netherlands.

Netherlands (The). 2008b. *Criminaliteit en rechtshandhaving.* Den Haag: Centraal Bureau voor de Statistiek.

Neumann, K. 1963. *Die Kriminalität der italienischen Arbeitskräfte in Kanton Zürich.* Zürich: Juris Verlag.

Newman, G.R., Freilich, J.D. and Howard, G.J. 2007. 'Exporting and Importing Criminality: Incarceration of the Foreign Born'. Pp. 31–51 in *Crime and Immigration,* eds J.D. Freilich and G.R. Newman. Aldershot – Burlington, VT: Ashgate.

OECD. 2003. *GDP Deflators.* Paris: OECD.

Palmer, D. 1996. 'Determinants of Canadian Attitudes towards Migration: More than Just Racism'. *Canadian Journal of Behavioral Science,* 28: 180–192.

Pareto, V. 1916. *Trattato di sociologia generale.* Firenze: La Barbera.

Park, R.E. 1928. 'Human Migration and the Marginal Man'. *The American Journal of Sociology,* XXXIII (6): 881–893.

Park, R.E., Burgess, E.W. and McKenzie, R.D. 1925. *The City.* Chicago: The University of Chicago Press.

Parsons, T. 1951. *The Social System.* Glencoe, IL: The Free Press.

Paternoster, R. and Mazerolle, P. 1994. 'General Strain Theory and Delinquency: A Replication and Extension'. *Journal of Research in Crime and Delinquency,* 31: 235–263.

Penninx, R. 1984. *Immigrant Populations and Demographic Development in the Member States of the Council of Europe.* Strasbourg: Council of Europe.

Peters, W. 1971. *A Class Divided.* New York: Doubleday and Company.

Petersilia, J. 1985. 'Racial Disparities in the Criminal Justice System: A Summary'. *Crime and Delinquency,* 31: 15–34.

Petilli, S. 1993. 'Il ruolo del diritto nella regolazione del conflitto'. Pp. 627–657 in *Immigrazione in Europa – Solidarietà e conflitto,* a cura di M. Delle Donne, U. Melotti and S. Petilli. Roma: CEDISS.

Pitsela, A. 1986. *Straffälligkeit und criminelle Viktimisierung ausländischer Minderheiten in der BRD.* Freiburg: Max Planck Institut.

Pogrebin, M.R. and Poole, E.D. 1990. 'Culture Conflict and Crime in the Korean-American Community'. *Criminal Justice Policy Review,* 4: 69–78.

Portes, A. and Zhou, M. 1993. 'The New Second Generation: Segmented Assimilation and Its Variants among Post-1965 Immigrant Youth'. *Annals of the American Academy of Political and Social Science,* 530: 74–98.

Povey, D. (ed.) 2005. *Crime in England and Wales 2003/2004: Supplementary Volume 1: Homicide and Gun Crime*. London: Home Office.

Putnam, R.D. 1993. *Making Democracy Work. Civic Traditions in Modern Italy*. Princeton, NJ: Princeton University Press.

Putnam, R.D. 2000. *Bowling Alone*. New York: Simon & Schuster.

Quassoli, F. 2000. 'The Judicial System and the Social Construction of Migrants' Criminality: The case of Milan'. Pp. 203–216 in *Minorities in European Cities: The Dynamics of Social Integration and Social Exclusion at the Neighbourhood Level*, eds S. Body-Gendrot and M. Martiniello. Houndsmills and London: Macmillan.

Radzinowicz, L. and King, J. 1977. *The Growth of Crime: The International Experience*. Harmondsworth: Penguin Books.

Rawls, J. 1971. *A Theory of Justice*. Cambridge, MA: Harvard University Press.

Reid, L.W., Weiss, H.E., Adelman, R.M. and Jaret, C. 2005. 'The Immigration-Crime Relationship: Evidence across US Metropolitan Areas'. *Social Science Research*, 34: 757–780.

Remotti, F. 1985. 'La struttura sociale'. Pp. 39–53 in *Chi sono gli zingari*, a cura di E. Marcolungo and M. Karpati. Torino: Gruppo Abele.

Ribordy, F.X. 1970. *Conflit de culture et criminalité des Italiens à Montréal*. Thèse présentée à la Faculté de Sciences sociales, économiques et politiques. Montréal: Université de Montréal.

Robert, Ph., Bismuth, P. and Lambert, T. 1968. *La criminalité des migrants en France*. Paris: Compte général du Ministère de la Justice.

Rosenthal, R. and Jacobson, L. 1992. *Pygmalion in the Classroom*. New York: Irvington.

Rosoli, G. (a cura di) 1978. *Un secolo di emigrazione italiana, 1876–1976*. Roma: Centro Studi Emigrazione.

Rumbaut, R.G., Gonzales, R.G., Komaie, G. and Morgan, C.V. 2006. *Debunking the Myth of Immigrant Criminality*. Washington, D.C.: Migration Policy Institute.

Rumbaut, R.G. and Ewin, W.A. 2007. *The Myth of Immigrant Criminality*. New York: Social Science Research Council.

Salt, J. 2007. *Report of the United Kingdom Sopemi Correspondent to the OECD, 2007*. London: Migration Research Unit, UCL.

Sampson, R.J. 2006. 'Open Doors Don't Invite Criminals: Is Increased Immigration Behind the Drop in Crime?'. *The New York Times*, March 11: A27.

Sampson, R.J. and Wilson, W.J. 1995. 'Toward a Theory of Race, Crime, and Urban Inequality'. Pp. 37–54 in *Crime and Inequality*, eds J. Hagan and R.D. Peterson. Stanford, CA: Stanford University Press.

Samuel, T.J. and Faustino-Santos, R. 1991. 'Canadian Immigrants and Criminality'. *International Migration*, XXIX (1): 51–76.

Schulz, S. 2004. 'Problems with the Versatility Construct of Gottfredson and Hirschi's General Theory of Crime'. *European Journal of Crime, Criminal Law and Criminal Justice*, 12: 61–82.

Segre, S. 1993. 'Immigrazione extracomunitaria e delinquenza giovanile: un'analisi sociologica'. *Studi Emigrazione*, XXX (111): 384–416.

Sellin, T. 1938. *Culture, Conflict and Crime*. New York: Social Science Research Council.

Sessar, K. 1981. *Rechtliche und soziale Prozesse: einer Definition der Tötungskriminalität.* Freiburg: Max Planck Institut.

Shah, R. and Pease, K. 1992. 'Crime, Race and Reporting to the Police'. *The Howard Journal of Criminal Justice*, 31: 192–199.

Shaw, C.R. and McKay, H.D. 1942. *Juvenile Delinquency and Urban Areas.* Chicago: University of Chicago Press.

Shen, C.-J. 2002. 'Confucianism as a Control Theory Explanation of Crime among Overseas Chinese in Southeast Asia'. Pp. 297–312 in *Migration, Culture Conflict and Crime*, ed. J.D. Freilich *et al.* Aldershot: Ashgate.

Simmel, G. 1908. *Soziologie.* Leipzig: Duncker & Humblot.

Simon, R. and Alexander, S.H. 1993. *The Ambivalent Welcome: Print Media, Public Opinion, and Immigration.* Westport, CT: Praeger.

Skogan, W. 1990. *The Police and Public in England and Wales: A British Crime Survey Report.* Home Office Research Study No. 117. London: HMSO.

Smith, D.A. and Klein, J.R. 1984. 'Police Control of Interpersonal Disputes'. *Social Problems*, 31: 468–481.

Smith, D.J. 1997. 'Ethnic Origins, Crime, and Criminal Justice in England and Wales'. Pp. 101–182 in *Ethnicity, Crime and Immigration: Comparative and Cross-National Perspectives*, ed. M. Tonry. Chicago and London: The University of Chicago Press.

Solivetti, L.M. 1993. 'Tossicodipendenti e misure alternative'. *Bion*, 2: 43–46.

Solivetti, L.M. 1999. 'Empirical Aspects of Migration and Crime'. Pp. 1–27 in *Proceedings of the Int. Conference on Migration, Culture and Crime* (Kibbutz Ma'ale Hahamisha). Jerusalem: Ministry of Science.

Solivetti, L.M. and D'Onofrio, P. 1998. 'Some Quantitative Considerations on Migration, Crime and Justice in Italy'. Pp. 273–288 in *Migration and Crime: Proceedings of the International Conference on Migration and Crime*, ed. ISPAC. Milano: ISPAC.

Sopemi. 1991. *Continuous Reporting System on Migration. 1990.* Paris: Sopemi.

Sopemi. 1993, 1995, 2000, 2001, 2002, 2003, 2004, 2006, 2008. *Trends in International Migration. Annual Report.* Paris: Sopemi.

Spain. 1998 ff. *Anuario Estadístico del Ministerio del Interior.* Madrid: Ministerio del Interior.

Stevens, P. and Willis, C.F. 1979. *Race, Crime and Arrests.* Home Office Research Study No. 58. London: HMSO.

Stofflet, E.H. 1935. *A Study of National and Cultural Differences in Criminal Tendency.* New York: Archives of Psychology, *185*, May.

Stowell, J.I. 2007. *Immigration and Crime: The Effects of Immigration on Criminal Behavior.* New York: LFB Scholarly Pub.

Strozza, S. 2002. 'Gli scenari migratori internazionali'. Pp. 363–433 in *Economia e popolazione*, a cura di M. Natale. Milano: Angeli.

Suisse, Office fédéral de la police. 1985 ff. *Statistique policière de la criminalité.* Neuchâtel: Office fédéral de la police.

Suisse, Département fédéral de justice et police. 2001. *Groupe de travail Criminalité des étrangers.* Département fédéral de justice et police (DFJP).

Sutherland, E.H. 1924. *Criminology.* Philadelphia: Lippincott.

Sweden, The Swedish National Council for Crime Prevention. 2007. *Kriminalstatistik 1950–2006.* Metafile: The Swedish National Council for Crime Prevention.

Taft, D.R. 1936. 'Nationality and Crime'. *American Sociological Review*, 1: 724–736.

Tarde, G. 1895. *Philosophie pénale* (4 ed.). Paris: Cujas.

Thomas, W.L. and Znaniecki, F. 1918–1920. *The Polish Peasant in Europe and America*. Boston, MA: Gorham Press.

Tonry, M. 1997. 'Ethnicity, Crime and Immigration'. Pp. 1–29 in *Ethnicity, Crime and Immigration: Comparative and Cross-National Perspectives*, ed. M. Tonry. Chicago and London: The University of Chicago Press.

Tournier, P. 1997. 'Nationality, Crime and Criminal Justice in France'. Pp. 523–551 in *Ethnicity, Crime and Immigration: Comparative and Cross-National Perspectives*, ed. M. Tonry. Chicago and London: The University of Chicago Press.

Tournier, P. and Robert, Ph. 1991. *Étrangers et délinquances*. Paris: L'Harmattan.

Transparency International. 1995. *TI Corruption Index*. Berlin: Transparency International.

UK Home Office. 1989. *Victims, Suspected and Those Arrested*. Statistical Bulletin 5/89. London: Home Office.

UK Home Office. 2003. *Statistics on Race and the Criminal Justice System*. London: Home Office.

UK Home Office. 2008. *British Crime Survey: Measuring Crime for 25 Years*. London: Home Office.

UN. 1991. *Demographic Yearbook 1989*. New York: UN.

UN. 2001. *World Population Prospects 2000*. Vol. 1. New York: UN.

UNDP. 1992, 1993, 1996, 2002. *Human Development Report*. New York: Oxford University Press.

UNESCO. 2000. *Statistical Yearbook 1999*. Paris: UNESCO (www.unesco.org).

US Census Bureau. 2007. *Statistical Abstract of the United States*. Washington, D.C.: Department of Commerce, Bureau of the Census (www.census.gov/compen-dia/statab/cats/law_enforcement).

US Department of Commerce, Bureau of the Census. 1933. *Prisoners in State and Federal Prisons and Reformatories*. Washington, D.C.: US Government Printing Office.

US Department of Justice. 2006. *Criminal Victimization in the United States, 2005*. Washington, D.C.: US Government Printing Office.

US National Commission on Law Observance and Enforcement. 1931. *Report on Crime and the Foreign Born*, ed. E. Abbott. Washington, D.C.: US Government Printing Office.

US Senate Documents, Reports of the Immigration Commission. 1911. *Immigration and Crime*. Washington, D.C.: US Government Printing Office.

Valenzuola, A., Jr. 2006. 'New Immigrants and Day Labor: The Potential for Violence'. Pp. 189–211 in *Immigration and Crime: Race, Ethnicity, and Violence*, eds R. Martinez Jr. and A. Valenzuela Jr. New York and London: New York University Press.

Venchiarutti, A. 2001. 'Interventi legislativi per l'integrazione degli stranieri in Europa'. *ISIG Magazine*, X (2–3): 16–18.

Vijver, F.J.R., van de, Breugelmans, S.M. and Schalk-Soekar, S.R.G. 2008. 'Multiculturalism: Construct Validity and Stability'. *International Journal of Intercultural Relations*, 32: 93–104.

Villmow, B. 1993. 'Ausländerkriminalität'. Pp. 39–47 in *Kleines Kriminologisches Wörterbuch*, ed. G. Kaiser *et al.* Heidelberg: Müller.

Wacquant, L. 2005. 'Enemies of the Wholesome Part of the Nation: Postcolonial Migrants in the Prisons of Europe'. *Sociologie*, 1: 31–51.

Walker, M.A. 1987. 'Interpreting Race and Crime Statistics'. *Journal of the Royal Statistical Society*, ser. A, 150 (1): 39–56.

Wallis, C.P. and Maliphant, R. 1967. 'Delinquent Areas in the Country of London: Ecological Factors'. *British Journal of Criminology*, 7: 250–284.

Wanner, Ph. 2002. *Migration Trends in Europe*. Strasbourg: Council of Europe.

Westfeld, L. and Estrada, F. 2005. 'International Crime Trends: Sources of Comparative Crime Data and Post-War Trends in Western Europe'. Pp. 19–48 in *Transnational & Comparative Criminology*, ed. J. Sheptycki and A. Wardak. London: Routledge GlassHouse.

Whyte, W.F. 1943. *Street Corner Society: The Social Structure of an Italian Slum*. Chicago: The University of Chicago Press.

World Bank. 1996, 1999. *World Development Report*. New York: Oxford University Press.

World Bank. 1997. *Social Indicators of Development 1996*. Baltimore and London: The Johns Hopkins University Press.

World Bank. 1998, 2001, 2003. *World Development Indicators*. Washington, D.C.: World Bank.

World Bank. 2004. *Governance Indicators Dataset*. Metafile.

Yesilgöz, Y. 1995. *Allah, Satan en het recht: Communicatie met Turkse verdachten*. Arnhem: Gouda Quint.

Zimmermann, H.G. 1966. 'Die Kriminalität der ausländischern Arbeiter'. *Kriminalistik*, 20 (dez.): 623–625.

Zhou, M. 1997. 'Segmented Assimilation: Issues, Controversies, and Recent Research on the New Second Generation'. *International Migration Review*, 31: 975–1008.

Appendix I

Crime rates and foreign-borns in the USA

Table I.1 Robberies per 100,000 pop. in the States of the Union, foreign-born rate and some other determinants: Linear regression

Independent variable	Dependent variable: Robberies per 100,000 pop. 2000				
	Coeff.	Std. Err.	t	P>t	Beta
Foreign-borns % 2000	2.171	1.1569	1.88	0.067	0.203
Blacks % 2000	2.974	0.5146	5.78	0.000	0.466
Metropolitan pop. % 2000	1.433	0.3430	4.18	0.000	0.479
Unemployment rate 2000	9.913	4.9246	2.01	0.050	0.152
Constant	−74.654	28.1625	−2.65	0.011	

Number of obs	=	50
Multiple R	=	0.884
R-squared	=	0.782
Adj R-squared	=	0.763

Appendix II

Non-nationals and crime rates in Western Europe

Table II.1 Summary of the main indicators used in the longitudinal analysis of Chapter 4: Fixed effects model (1990–1994–1997–2000–2003)

Variable	Method	Mean	Std. Dev.	Min	Max	Observations
Homicides per	overall	1.451	0.6102	0.5	3.3	N = 90
100,000 pop.	between		0.5250	0.9	3.04	n = 18
	within		0.3302	0.851	2.771	T = 5
Rapes per	overall	9.602	5.9801	1.2	28.6	N = 88
100,000 pop.	between		5.3679	2.16	21.52	n = 18
	within		2.9806	−0.922	20.26	T-bar = 4.88
Robberies per	overall	92.524	67.1066	6	276	N = 86
100,000 pop.	between		67.3166	10.02	240.14	n = 18
	within		21.3947	35.82	155.12	T-bar = 4.77
Non-nationals	overall	6.883	7.8810	0.5	38.6	N = 90
%	between		7.9689	1.42	34.42	n = 18
	within		1.2086	1.063	11.06	T = 5
Population	overall	21461.6	24891.16	256	82532	N = 90
(,000)	between		25464.25	273.8	81628.2	n = 18
	within		533.20	19586.4	23833.2	T = 5
Urbanized	overall	74.561	13.2191	46.7	97.2	N = 90
pop. %	between		13.4721	51.1	96.86	n = 18
	within		1.1854	70.16	78.40	T = 5
Pop. in	overall	17.586	10.6013	0	38.50	N = 90
cities >1 MI %	between		10.8216	0	38.05	n = 18
	within		0.7375	14.51	20.40	T = 5
Daily	overall	287.288	149.996	32	603	N = 90
newspapers	between		149.430	52.4	578	n = 18
per 1,000 pop.	within		34.248	149.08	407.08	T = 5
Computers	overall	252.160	177.898	17	740	N = 87
per 1,000 pop.	between		120.289	48.6	486.33	n = 18
	within		137.302	−80.23	576.76	T-bar = 4.83
Cars	overall	416.177	93.4496	162	638	N = 90
per 1,000 pop.	between		82.4914	249.8	565	n = 18
	within		47.2635	258.97	567.97	T = 5

Table II.1 (Cont.)

Variable	Method	Mean	Std. Dev.	Min	Max	Observations
Cell phones per 1,000 pop.	overall	364.266	363.835	1	1198	N = 90
	between		56.288	261.4	454	n = 18
	within		359.653	−50.33	1145.6	T = 5
GDP PC ($US)	overall	22507.8	8009.83	8184	46659	N = 90
	between		7708.95	9348.8	38510	n = 18
	within		2720.35	14071.8	30656.8	T = 5
GDP PPP PC ($US)	overall	25495.7	7370.4	14183	61641	N = 90
	between		6490.72	16244	46622.6	n = 18
	within		3753.23	11191.1	40514.1	T = 5
Agriculture, employment (% of total employment)	overall	6.280	4.6292	1.2	23.9	N = 87
	between		4.7161	1.76	20.37	n = 18
	within		1.3740	2.380	11.08	T-bar = 4.83
Agriculture, value added (% of total GDP)	overall	3.815	2.7166	0.6	11.8	N = 90
	between		2.5758	1.04	10.46	n = 18
	within		1.0213	0.715	7.17	T = 5
Education, public expenditure (% of GDP)	overall	5.413	1.3404	2.4	8.4	N = 90
	between		1.2775	3.096	7.92	n = 18
	within		0.4879	4.103	7.21	T = 5
School expectancy years, primary to secondary	overall	13.141	1.0015	10.74	15.88	N = 90
	between		0.6624	11.83	14.01	n = 18
	within		0.7642	11.08	15.07	T = 5
Human development index	overall	0.917	0.0238	0.849	0.963	N = 90
	between		0.0152	0.880	0.940	n = 18
	within		0.0187	0.879	0.956	T = 5
Long-term unemployment, males (% of males)	overall	2.756	2.1892	0.156	10.06	N = 87
	between		1.7796	0.477	5.94	n = 18
	within		1.3406	−1.226	6.87	T-bar = 4.83
Unemployment, youth males (% of m. labour force 15–24)	overall	13.925	7.8045	2.7	37.4	N = 90
	between		6.7379	4.96	25.96	n = 18
	within		4.1894	1.145	27.84	T = 5
Social benefits PC (Euro)	overall	5691.0	2505.49	823	12470	N = 90
	between		2125.95	1870	8374.4	n = 18
	within		1400.34	2019.6	9786.6	T = 5
Total benefits PC (Euro)	overall	6409.6	3024.96	939	13764	N = 90
	between		2525.40	2049.4	10608.8	n = 18
	within		1749.11	1651.6	12056.6	T = 5

Continued

Table II.1 (Cont.)

Variable	Method	Mean	Std. Dev.	Min	Max	Observations
Divorces	overall	1.898	0.7646	0	3.0	N = 90
per 1,000 pop.	between		0.7490	0.28	2.72	n = 18
	within		0.2208	1.238	2.53	T = 5
Infant mortality	overall	5.438	1.6368	1.4	11.3	N = 90
per 1,000 living	between		1.0045	3.26	7.52	n = 18
births	within		1.3097	2.61	9.21	T = 5
Tuberculosis	overall	17.112	12.7651	2.5	67.5	N = 90
per 100,000	between		12.3358	4.2	53.76	n = 18
pop.	within		4.1969	4.05	31.47	T = 5
Gini	overall	30.059	3.8881	22.8	39.2	N = 87
index	between		3.7294	24.5	35.84	n = 18
	within		1.5532	26.22	34.27	T-bar = 4.83

Table II.2 Crime rates, non-nationals and other determinants: Fixed effects linear regressions (1990–1994–1997–2000–2003)

Indep. Variable	Dependent Variable: Homicides per 100,000 pop.			
	Coeff.	*Std. Err.*	*t*	*Prob.*
Non-nationals	−0.08584	0.030788	−2.79	0.007
Constant	2.04198	0.215134	9.49	0.000

R-sq: within = 0.0987
   between = 0.0258
   overall = 0.0255

Prob > F = 0.0068

Number of obs   =   90
Number of groups   =   18
Obs per group: min =   5
     avg =   5.0
     max =   5

Indep. Variable	Dependent Variable: Homicides per 100,000 pop.			
	Coeff.	*Std. Err.*	*t*	*Prob.*
Non-nationals	−0.111237	0.033979	−3.27	0.002
Gini index	−0.056741	0.023882	−2.38	0.020
Divorces	0.391840	0.184409	2.12	0.037
Constant	3.218095	0.734972	4.38	0.000

R-sq: within = 0.2162
   between = 0.0827
   overall = 0.0948

Prob > F = 0.0010

Number of obs   =   87
Number of groups   =   18
Obs per group: min =   2
     avg =   4.8
     max =   5

Table II.2 (Cont.)

Indep. Variable	Dependent Variable: Ln Homicides per 100,000 pop.			
	Coeff.	*Std. Err.*	*t*	*Prob.*
Non-nationals	−0.03347	0.033363	−1.00	0.319
GDP PPP PC	−0.00007	0.000025	−3.09	0.003
Ln GDP PPP PC	2.93661	0.778825	3.77	0.000
Infant mortality	0.06872	0.030200	2.28	0.026
Constant	−27.53466	7.473091	−3.68	0.000

R-sq: within = 0.2461   Number of obs   =   90
          between = 0.0130   Number of groups   =   18
          overall = 0.0415   Obs per group: min   =   5
                                                                  avg   =   5.0
Prob > F = 0.0006   max   =   5

Indep. Variable	Dependent Variable: Rapes per 100,000 pop.			
	Coeff.	*Std. Err.*	*t*	*Prob.*
Non-nationals	0.399569	0.292031	1.37	0.176
Constant	6.834348	2.053385	3.33	0.001

R-sq: within = 0.0264   Number of obs   =   88
          between = 0.0034   Number of groups   =   18
          overall = 0.0024   Obs per group: min   =   4
                                                                  avg   =   4.9
Prob > F = 0.1757   max   =   5

Indep. Variable	Dependent Variable: Rapes per 100,000 pop.			
	Coeff.	*Std. Err.*	*t*	*Prob.*
Non-nationals	−2.08250	0.35693	−5.83	0.000
Social benefits PC	0.00199	0.00032	6.19	0.000
Urbanization	−0.92748	0.35429	−2.62	0.011
GDP PPP PC	0.00039	0.00012	3.17	0.002
Divorces	3.59898	1.44627	2.49	0.015
Constant	64.79409	24.69862	2.62	0.011

R-sq: within = 0.5510   Number of obs   =   88
          between = 0.0287   Number of groups   =   18
          overall = 0.0060   Obs per group: min   =   4
                                                                  avg   =   4.9
Prob > F = 0.0000   max   =   5

Continued

Table II.2 (Cont.)

Indep. Variable	Dependent Variable: Ln Rapes per 100,000 pop.			
	Coeff.	*Std. Err.*	*t*	*Prob.*
Non-nationals	−0.099655	0.030807	−3.23	0.002
GDP PPP PC	0.000045	0.000012	3.64	0.001
Urbanization	−0.089587	0.032597	−2.75	0.008
Infant mortality	−0.165460	0.038618	−4.28	0.000
Tuberculosis	0.035192	0.010972	3.21	0.002
Cell phones	0.000349	0.000125	2.79	0.007
Constant	8.450885	2.409749	3.51	0.001

R-sq: within = 0.5957	Number of obs	=	88
between = 0.2432	Number of groups	=	18
overall = 0.1454	Obs per group: min =		4
	avg =		4.9
Prob > F = 0.0000	max =		5

Indep. Variable	Dependent Variable: Robberies per 100,000 pop.			
	Coeff.	*Std. Err.*	*t*	*Prob.*
Non-nationals	0.51506	2.13447	0.24	0.810
Constant	88.94829	15.04559	5.91	0.000

R-sq: within = 0.0009	Number of obs	=	86
between = 0.0144	Number of groups	=	18
overall = 0.0156	Obs per group: min =		3
	avg =		4.8
Prob > F = 0.8101	max =		5

Indep. Variable	Dependent Variable: Robberies per 100,000 pop.			
	Coeff.	*Std. Err.*	*t*	*Prob.*
Non-nationals	−6.07594	2.73466	−2.22	0.030
Newspapers	−0.15002	0.06863	−2.19	0.033
Agric. value added	12.81820	3.90292	3.28	0.002
Cell phones	0.03333	0.01200	2.78	0.007
Cars	0.19122	0.11668	1.64	0.106
Constant	36.34944	52.07393	0.70	0.488

R-sq: within = 0.2904	Number of obs	=	86
between = 0.0308	Number of groups	=	18
overall = 0.0371	Obs per group: min =		3
	avg =		4.8
Prob > F = 0.0005	max =		5

Table II.2 (Cont.)

Indep. Variable	Dependent Variable: Ln Robberies per 100,000 pop.			
	Coeff.	*Std. Err.*	*t*	*Prob.*
Non-nationals	−0.090306	0.025046	−3.61	0.001
Social benefits PC	0.000132	0.000025	5.24	0.000
Agric. value added	0.089012	0.031668	2.81	0.007
Cars	0.002016	0.000843	2.39	0.020
Constant	2.893064	0.380562	7.60	0.000

R-sq: within = 0.4504
    between = 0.0950
    overall = 0.0636

Prob > F = 0.0000

Number of obs =	86
Number of groups =	18
Obs per group: min =	3
avg =	4.8
max =	5

Appendix III

Non-nationals in prison and characteristics of the various European countries

Table III.1 Summary of the main indicators used in the longitudinal analysis of Chapter 6: between effects model (1991–1995 and 1996–2000)

Variable	Method	Mean	Std. Dev.	Min	Max	Observations
Relative index of incarceration (1991–95 & 1996–2000)	overall	3.12	1.96	0.44	8.69	N = 36
	between		1.95	0.725	7.30	n = 18
GDP spent on food (%)	overall	8.69	3.64	4.0	22.1	N = 36
	between		2.87	5.75	16.2	n = 18
Inflation rate yearly (%)	overall	3.10	2.34	0.8	14	N = 36
	between		1.92	1.76	9.76	n = 18
GNP per capita of the poorest 10% of the population	overall	7937.5	3562.83	2200	15940	N = 36
	between		3541.35	2552	15813	n = 18
Ratio income richest 20% to poorest 20% of the pop.	overall	4.53	1.22	3.0	7.4	N = 36
	between		1.22	3.05	7.1	n = 18
Public expenditure on social protection per capita (total)	overall	5817.6	2339.28	1519	10080	N = 36
	between		2153.04	2058	8699	n = 18
Pop. (25–64 yrs) that completed senior sec. school (%)	overall	63.54	17.44	19.6	85.5	N = 36
	between		17.66	19.75	84.5	n = 18
Daily newspapers per 1,000 pop.	overall	287.53	150.87	50.8	602.3	N = 36
	between		150.37	59.1	592.0	n = 18
Personal computers per 1,000 pop.	overall	229.90	107.05	34	426	N = 36
	between		103.15	41.5	384.5	n = 18
Corruption control index	overall	7.64	1.82	2.99	10	N = 36
	between		1.81	3.79	9.66	n = 18
Rule of law index	overall	1.69	0.41	0.74	2.22	N = 36
	between		0.41	0.745	2.13	n = 18
Freedom from business regulations	overall	7.18	1.16	4.4	8.9	N = 36
	between		1.05	5.15	8.85	n = 18
Hidden economy, share of GDP	overall	15.24	6.32	5.9	28.7	N = 32
	between		5.35	7.75	27.95	n = 16

Table III.1 (Cont.)

Variable	Method	Mean	Std. Dev.	Min	Max	Observations
Non-national population, variation	overall between	20.29	24.44 20.63	−8.7 −4.05	84.2 66.85	N = 36 n = 18
Non-nationals aged 0–4 yrs (%)	overall between	5.78	2.14 2.06	0.3 0.5	9.8 9.25	N = 36 n = 18
Illegal immigration, estimated level	overall between	1.72	0.81 0.81	1 1	3 3	N = 36 n = 18
Non-nationals from non-European countries (%)	overall between	34.30	18.94 18.83	3.1 4.05	71 70.8	N = 36 n = 18
Non-nationals from non-European LDC (%)	overall between	29.45	18.11 18.09	2.0 2.8	64.7 63.6	N = 36 n = 18
Non-nationals from non-European LDC & their variation over time	overall between	0.00	1.09 1.05	−1.590 −1.426	2.587 1.924	N = 36 n = 18

Table III.2 Selected independent variables and the relative index of incarceration of non-nationals (1991–1995 and 1996–2000, controlling for gender, age groups differences and illegal immigration): longitudinal linear regression (between effects), t-scores and probability; factors and factor scores

Independent variable	Dep. variable: Relative index of incarceration	Factor analysis		
	t-scores (prob.)	1st factor	2nd factor	3rd factor
GDP spent on food (%)	3.37 (0.004)	−0.364	−0.571	0.247
Inflation rate yearly (%)	3.30 (0.005)	−0.214	−0.656	0.101
GNP per capita of the poorest 10% of the population	−3.40 (0.004)	0.319	0.728	−0.506
Ratio income richest 20% to poorest 20% of the population	2.82 (0.012)	−0.389	−0.748	0.260
Public expenditure on social protection per capita (total)	−2.54 (0.022)	0.359	0.746	−0.351
Pop. (25–64 yrs) that completed senior sec. school (%)	−3.06 (0.007)	0.539	0.472	−0.565
Daily newspapers per 1,000 pop.	−3.15 (0.006)	0.745	0.490	−0.346
Corruption control index	−6.05 (0.000)	0.746	0.277	−0.270
Rule of law index	−5.97 (0.000)	0.563	0.410	−0.395
Hidden economy, share of GDP	5.29 (0.000)	−0.394	−0.254	0.289
Freedom from business regulations	−4.26 (0.001)	0.775	0.226	−0.184
Personal computers per 1,000 pop.	−4.65 (0.000)	0.622	0.513	−0.365
Non-national population, variation	3.62 (0.002)	−0.104	0.033	0.187

Continued

Table III.2 (Cont.)

Independent variable	Dep. variable: Relative index of incarceration	Factor analysis		
	t-scores (prob.)	1st factor	2nd factor	3rd factor
Non-nationals aged 0–4 yrs (%)	−3.04 (0.008)	0.329	0.725	−0.157
Illegal immigration, estimated level	7.35 (0.000)	−0.747	−0.163	0.322
Non-nationals from non-European countries (%)	2.29 (0.036)	−0.064	−0.104	0.972
Non-nationals from less dev. non-European countries (%)	2.67 (0.017)	−0.155	0.005	0.971
Non-nationals from less developed non-European countries & their variation over time	3.94 (0.001)	−0.061	−0.134	0.751

Index

For Product Safety Concerns and Information please contact our EU
representative GPSR@taylorandfrancis.com
Taylor & Francis Verlag GmbH, Kaufingerstraße 24, 80331 München, Germany

www.ingramcontent.com/pod-product-compliance
Lightning Source LLC
Chambersburg PA
CBHW050437280326
41932CB00013BA/2154

9 780415 697743